| | | | | | | |

Taking Risks

| | | | | | | |

TAKING RISKS

literary
journalism
from
the edge

INTRODUCTION BY **MICHAEL IGNATIEFF**
EDITED BY **BARBARA MOON** & **DON OBE**

BANFF CENTRE PRESS
BANFF, ALBERTA

Grateful acknowledgement is made to those writers
who granted permission to reprint the selections in *Taking Risks*.

Canadian Cataloguing in Publication Data
Main entry under title:
Taking risks

Essays from the Banff Centre for the Arts'
Creative Non-fiction and Cultural Journalism program.
ISBN 0-920159-57-5

1. Canadian essays (English)* I. Moon, Barbara.
II. Obe, Don. III. Banff Centre for the Arts.
PS8373.T34 1998   C814'.5408   C98-910987-9
PR9197.7.T34 1998

| | | | | |

Edited by Barbara Moon and Don Obe
Design and photography by Janine Vangool, Vangool Design & Typography
Printed and bound in Canada by Hignell Book Printing Limited

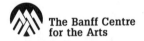

**The Banff Centre
for the Arts**

Banff Centre Press
The Banff Centre for the Arts
Box 1020 – 50
Banff, Alberta, Canada T0L 0C0

Table of Contents

| | | | | | |

At Banff

| | | | | | |

Michael Ignatieff

| | | | | | |

E VERY MORNING YOU GO OUT TO A STUDIO AT THE END of a wood-chip path among the pines. There are few distractions. Sometimes elks calve in the woods around you. Otherwise it is silent and cool. A storm may blow down off the mountains. There are other writers out there, and occasionally they drop by, but usually it's just you, face to face with the screen. You meet three times a week with the others, seven besides yourself, plus two editors and the program chairperson. You came with an idea: over four weeks, you watch it grow or vanish or turn into something entirely different.

The time at Banff is kept as unreal as possible. You are exempt from ordinary life. You don't have to go to the store or look after your children or visit your relatives. The obligations—and the excuses—that keep you from writing are taken out of the frame. The result is that your writing often ends up surprising you. In the rest of your life, you're working on commission: word lengths, subjects, deadlines are all given. You're a taxi: you pick up the fare, you take it to the destination by the best route you know. Here you choose your own destination. You have a month. Five thousand words. Some go further than they have before; others manage to go places they didn't know existed; still others get lost and have to struggle back onto the path. You can't afford to stay lost at Banff. The program editors are there to help you find your way back. Before you leave, you must have a result—a finished piece of writing in a publishable state.

As chairman, I did not create this regime. I inherited it and hope to turn it over to the next chairperson in the shape I found it. But the regime has had an effect on me. It has made me think about writing as such. Most of the time, I don't think about it at all. I am a working writer. I get up every morning, sit at a machine, and make sentences, paragraphs, articles, and books. I'm usually too busy trying to fix my mistakes to ask myself why I keep making them. In Banff, I do think about my mistakes. I do so when we meet in the afternoons to talk about one writer's draft and how it could find its best shape. All of the pieces in this book, seven of which slowly came into shape on my watch, five on the watch of my predecessor, Alberto Manguel, have made me go back to the fundamentals. I think about what works, what doesn't. I learn from our writers' mistakes. Sometimes I can help. Sometimes I can't.

In a form that is so constantly being reinvented, it may seem absurd to speak about the rules of non-fiction, but it does have a few. You can't make up facts or invent dialogue; well, you can, but it usually doesn't work. The facts usually turn out to be a good deal stranger than fiction, and you do best if you think hard about what makes them strange. Of course, you do get to choose the facts and the voice of the storyteller who gives them their shape. It doesn't have to be your own voice. It just has to be true.

Readers often fail to appreciate that the voice that tells a true story needn't be the writer's own. Choosing a voice is the heart of the business, and it is easy to get it wrong. Mostly, this comes down to deciding what elements of your self need to be disclosed in order to give the story its effect. The temptation is to tell everything, but candour can be a bore. There is actually no obligation to disclose everything. Most of what writers might want to say about themselves turns out to be strictly irrelevant to the stories they happen to be telling. What needs disclosure is the reason the story needs telling. But writers don't need to enter the confessional box to give a plausible answer.

Finding the voice for a piece is also about establishing your authority, your right to tell the story. Authority comes in many guises, from command of complex facts, or mastery of a register of irony or humour, even the authority that comes from a perfect impersonation of someone else's voice. There are styles and fashions in these matters, and it is a good thing to avoid being too fashion conscious.

The trick is to make it seem natural and, of course, nothing comes naturally. Writing belongs in the mysterious category of experiences that must be learned yet cannot be taught. Those who supposedly teach writing do so by learning from those they teach. I certainly have. Learning from envy, an emotion I have learned to trust.

It's pleasing but not necessarily helpful to think of nonfiction writing as an art. Craft will do. When I enjoy writing, I feel as if I am planing wood, smoothing it down so that it feels good under my hand. A writing class is not really best understood as a workshop in the making of art. It is a place where you consider the rules of a craft and where you conduct experiments in how human messages go astray. For this is the most baffling aspect of the exercise: how words and combinations of words mysteriously fail to hit the mark. "This works for me," someone says in one of our afternoon sessions. "Not for me," says another. Figuring out why we miss is painful. Sometimes it is because what has been left unsaid—and managing the unsaid is hard. Sometimes it is because the words don't mean to me what they mean to you. Sometimes it is because there simply isn't enough craft in the marshalling of the words on the page. And so the revisions begin, in an ongoing struggle to reduce the distance between what a writer intends and a reader understands.

The Utopia that writing lives for—and it is a Utopia—is that this distance can be obliterated. Perfect communication. Transparency between human thoughts and feelings. Such a Utopia is a morality as well. There may be other arts in which an artist can afford not to care about being understood. Meaning is not a problem for a saxophone player or even for a painter: messages in these media don't necessarily have to carry meanings. Writing can be elusive, but it has to be elusively meaningful, and if there is only wilful obscurity, however artful, it isn't worth a reader's time. In writing, the test is that it mean to a reader approximately what it means to a writer. A writers' workshop lives by that ethic: if the meaning isn't getting across, the writing has to be fixed.

The sessions at Banff between writers and editors and between writers and writers are not surrogate psychoanalysis. We are in the business not of teaching people how to live but of helping writers write better. Yet we have to deal with the murky world of emotional truth. Bad writing seems to come from not caring enough about the singularity of experience. Bad writing describes facts in ways that blur their singularity, in ways that make them seem as if they could have happened to anybody. Language being what it is, it is hard to be original. But it is possible for any determined language user to be singular—to put ordinary words together in sequences that make it plain that an experience had a particular shape and no other.

It can feel wonderful when you get it right. There is nothing like the validation that comes from having found the words that make experience singularly your own. Yet this validation doesn't come easily. I have some experience with these issues, but there are no experts in emotional truth. So at Banff I learn more than I teach.

The writers are doing the same: Banff gives them time to think about what they do for a living. Several pieces in this anthology take this form. Brian Johnson makes his living interviewing celebrities for a magazine. Here he gets to think about the curious transaction of the celebrity interview and the strangely melancholy results of living in the penumbra of fame. Marni Jackson looks back on her experience as a host of a television book show to think about the flattening impact of the medium on the messages it transmits. David Carpenter considers the issue of borrowing from other writers. The essay invites us to reconsider both the nature of originality and the ambiguous flattery implied in imitation. In all these pieces, writers used the month in Banff to stand outside themselves, to stop their particular game and think again about its rules.

This anthology includes three pieces about music: by Ian Pearson, Kim Echlin, and David Hayes. They are about the embarrassment of being a devoted, even obsessive fan, about the transmission and transmutation of musical traditions, and about the self-destructive life of artists who work on the edge of personal disaster. Another piece, by Kyo Maclear, is about the way in which Japanese cultural artifacts, from cartoons to karaoke to Tamagochis, are sweeping through North American popular culture. But all of these pieces are oblique exercises in self-portraiture: for Maclear, an opportunity to think about what it means to be of mixed Japanese Canadian origins; for Echlin, an opportunity to reflect on the inspirational power of artistic traditions in general. So there is memoir and self-revelation in all—but indirectly, through the revelation of something larger. Dan David's piece takes us through the Oka siege as seen from what was, for most Canadians, the other side of the barricades. Obliquely, he offers us a portrait of a writer whose terms of accommodation with Canada were put in painful question by the siege. Joan Skogan's essay builds on her experience on board BC fishing boats in order to address the subject of the Virgin Mary and her manifold incarnations in the roadside shrines, the churches, and the private icons of a Canada that seems to seek Mary's guidance more often than it wishes to admit.

All of these essays explore the wellsprings of inspiration and creativity. Two additional essays in this volume touch on this theme indirectly: the one, by Mark Abley, on what the whole world loses when an Aboriginal language dies out; and the other, "Lise Meitner's Walking Shoes," on the strange and unintended paths that human creativity takes when it innocently imagines the means of its own destruction. A third piece, by Stan Persky, ostensibly about a trip to Albania after the fall of communism, is actually about devotion to the word: how faithful translation and the compilation of honest dictionaries kept two men from losing themselves completely to the tyranny of a communist dictator.

All of the pieces in this volume have the virtue of being by writers more interested in the world than they are in themselves. They all manage to imply that the world out there is a good deal more fascinating than anything writers have yet managed to say. For that is what writing is supposed to do for us as readers: not to reduce us to admiring silence, but to turn us back to the world to see and feel it anew.

| | | | | | |

Turning into Talent
A Writer on TV

| | | | | | | |

Marni Jackson

| | | | | | | |

If the work of the city is the remaking or translating of man into a more suitable form than his nomadic ancestors achieved, then might not our current translation of our entire lives into the spiritual form of information seem to make of the entire globe, and of the human family, a single consciousness?
—MARSHALL MCLUHAN, *UNDERSTANDING MEDIA*

Television is at its most trivial, and therefore, most dangerous when its aspirations are high—when it presents itself as a carrier of important cultural conversations.
—NEIL POSTMAN, *AMUSING OURSELVES TO DEATH*

If we treat TV as a real place, it will rise to the occasion.
—DOUG RUSHKOFF, *MEDIA VIRUS*

UNTIL I HAD TO GO ON TV—I THINK OF IT AS THE media version of being drafted—I was an unrepentant print person. If movies had subtitles, so much the better. If a book wasn't handy, a supermarket bulletin board would do. Like a baleen whale sifting through seas of plankton, I required a lot of print every day just to feel vaguely nourished. And, like any other writer born before TV, my attitude toward television was both fearful and dismissive. For us, TV is still the interloper, the dopey cousin who came to stay for the weekend and then took over the living room.

So . . . when TV came calling, why did I say yes?

In a way, I blame John Updike. I began my book-reviewing career, if that's not an oxymoron, with a university paper on Updike, long before he wrote his forty-eight (and counting) books. The gist of it was that you can't talk about content without analysing form—to describe Updike's language is necessarily to wrestle with his ideas. His Dutch-master realism is the embodiment of his fictional worlds, in which characters caught in the rich and sticky materialism of middle America also long to transcend all that surface detail. The idea I was groping toward was some version of "the medium is the message," although, alas, that phrase eluded me. But that was before TV had insinuated itself into my critical life or, indeed, my personal one.

When Neil Postman began to write about television in the 1980s, he harped on the old form/content problem too, pointing out that everybody talks about the content of TV (ad nauseum) without tackling its epistemology. TV may be more than fifty years old, but our analysis of it is still in its infancy. Oddly enough, Updike—Mr. Gutenberg—made me think my first TV thoughts.

Time passes. I become a journalist. Updike types madly away. The lines between print and electronic media overlap and blur; hyper-shy authors begin tweezing facial hairs and hauling on pantihose to go on TV to talk about their books.

In 1995, the executive producer of *Imprint*, a book show on Ontario's public network, called me up. Would I like to audition for the job of host—the same job that had caused two previous writers and virgin TV types such lacerating embarrassment and bad reviews?

"But I have stage fright," I said.

"We can deal with that. There'll be training."

A job. It had a certain allure, what with being paid and all. Maybe TV could be my form of tenure, the thing that would let me go on writing. It never occurred to me that doing TV would install a new sort of V-chip in my brain—one that blocks the writing impulse. Then, in the course of our talk, the executive producer mentioned Updike—his favourite author, as it turned out. We'd get him on the show! How bad could it be, I thought, to chat with writers in front of a camera?

My first mistake was to assume that TV was child's play and could be tacked onto the bottom of my résumé. I didn't realize then how transformative—how biological even—the whole experience of passing through TV's digestive system would be.

| | | | | | | |

IT WAS OUR FAMILY VACATION. TRYING NOT TO WRINKLE my ironed shirt, I drove down from our rented cottage to do the audition, an interview with Oakland Ross, a journalist turned fiction writer. A producer met me at the door and led the way through a labyrinth of halls into the depths of the building, where TV studios always lurk, like mushroom farms. I was nervous in a high school-dance sort of way. I knew that it wasn't my skill as a journalist that was going to be judged so much as my "presence," and there wasn't much I could do about that. Either TV likes you, or it doesn't. It's not an audition; it's a blind date. Or maybe an X-ray. I myself had sat in rooms full of normally kindly women, watching *The Journal* and making snide remarks about Hana Gartner's jewellery. TV objectifies. Watching TV hosts turns everybody into a construction worker, circa 1961, rating the babes who walk by.

In the makeup room, I had a plastic cape tied around me like a giant bib, with Kleenexes tucked in my collar for any Pablum spills. The makeup artist was a pleasant woman with a German accent who made expert conversation with me. Why couldn't she be the host? With sticks and wands, she gave my face bolder, simpler outlines. TV requires high definition—lipliners, eyeliners, one-liners. We plucked at my hair, spraying down the more rebellious strands, and swabbed my hands with foundation so that they would match my face. A great deal of artifice is required to "just be yourself."

Another producer led me down the hall into the studio—a dark, cool, hermetic capsule that runs on its own time. There you quickly lose touch with the weather outside and the events of the day. The room has a peaceful, morguelike feeling, as if something vaguely forensic is going on.

The floor director, gracious as a maître-d', seated me at a round table on a dais stapled with a shiny piece of carpet. Two operators sat behind big ungainly cameras, gliding them around the floor like silent Zambonis. A soundman came over and helped me to thread a microphone up through my shirt. Then the decoy author was ushered in. Like candidates on *The Love Connection*, we greeted each other with wavering smiles across the table.

The producers sitting in the control room signalled the floor director that things were ready to roll. Using his fingers underneath the lens of the camera, the floor director counted us down, and we began. I looked toward the red light, warmly greeted my nonaudience, and turned to my fake guest.

"Welcome to *Imprint*, Oakland," I said, smiling what I felt to be a vast, vulpine, Jack Nicholson-sized smile, but which in truth barely turned up the corners of my mouth.

"Thank-you for having me," he said, eyes a-twinkle.

"You're a journalist who left a great job as a foreign correspondent to write short stories instead. What does fiction do that journalism can't?"

The Frisbee was in the air, and like a good dog he grabbed it and dashed off. Luckily, my decoy was both a good writer and a nimble talker. Meanwhile, in their cockpit, the producers observed us on a wall of monitors. I caught a glimpse of myself on the studio monitor and didn't like what my shoulder pads were doing. They were migrating. I looked down at my sheet of questions (grey so they don't reflect the light, stiff so they don't slip off your lap), which now seemed too written and wordy. We had the out-of-body experience that passes for a normal TV interview, and in a trice the ten minutes was up.

I was led to yet another door. With cheerful opaqueness, one of the producers said they were looking for a cohost too, some yet-to-be-determined male. They would be in touch. Then I got in my car and drove back up north, feeling disembodied and off-kilter. It had all gone smoothly enough, but . . . it left a strange, soul-snatching aftertaste. Where had I felt this before? Oh, yes, I realized, it was back in the early 1970s, after a bout of bad sex with a relative stranger.

But by the time I reached the cottage, the penumbra of TV had lifted and I was back inside myself.

"How did it go?" my husband asked.

"Okay," I said, but I thought I hadn't "occupied space," as they say in TV. On the contrary, I felt TV had occupied me.

So it was surprising when the call came the next week offering me the job as one of two hosts. And even more surprising that I said yes. As with any seductive new relationship, I thought that maybe I had misjudged TV—deep down, it probably meant well. It just had to get to know me better, that's all. Plus my vanity was now in play. Perhaps I could get to be good on TV. It was rumoured to be fun, after all, something writing never gets accused of being.

My husband does TV occasionally as an offshoot of his job as a film critic. And he enjoys it, although he warned me that being on TV has the same pitfalls as writing in the first person: first it liberates, and then the experience threatens to congeal into a "persona" that must be groomed and barbered, like a poodle. "Except that TV is really worse than writing in the first person," he said. "TV is the first person squared."

His other homily regarding television, one that came to haunt me, was that "It's better to go on TV than to be on TV." In other words, going on TV in the role of a guest, as somebody with content, can deliver a refreshing jolt of adrenalin. But when you become a TV host—even on a modest little book show on public TV—you become generic. You end up being composted into the medium itself.

| | | | | | |

The audience participates in the inner life of the TV actor as fully as in the outer life of the movie star. . . . With TV, the viewer is the screen.
—MARSHALL MCLUHAN, *UNDERSTANDING MEDIA*

I came to understand Charlie's Angels *when I realized that the entire show was about hair.* —NEIL POSTMAN, "SHE WANTS HER TV! HE WANTS HIS BOOK!", HARPER'S, MARCH 1991.

FOR TWO YEARS, UNTIL I QUIT, I WAS A COHOST OF *IMPRINT*. I was always a little ambivalent, and, as I quickly learned, you can't be coy with TV. It wants all of you. Television doesn't simply hire your skills; it hijacks your molecules. At the same time that it dematerializes you, reducing you to a dance of pixels on the screen, it dwells with a special ruthlessness on your physical appearance. You walk away from "doing TV" feeling both amplified and emptied out. I was hired to be this strange television entity known as The Host. What the heck is a host anyway? Isn't it just a matter of reading the TelePrompTer without stumbling?

McLuhan warned us that new media always cannibalize the conventions of the medium they replace. The convention of the host is proof of this—a security blanket for TV sceptics, an unnecessary figure who mediates between viewer and program like the device of the Victorian author who addresses the "Gentle Reader." The host is a ghost, a spectre of print authority—the omniscient, editorial voice, the Alistair Cookes of *Masterpiece Theatres*. Even though news anchors are the pillars of television (Holy Hosts), they strike me as anachronistic and vaguely anti-TV. Television is about moments and emotion, not analysis or reflection. Utterly artificial "reality-based" shows such as *Hard Copy,* or the hostless flow of *C-Span,* are, for better or worse, the future of TV, the syntax that truly belongs to the medium.

Toronto's CITY-TV executives understood this early in the game; their "hosts" are more like technicians with pretty faces—videographers who remind us that we are watching TV, its own breed of reality, not life mediated by TV. Their arts programming is more often unhosted—which is cheaper and perhaps more respectful of the viewer. The literate ideals of public television, with its lingering mandate of education, mean that it is more likely to duplicate conventions from plays, newspapers, or books. The proscenium arch is still lurking in the wings of much public television, where pure TV is feared as a barbaric medium that brutalizes ideas.

But as media critic Doug Rushkoff wrote in his book *Media Virus*, TV often uses trash to slip its most potent ideas by us. For many years, the best critique of TV was not to be found on PBS or TVO but in the mouths of babes (children, that is) on a cartoon show: *The Simpsons*. Rushkoff's theory is that TV doesn't act like a virus; it is a virus, one that glides past our intellectual defences disguised as something innocuous—a cartoon, a glib talk show, somebody's homemade video footage. What is loose in the culture will find its way onto TV through the strangest routes—as a shopkeeper who captures the imagination of the public on *The Late Show with David Letterman,* or in the jaw-dropping vulgarity of *The Jerry Springer Show,* one of the most watched programs on TV. Springer's show has become a daily ritualized subversion of the authority and presence of its host, as the guests overturn the traditional talkshow format and stage fake brawls, like some gabby new breed of pro wrestling. Jerry, the mild and weary, the sidelined voice of reason, controls nothing. He's just there as a viewer surrogate, alternately amused and shocked, until the conclusion of the show, when he delivers a surprisingly thoughtful little sermon (another "Gentle Reader" anachronism). The moral authority of a Walter Cronkite belongs to the early days of television, when the medium merely recorded life instead of replicating its own reality.

It's interesting that "host" is a viral term too. In biology, a host supports parasitical life or acts as the carrier of a virus. A TV host is a carrier, the face that delivers TV's agenda into your living room. The host is just a ghost, and that's exactly how people look at you when they vaguely recognize you from somewhere. In *Understanding Media*, McLuhan tells a little story about the actor Joanne Woodward. She was describing to someone the difference between being in the movies and being on TV. "When I was in the movies," she said, "I heard people saying 'There goes Joanne Woodward.' Now they say 'There goes somebody I think I know.'"

Her point, and McLuhan's, is that personal identity gets subsumed in the powerful relationship people have to the performer on TV. When you go on TV, you become TV's property. What you say becomes inseparable from who you are, which is sometimes indistinguishable from what you wear. (I remember one *Imprint* viewer who came up to me and said, "I loved your interview with Lewis Lapham—you should wear that shade of blue more often.") The declension of the TV host goes like this: from a person, to a personality, to a persona. The successful television presence is someone who is, or learns to project, a construct—a simulacrum of himself or herself. Sincerity's not enough—it melts like a chocolate bar in the heat of the studio. Sincere guests are fine, and fresh TV virgins are always required for talk shows. But the host must remain generic, like the Barbie and Ken high-hostness of the entertainment newsmagazines such as *Entertainment Tonight*. Too much nuance, too much idiosyncrasy, and the transparency of the host no longer works. The host is a television convention that we accept with an unthinking innocence—just part of TV's dollhouse furniture.

Needless to say, nothing about being a writer prepared me for this new role. Being a TV virgin reminded me of when I started out in journalism and first-person writing was considered artless and unprofessional. Journalism mistrusted "voice" in the same way that TV now mistrusts the raw, unscripted moment, or "dead air." First they hire you for your "voice" then they suggest you have your vocal chords removed.

Despite the fact that I'd been a journalist for twenty-five years, dreaming up my own questions, in the first year of the show I was supplied with a set of "greens" before each interview—a list of possible questions provided by the producer in charge of the item. I could amend the list or add to it, but the producers wanted to know in advance how the conversations would go. This baffled me. Wasn't the whole idea to capture fresh moments? Real talk? No. Evidently, the idea was to adapt to the existing technology—a fake-cozy set in a studio with two or three cameras. The technology defined the parameters of how the interviews were conducted.

It felt, in fact, like the opposite of writing—TV was scripting us. This arose not from the medium itself but from the show's old-fashioned production conventions, which worked against TV's great strength: its ability to capture the unrehearsed moment. I was told that interviews should have "three acts" and that my second acts could use some work. It reminded me of all those screenwriting workshops that basically recycle Aristotle and find new ways to tell people that things need a beginning, a middle, and an end. Aristotle is still applicable to almost anything remotely dramatic. But conventions belonging to literature and print restrict the free play of TV's vitality.

This may be especially true of "highbrow" TV, with its roots in education. As TVO has demonstrated, public television's great strength is in programming—documentaries, shows for children—not in redefining the medium itself. This is true of other networks too. In *Hotel America*, a dapper little screed about the decline of American civilization by Lewis Lapham, the author talks about what it was like to be the host of an American book show called *Bookmark*, on PBS. "Instead of offering an alternative to the Roman circus of commercial television," he writes, "they presented a show of slightly less expensive lions. . . ." Lapham thinks public TV could be truly exciting if it went out to the places where people still talk and argue and hold forums and discuss ideas. You don't put public discourse inside the belljar of the studio and then squeeze the life out of it—you take TV to where people are talking, and record it.

With the rampant cell division of television channels, the experience of going on TV has become less rarified. The day may come, in fact, when everybody's life is potential TV fodder—a concept explored in the recent movie *The Truman Show,* in which the hero, played by Jim Carrey, discovers that the minutiae of his daily life are, in fact, the content of a TV show secretly watched by the rest of the planet. It takes a familiar narcissistic fantasy—the desire to be the star of your own show—and plays it out. The horror of this dark comedy is the prospect of the isolation it entails. Is this going to be the fallout of a world divided into the watchers and the watched? What kind of collective loss of innocence are we undergoing? My stint on TV made me aware of the self-objectifying powers of the medium.

When you're a writer or a journalist, you lose your innocence in several stages, like a space launch. You may write away for a while with no discernible relationship to your readers. But if you become a columnist or publish a memoir, you create a public persona that both is and isn't you. The tension between these two selves may even be the tension out of which writing spins. When novelists publish their first book, they go through a similarly intense feeling of exposure; even glowing reviews aren't a salve for the feeling of having handed over a few of your internal organs to perfect strangers. This is part of the job of writing, apparently, and for better or worse, it is a searing passage.

Going on TV is another radical loss of innocence, one that more and more of us must undergo in the course of a career in the arts. Journalists who appear on panels, authors who go on book tours, experts who appear on the news—they all experience the strange conflation/deflation of self that TV brings about. You see yourself on tape, in the round—not as an image in the mirror, but as a set of behaviours and gestures. The way others see you, in fact. You forever lose a certain innocence about yourself. It's the same as astronauts going into space and getting their first glimpse of Earth as this blue swirling marble in space. But writing, it seems to me, is about not seeing yourself in the round—that sort of writerly self-awareness has a blind spot in the middle. It supplies some of the courage and fool-ishness required to write, and the unfinished puzzle of identity is what drives many authors on. Writing feeds on distortion, prejudice, and eccentricity. Honing your TV self, on the other hand, requires a sleek and calculated brand of self-consciousness.

And self-consciousness, as the poet and novelist Michael Ondaatje once muttered in an interview, is the enemy of writing. On TV, the host has a fitted earpiece so that, if something goes wrong, the producer in the control room can tell him what to do and say. In writing, an author deliberately turns down the volume of the world around her, so that she can detect the inflections of her own voice.

The exhilaration of TV is its potential for democracy—its levelling effect. The danger lies in the way it likes to turn people into smooth, simple shapes, like soapstone carvings.

By the end of my first year on TV, the show had been subjected to a focus group, one of those marketing tools that tries to evaluate what the "public" wants. I was designated Host B. "Host B's style," the report stated, "was either liked or disliked." This sums up most of the wisdom concerning who works on TV.

The way strangers relate to you is illuminating too. Being the host of a book show with 35,000 viewers (on a good night) is minor celebrity indeed, but it did happen that people would give me puzzled, do-I-know-you looks at the Y or sly smiles in the parking lot. And what they said is revealing: not "I liked your conversation with Grace Paley" but "I saw you on TV!" It's like you're a raccoon that wandered into their living room—a refugee from the wilderness of TV, come down their chimney. When people say "I saw you on TV," they're saying, "We have a history now—we're connected." What *they* feel is the powerful, indiscriminate relationship people have to faces on TV. What *you* feel is the curious blend of being visible and erased at the same time.

Now, two years after leaving my TV job, I begin to have some inkling of why I toyed with TV and what it has to do with the writing life. My theory involves eating disorders and our old friend Marshall McLuhan. Bear with me one more time.

More than thirty years ago, McLuhan was unbelievably prescient—if slightly Utopian—in what he wrote about TV in *Understanding Media*. He too was a print person, but one who didn't resist the incoming tide of the electronic age. Instead, he got into the swim. He played in the new media currents like a dolphin. But what kept his thinking from evaporating into the fibre-optic future was, of course, his bookish side—his literacy and erudition, and the way he played his hot print mind off the cool media he wrote about. In a word, he had content. The problem with contemporary media analysis is its cannibalism—it must feed upon itself, with less and less reference to the world of extra-media events (reality, I think it's still called).

Critics see this as a sign of cultural narcissism. Well, it is that. But perhaps it is also a necessary passage in our electronic adolescence. We still lack the appropriate language and attack for analysing the passage we're in right now. Like teenagers adjusting to new bodies, we become self-absorbed, staring into the media mirror for hours on end. We're stuck in the transformative tunnel between the old print realities and a new firmament we don't entirely trust. As McLuhan said, first we shape the tools, and then the tools shape us.

McLuhan's most famous prophecy was that the electronic media would serve as an extension of our consciousness and an amplification of our senses. McLuhan claimed that this new technology was not armour, or antinature, but our new skin and nerves. In the future, he said, we would wear our brains and nervous systems on the outside. In his vision, TV is just part of our evolution as thinking, fact-gathering, Letterman-watching *Homo sapiens.*

But if TV in some sense incarnates us, could this explain why it both rivets and repels us? Is this why we try to ration our TV consumption, like image bulimics, and then guiltily binge-watch ur-TV programs such as *Hard Copy?* If it's true that the electronics media are carving new neural pathways, then what sort of horrible new body-image problems are we in for now?

We live inside the skin of TV—it shapes culture even if we refuse to watch it in our homes, and our attitudes toward it are as vexed and emotional and muddled as our attitudes toward our own bodies. We're forever trying to improve TV's diet, to get TV into shape, but it remains carnal, impudent, voracious, shameless. Like weight watchers on a futile series of diets, we try to control the calorie content of TV, watching our intake of violence or fattening game shows. We fight flesh, and resist TV, instead of confronting the nature of our relationship with both.

Some say that the electronic media are slowly disembodying our culture, but the reverse could be true. We watch TV as if gazing into a new kind of mirror, and, although what we see often troubles us, we find it hard to turn away. On we go, gorging and purging, disowning TV even as it rivets us with ur-TV imagery—O. J. Simpson in the white Bronco racing toward his mother, the Rodney King videotape, Monica Lewinsky beaming at Bill Clinton in her beret. In those moments, we inhabit TV as vividly as we inhabit our bodies. And we often hate it in the same way too.

This may explain my retrograde sense of being back in high school when I was on TV. It only appeared to be about doing well and getting good marks. In fact, it was about popularity, and hair. Of the many trenchant criticisms I received when I first went on the air, the one I remember most vividly was "Your hair looks like a pine-apple." On TV, hair rules.

Michael Ignatieff can talk about the morality of ethnic nation-alism on air, but if he has an Alfred E. Newman sprig of hair waving around, no one will hear a word he says. This is not the same thing as calling TV shallow. Our response to people on TV is visceral and immediate, and how people look is inseparable from their "content." In the Mike Nichols movie *Primary Colors,* people in a bar watch Emma Thompson playing the first lady on TV as she gives a sombre press conference about (what else?) the integrity of the president. When it's over, one of the women watching gives her considered response. "I like her hair better that way," she muses. "Yeah," someone else says, "it softens her face." This scene strikes a chord because it is true to the way we all watch TV, if we're honest with ourselves. It's part of the new epistemology of TV that Neil Postman was waiting for.

More hair evidence: was it just coincidence that Kramer, of the unique high hair, was the most beloved character on *Seinfeld?* Even the first host of TVO's *Imprint,* writer and broadcaster Daniel Richler, ran the hair gauntlet when he first went on the air. The early reviews entirely focused on his spiky, unblow-dried, anti-TV hair. (Revenge was his; now he's the host and coproducer of *Big Life* on CBC's *Newsworld.* This may be proof that "hair reviews," positive or nega-tive, are a reliable sign of telegenesis.)

AT THE AGE OF FIFTY, I WAS JUST BEGINNING TO SHED, with great relief, a lifetime of negotiation with my looks and image. I'm sure that's part of why I became a writer in the first place—to escape the conventions that being female imposed back in the 1960s. Discarnate, I felt much freer. But when TV came calling, the prospect of putting my writing voice together with the rest of me was seduc-tive. I could be whole again—if only on TV. The Church of TV promises to heal.

The media as faith healer is one of the themes of *The Beauty of the Lilies,* John Updike's forty-seventh book. It came about that I was going to talk to the author about his novel for *Imprint.* I was back in

Updike country again, where I began. We were going to tape an hour of conversation—it eventually ran to something like thirty minutes, an eternity in TV time. The book ends on TV, with an apocalyptic scene that unfolds on the six o'clock news. The hero, a Presbyterian minister whose faith has deserted him, watches a news item about a Waco-like cult shoot-out in which his own grandson dies. This wasn't just the conclusion of his book, Updike hinted, but the end of all books, on TV. A ripe subject for a conversation with an author on television.

Updike's writing is at the antipodes of TV style—his language is as close to stucco as words can get. His novel presents movies and TV celebrity as part of the withering of faith and shrinkage of life that he detects toward the close of the century. There is also the notion, not exactly original, of the cult of celebrity as the new Western religion. In Updike's book, not only does the Church of TV heal, but Hollywood is literally heaven—that old-fashioned notion of the virtual self.

We set up for the interview in a downtown hotel. I wore a white shirt under a black jacket—neutral, almost typographic. As I waited for Updike and the publicist to arrive, I thought it odd that all the thoughts and questions arising from a twenty-five-year relationship with a writer's work, which amounts to a unique, weirdly intimate connection, were going to be consummated in a hotel suite in the cold bonfire of television.

Updike arrived, bushy eyebrowed and worryingly thin in the haunches. He's a striking-looking man, with a slight resemblance to a Greek satyr, as well as a genuine air of humility.

"I like your shoes," he said as we sat down toe to toe. I was wearing rather prim lace-up Victorian boots. We both looked down at my feet as he continued. "It's so hard to find boots that work in the snow and in . . . this sort of situation."

The soundman wired him up, and we began our conversation. He was smiling and responsive, although I thought I detected a lurking stutter; if one word threatened to trip him up, he would take a different tack. His voice was soft and low. We talked with ease about the themes of the novel, but it was the mention of one tiny detail that seemed to animate him—a metaphor in which the minister's faith deserts him, like a stream of champagne bubbles ascending up into the air.

"That was how the book began," Updike said, his fingers bubbling. "I don't know . . . the image just came into my mind...." For an instant, his astonishing fluency deserted him, and he was remembering what it was like to write. Then we went back to the business at hand.

| | | | | | |

IT IS EASIER, I NOW CONCLUDE, TO PUT BOOKS ON TV THAN it is to anatomize television on the page. The face of TV remains maddeningly fuzzy, like the dancing blue blob that protects the identity of the accused on newscasts. When I began to write about it, every time I tried to capture its likeness in words, it would go swimmy in the centre. I had to quit TV and go back to my desk to get any sort of grip at all.

I still get the odd twinge of phantom pain in the part of me that television lopped off, but I'm sure that will fade. Even McLuhan predicted that, before the amplification of the senses, we would pass through a period of numbness and amputation. I'm even optimistic about TV. As soon as it stops mimicking print and theatre, its own pagan intelligence will shine through.

And, now that I'm back on the other side of the screen, I've discovered how to watch TV. You simply treat every channel as a nature documentary and the people on it as a new species, evolving.

With Updike, this would be a metaphor. On TV, it could turn out to be true.

1996, revised 1998

| | | | | | |

All My Relations

| | | | | | |

Dan David

| | | | | | |

The old man stands by the edge of the woods, at the far end of the cornfield behind my sister's house. He wears a long, flowing shirt and a *kastowah*, a Mohawk headdress. It's made of a brimless cap circled by a flurry of small, curled, white partridge feathers and topped by three eagle feathers. A leather medicine bag hangs from his braided belt. He holds a staff at the end of one outstretched arm. The staff is carved like a condolence cane. It has a series of symbols representing events in history mixed with others signifying the laws and ceremonies.

He stands there, looking toward my sister's house. He turns slowly and points his staff in the direction of the Pines. After a few moments, the old man turns once more and begins walking toward my sister, who watches from her kitchen window. The old man crosses the field, getting closer. She knows this man somehow. Then he disappears.

My sister knew the old man's appearance that day was a warning. Something more terrible than anyone could imagine was about to happen. But she also knew there was something else the old man wanted her to know. Our ancestors were there, and they would protect the people from harm. For the first time, Linda says, she felt no doubt about the Mohawk occupation in the Pines.

| | | | | | |

ANYONE COULD TELL SOMETHING WAS ABOUT TO HAPPEN at Kanehsatake that summer. You read the newspapers or listened to the radio, and you just knew. But nobody could have predicted the tidal wave of discontent and rage that would roar across the country, picking up strength as it went until it finally subsided.

The facts you may remember. On the morning of July 11, 1990, hundreds of riot police moved in to remove a Mohawk barricade at Kanehsatake in an area called the Pines overlooking the town of Oka. The "barricade" was nothing more than a low mound of earth on a rarely used, sandy side road into the Pines. The Mohawks put it there to stop the mayor of Oka from bulldozing the Mohawk cemetery— where my great-grandfather is buried—and cutting down the Pines, a pine forest planted about a 100 years ago in order to expand an exclusive, whites-only golf course.

A thirty-second firefight exploded between Mohawk Warriors and the Sureté du Québec. One officer was killed. Hundreds of police officers and thousands of Canadian soldiers descended upon a handful of rebellious Mohawks. After a seventy-eight-day standoff, the Mohawks walked out. Our job is done, they said, and we're going home. The problem was that some didn't know where home was anymore.

I know how they felt. When I went behind the barricades, I had no inkling of the sheer power of the forces at work at Kanehsatake that would sweep me away. At times, I felt helpless; swirls and eddies trapped me, pushing and pulling me in one direction and then another, ramming me against things lying just beneath the surface. Occasionally, I found myself floating in pools of such serenity that I doubted the anger and hatred raging outside. Nor could I guess where these currents would eventually deposit me.

There were times when I saw no future. The obvious threat came from men dressed in official uniforms as well as those dressed in army surplus. They wielded power over life and death, power that came from the weapons they held in their hands. Too often, they were far too ready to use them. But there was another threat, more subtle and harder to identify. This threat attacked my perception of reality. It weakened my sense of identity. People I grew up with, worked with, called my friends, even aunts and uncles, condemned me because I stayed behind the barricades. It left me uncertain, full of doubt, about why I was there and why I stayed. It battered me and left me feeling betrayed.

Despite several trials and inquests, no one knows for sure who started shooting first. The police fired at unseen Warriors in the woods and anything else that moved. The Warriors shot back. Together, they fired thousands of rounds. About two dozen Mohawk women and children were caught in the crossfire.

| | | | | | |

THREE OF MY SISTERS AND TWO OF MY NIECES ARE IN THE Pines that morning. My younger sister, Kasennenhawi, Gussy for short, hears bullets snap by her, sees sand kick up around the other women and the children as they dive for cover, feels the splinter of bark as bullets gouge the trees they hide behind. Later, she wonders why no one else is killed.

Standing there with the other women only yards from the police, Gussy is afraid at first—but not of dying. There's something else in the Pines that morning. She can't describe it to this day. The police aim at women with tear gas and concussion grenades. These explode all around them. The women should be wounded, but they aren't. A sudden wind springs up, blowing tear gas meant to render the women weeping and powerless back toward the police. The women feel a strange calm settle over them. They know someone or something is watching over them. But Gussy can see only death in the eyes of the police. She knows someone will die that day.

I'm afraid it might be Gussy or someone else in my family after I hear the gunfire on the radio that morning. I know my family must be in the middle of everything. I throw a tape recorder and a camera into my car along with some spare clothes. I speed out of Maniwaki, the reserve north of Ottawa where I live. It's a three-hour drive to Kanehsatake. Most of the way, I swing between fear and rage. I can't get rid of the image in my mind of one or another of my brothers or sisters lying in the sand, bleeding. I'm almost home when I hear that no Mohawk is wounded but that one policeman is dead.

I don't see the police roadblock until I'm almost upon it. By then it's too late to do anything but slow down, open the window, and put both my hands in clear view high on the steering wheel. One officer motions me to stop at an imaginary line on the highway. Another officer points toward me and says, "C'est un Warrior." I hear a flurry of rifle bolts jamming bullets into chambers. Half a dozen police officers aim their rifles at my head.

Things we say in the sweat lodge ceremonies play over and over in my mind. We say "all my relations" when we enter the lodge to sit. We say "all my relations" when we invite the spirits in. We say it again whenever we end our prayers. And we say "all my relations" when we break the circle to leave the sweat lodge.

Other words come to me as well from some of those prayers. Clean the rock with cedar. Hold the sage close. Douse the rock with water and feel the steam burn. Take some of the sacred tobacco and sprinkle a bit over the hot rock. Say the words that your heart demands and pray for guidance.

Mine are simple. In every person's life, the elders tell us, there are forks in the road: choices to make, directions to choose. One fork represents the easy road, the path of least resistance, the road away from the people, the road of personal gain, of escape from life and into whatever personal hell one chooses. The other fork represents the red road, the more difficult road, full of adversity and hardship, the road back to the people and their beliefs, the road to life and all of the pain, anguish, and joy that life demands as the price of admission. Guide me. Help me to know the difference.

All my relations.

I KNOW THERE'S NO TURNING BACK ONCE I CROSS THAT imaginary line at the roadblock. I worry about what the Warriors may do when they see me behind the barricades. I know them from the civil war at Akwesasne, near Cornwall, between the Warriors and the anti-Warriors the summer before. They know me from the stories I write about the smuggling, the guns, and the violence that seems to follow them. Some have threatened me for those stories, and I wonder what they'll do when they see me. I even have to worry about some of my relatives who hate my family—just because. I don't know how they'll react. I have no idea what I'm getting into except that these are my people, my relatives, my father and mother, my brothers and sisters. The cop waves me through.

Once in the Pines, I find people from all over the territory, all ages, all families, all factions, walking around in elation, confusion, and fear. Most are caught up in the euphoria of the moment; they've survived the police raid and driven the attackers off their land. Others just wander around, aimless and dazed. A few prepare themselves in personal ways to kill or to die in anticipation of the next attack, which they're sure will come.

> I stumble around the Pines, searching for my family. I see someone crouching in a shallow trench near the golf course. He looks familiar. "Joe?" I ask, uncertain. The man is wearing black cargo pants, an army-fatigue jacket, and a bandanna hiding his face under a dark green military cap. He's cradling an AK-47. Two fast-load magazines are jammed into his jacket pockets. My little brother turns and says, "Yep. I know. I don't believe it either."

> In my family, Joe's the one blessed with that rare gift which allows him to stare at a rock, hear muted voices within, and chisel away the excess until only the rock's inner spirit remains and is set free. He can look at a blank canvas and, with splashing colours and gentle strokes, make a dream dance upon its surface. He hates guns and war and violence. That's when I decide—no matter what—I will not pick up a gun.

THE SECOND ATTACK NEVER COMES, AND A TENSE TRUCE settles over the barricades. As long as you stay inside, you're safe. The moment you try to leave, however, almost anything can happen. The police pull a young couple from their car and force them at gunpoint to strip in the middle of the road and in front of dozens of people in their cars. Little kids in the back seats of cars cry while cops hiding behind sandbags shout insults and aim assault rifles at their parents. The police tear groceries for hungry families out of people's arms and throw them into the ditch. I won't pick up a gun. I become a food smuggler instead.

I hear about the cops playing Russian roulette with helpless captives in abandoned barns. I feel sick when teenagers describe how the police burn tattoos into their chests with cigarettes in empty parking lots. A man, a gentle man, a peaceful man, a drunk, tells me he can't walk very well. His testicles are swollen to the size of small grapefruit after the police beat him because he refuses to sign a blank confession. I begin working with the human rights observers.

At the checkpoints, I take down names, ranks, units, and whatever other information I can gather—especially when things get hot. The army decides one day, without warning, to move its line 100 metres or so into Mohawk territory. People start yelling and screaming at each other over the razorwire stretched across the road. A Warrior yells "lock and load." A machine gun on one of the armoured personnel carriers swivels toward everyone standing on that exposed piece of highway on the Mohawk side of the line. There are women and children here as well as Warriors. "Excuse me, corporal. Can I have your name and unit please? I'm with the observers." The corporal looks at me and stops screaming for just a second. Sometimes that's all it takes.

I hate these people and their guns. One kid—he must have been about fourteen years old—stops my car on my way into the Pines. It's near the end of the summer. We all know the army's going to sweep through the territory any day. Everybody's tired and on edge. Things are extremely tense. Some of the Warriors have been out here at checkpoints like this one for days without rest. But I need to get my dad out of the Pines. The kid tells me to turn my car around and go back. That's it. I've had enough. I tell him to fuck off. I get out of the car to tell him these are my Pines. This is my land. And I'm going in to pick up my dad.

He raises his AR-15 and aims it at my gut. I think: This is strange. I know what kind of rifle he's holding. I know what it can do. So does my five-year-old nephew. He can quote the calibre of shell the rifle fires, its range, and even the number of bullets its magazine carries. We didn't know any of this before this summer. I look into the kid's eyes. They're empty. He could blow me away without a pause, without a flicker of concern. The look in his eyes isn't much different from the look I've seen all summer at the police and the army roadblocks. It's the look of people too whacked out by a military mind-set, fatigue, or dope to care anymore. For the first time inside the barricades, I'm scared. I ease back into my car, shift into drive, and move forward slowly, very slowly, leaving the kid standing there. Nothing happens. Around the corner and away from the checkpoint, I stop the car and light a cigarette. I can't smoke it. I'm shaking too hard. I stay this way for about ten minutes until I stop shaking enough to go pick up my dad.

It may sound strange, but that summer I feel I've found home for the first time in a long while. I'd left years before to get away from people grown used to silent resignation. I return to find people filled with pride, hope, and even dignity. Inside the barricades, people who haven't spoken to each other in decades over long-forgotten arguments hold hands and stand together in one great circle under the Pines. For at least a little while, they bury the old hatreds. They're just grateful to be alive and free. At times like this, they believe that almost anything is possible. So do I.

There is such peace behind those barricades. It's easy sometimes to forget the stone-throwing mobs outside. I sit for hours in the Pines and never hear a car break the silence. I listen under those trees while my soul dances to the sound of Mohawk, Mi'kmaq or Kwakiutl voices weaving themselves into the beat of a drum. I don't remember the northern lights being so bright, so intense, so green. My sister's right—the spirits are with the people in the Pines.

My summer is like that: periods of tremendous peace and hope punctuated with flashes of anger, fear, and deep despair. Few on the outside realize what we, the people caught in the middle, are going through. I remember one interviewer asking me why—as a journalist—I couldn't be "objective." I hear explosions in the Pines even as the question is asked. I know my little brother might be dying at that very moment. I nearly break down on-air. I manage to mumble some stupid answer that doesn't make much sense. All I can think is how much I hate the person asking that question.

On September 28, 1990, after two and a half months, my brother puts down his weapon and "walks home" with forty-six other holdouts, men and women, out of the barricades and into army detention. I go back to my former wife's reserve north of Ottawa. Too much hate. Three packs of cigarettes a day. A bottle of aspirin and two hours of sleep a night for weeks on end. I collapse. A couple of months later, on a job-hunting expedition to Toronto, a helicopter bursts over the buildings, the sound exploding overhead. I find myself crawling under the back of a parked car. I'm a stumbling, mumbling example of Kanehsatake after the standoff.

The decision to go down one road or the other requires an individual leap of faith into the unknown. It doesn't matter if it is a considered choice or results from the flip of a coin; there's no guarantee the choice is the right one. The signs before the choice and afterward are deceptive, contrary, and confusing. There's often no one to provide a gentle nudge in one direction or the other. Every now and then, however, the voice of an ancestor whispers in your ear, barely heard and rarely recognized. All my relations.

NOTHING MAKES SENSE ANYMORE. THINGS I'VE SEEN AND heard are called illusions and lies. I'm condemned as both a brain-washed hostage and a terrorist at the same time. I'm handcuffed by doubts about why I returned to Kanehsatake and why I stayed there. I wonder if I've been deluding myself, seeing those behind the barri-cades with false nobility? I can't tell right from wrong anymore.

I see so much hope crushed so completely afterward. Dreams of freedom become plans to expand a criminal empire of smuggling, gambling, and guns. Good people who gave so selflessly are singled out for retribution. No one seems to notice how those who began the summer as gun-toting Warriors, crying out for blood, miraculously transformed themselves into police informers and witnesses. Those who deserted the community and its people are hailed as heroes. I should know, but I can't tell who's right anymore. I just want to forget it all.

"Why are you calling me?" I ask a woman I know from my days at CBC in Toronto. She says she's writing a series of stories about Aboriginal people for private radio. She remembered me and tracked me down by calling people at our old program. She's looking for a narrator. She thought about me. I need the work. I'm broke. The jobs aren't there anymore. "But I spoke with the executive producer where we used to work," the woman continues, "and he told me not to hire you because you're a Warrior spokesman. So, do you know anybody else I can ask?"

I GET A PHONE CALL ONE NIGHT FROM AN OLD FRIEND AND teacher. He's putting my name in for a Commonwealth Fellowship. If I get the award, it means going to London for a couple of weeks, having an audience with the queen, and then heading off to the South

40

Pacific for a month. Paradise. I hesitate before answering. I don't have a Canadian passport. I'll have to apply for one. But I'm not sure I want to get into another fight over my Mohawk citizenship. My soul is sore and tired.

The problem boils down to this: I was born in Syracuse, New York. However, my parents are both from Canada. My mom is from Kanehsatake. My dad is from Akwesasne. Technically, that allows me dual citizenship, Canadian and American. But I'm also Mohawk. Canada doesn't recognize the Mohawk as an "internal, sovereign but domestic nation" as the United States does. The Canadian government wants my parents to declare themselves Canadian citizens before it will give me a passport. In effect, Canada wants my parents to surrender their Mohawk citizenship. Canada has no idea what it's asking. Demanding.

No declaration of Canadian citizenship by my parents, the Canadian government says, no Canadian passport for me. The clock is running. My award is in jeopardy. I can almost hear the boarding call. The bureaucrats in Ottawa grow more insistent. Just get my parents to sign a letter stating they were born in Canada, they nudge. It's just a formality. Just a piece of paper.

"Mom, what are these cheques?"

Uncashed family allowance cheques, sent to every Canadian family and a universal benefit of Canadian citizenship, are stacked in a small pile, bound by a rubber band, and stuffed into the back of a dresser drawer. Like her mother before her, my mom won't cash a single one. To do so would imply her surrender of Mohawk citizenship, identity, principles, and beliefs. She refuses to vote in any Canadian election—especially band elections—for the same reason.

"Some of them have your name on it," mom says, pointing her chin toward the drawer and at the pile of cheques. "Cash them if you want."

We are eight kids, running around in torn and patched hand-me-downs. Church charity. I wear shoes with soles that flap and shout my shame despite the staples and glue. Each night, I wash my "favourite" shirt for school the next day because it is really the only shirt I own without holes. I look at the pile of cheques and dream of that warm sweater hanging in a department store window.

I look at my shoes and think about a pair of shiny white sneakers that are guaranteed to make me run faster. A choice. A fork in the road. Cash the cheques. Or be your great-grandfather's grand-daughter's son.

Years later, I remember seeing those cheques again. Uncashed, they lay in the kitchen cupboard, a reminder of a mother's choice passed on to her children and their children and the children to come.

| | | | | | |

I COULD FIND COPIES OF MY PARENTS' BIRTH CERTIFICATES or wrangle some official-looking document from the band council without my mom's or dad's knowledge. I don't. I can't do it—not to them. Perhaps it's something in the voices of those bureaucrats that grates, an attitude, an arrogance maybe. How dare they say citizenship is just a formality and a passport just a piece of paper. Then again, maybe it's the voice of an ancestor whispering in my ear.

Late one night, when I've all but given up hope of going to London, I get a hushed phone call from a senior official at External Affairs. "Don't worry about the award," he almost whispers. "Get the American passport. Fly to London. We'll straighten things out when you get there. As far as we're concerned, you're Canadian, and you're going on this fellowship." That's how I become the only "American" ever to represent Canada as a Commonwealth Fellow.

Peter Donigi is a lawyer from Papua New Guinea. James Gitoho is Kikuyu, an architect from Kenya. I am Mohawk. We come from homelands thousands of kilometres apart, different ends of the world. Yet we are alike in so many ways. We share similar values that spring from our distant and different tribal memories and from a shared colonial heritage. They are proud, independent, and strong. I am wounded. They sense this and let me hobble along beside them.

We talk, trade ideas, and share experiences. Our nations were once part of a mighty empire, allies loyal to the British crown for reasons of our own or held in submission by force. But the empire has dissolved, and its might has faded. True believers in the old empire, we discover, contend that our nations remain loyal to the Commonwealth because we revere the crown and treasure the "civilizing influence" of Westminster laws and parliament. We, on the other hand, see the Commonwealth as an evolutionary process from slavery and exploitation to freedom. The laws, and the values they represent, are foreign to us. Nor do we have great love for any person living in Buckingham Palace. The attraction, the tie that binds, is economic. It pays to remain a part of the Commonwealth in training, trade, and aid. Still, we admit to each other, it'll be nice to finally meet the lady at the centre of the Commonwealth. We've never met real royalty before.

But I've met Lena. She's Algonquin. For some reason I can't understand at the time, her people have picked her to represent them at some parliamentary hearings into Aboriginal rights in Ottawa. She doesn't speak English or French very well, but she knows three or four Indian languages. The Algonquins try to reassure me. They don't succeed.

I've worked in Ottawa. People there only respect high-priced lawyers in three-piece suits and wealthy old politicians with powerful connections. They talk a certain language. They communicate in a strange code. All the other Indians hire high-priced guides in three-piece suits to represent them, I explain. They tell me Lena built her own cabin and raised a large family on her own. She killed a moose with one shot. Then she hauled the drawn carcass in pieces, back and forth, the six kilometres to her cabin. She's lived on the land all her life.

I finally meet Lena and see a small, old lady in a faded flower-print skirt and a tattered babushka wrapped around a grey head. She has a kind, deeply etched face. She ambulates with that peculiar slow walk, swaying to and fro, called the James Bay waddle.

A month or so later, I'm in that Ottawa hearing room watching hangers-on and the not-so-influential navigate around those with power and authority. They show much deference: lowering of heads and baring of teeth. Dog language. They chatter around the doorway, making it difficult for anyone else to enter or converse. Suddenly, a strange hush falls over the room. People used to being at the centre of great power and authority in this country go quiet and draw apart. As though on instinct, like a school of fish sensing a change in the current or the presence of a predator, they clear away from the door, fashioning a corridor from the hallway into the hearing room. Lena enters this corridor. She's wearing a faded but neat flower-print skirt and a new babushka, walking with that familiar swaying motion.

That's royalty, I tell my friends, not some false notion of power that comes with a job, a title, or wealth. It's a majesty that glows from inside a person and comes from strength, dignity, and pride. Those people in Ottawa recognized that somehow. My friends nod in agreement. We talk about other such people we know in our separate back homes long into the night. After we part, I carefully press my scarlet ribbon shirt and breechcloth, fuss over the feathers in my *kastowah*, and lay out my medicine bundle. I think about what I'll say to the queen. And I think about my great-grandfather, who preceded me here nearly ninety years before.

| | | | | | |

THE NEWSPAPERS CALL HIM CHIEF KENNATOSSE AND, IN understatement typical of newspaper writing of the time, describe him as a man who "has made the situation at the reserve of the Okas near the lake of Two Mountains exceedingly interesting." The priests of the Seminary of St. Sulpice call him Joseph Gabriel. The federal government, and the Department of Indian Affairs in particular, call him a "ringleader of Mohawk rebelliousness." People in Kanehsatake call him Kanawatiron. He's a Mohawk farmer, a faithkeeper, and a fugitive. He's my great-grandfather.

Growing up, I hear little about Kanawatiron except for the odd snatch of conversation between my mom and her mother. For some reason, he remains this mysterious person until the day I spot some railway tracks, overgrown and barely visible, from my school bus window. The tracks seem to come from nowhere and to go nowhere.

That evening, I ask my mom why those tracks end right there by that road on the way to Pointe Calumet. "Oh," she says matter-of-factly, "that's because of your great-grandfather, Joseph Gabriel. He was my mother's father. They were going to build a railway through our land. He said we'd lost enough land already and the railway would destroy whatever was left. So your great-grandfather and about forty other Mohawks from here picked up their rifles, got on their horses, and rode out to where the railroad crews were laying tracks. They never used their guns, but they scared the railroad crew off. That crew never came back. That's why the tracks stop right there."

For years, it's just a story told under the dim glow of a kerosene lamp at our old, enamel-topped kitchen table. Until, that is, the day a friend hands me a stack of photocopies of old newspaper clippings. The clippings are almost all about Kanawatiron. One almost jumps out, a story from the front page of the *Montreal Daily Star*, dated 1911:

INDIANS THREATEN WAR AGAINST RAILROAD MEN.

Witnesses say that there were at least forty braves armed with shotguns, revolvers and bludgeons, who with regular war cry accompaniment, informed the railroad laborers that they could proceed at their peril, as the property they were about to cross belonged to the Iroquois. The navvies are said to have retired gracefully. . . .

That's my great-grandpa. Here's proof that those stories, or at least some of them, are more than fanciful tales told to children around the kitchen table. It's oral history—my family's history—passed down through the generations. The facts of the story are kept faithfully intact, but the viewpoint is much different from the newspaper accounts. It's as though Kanawatiron is reaching across the passage of time at the very moment I need to believe.

MY HISTORY TEACHER PACES UP AND DOWN THE AISLES IN my grade 7 class while describing the Lachine Massacre. We have our books open to that section and to the illustration that accompanies it. The picture shows a French woman with one hand raised as if to stop the Iroquois warrior above her, and her other hand shields two children behind. The woman holds her chin high, defiant, brave. The children's faces are contorted in fear. The Iroquois warrior holds a war club above the woman, poised to strike. His face is painted, twisted, demonic. One of the kids sitting in the row beside me lifts his face from the book and whispers, "Damn savage."

Sometimes, after class, the kids take revenge. They wait for me to turn a corner, surround me, call me names, pound and kick me. Just the same, I know these kids are my problem. "Don't come crying to me," mom says. "You've got to learn how to defend yourself. There's always going to be people like that around." I learn to fight back with my fists.

The teachers, though, are another matter. "The Lachine *Battle*," mom says that evening, emphasizing the word, "was against a defended village and in retaliation for Champlain's massacre of hundreds of Mohawk women, children, and old people the year before. That bastard burned five villages to the ground. The men were off trading with the British." Then mom reaches into one of those stacks of paper, or into a box full of clippings, and pulls out the document she wants. "Here," she says, shoving the paper at me, "go back and tell your teacher that side of the story. And tell him to do his homework. If you have any problems, come back and tell me."

Mom is like that: never one to back down from a fight, proud, and exceedingly stubborn. Fight with your mind too, she teaches. She says she's this way because she's just like her mother, Lena TewateronhiaKotha Nicholas. Grandma was just as ready to fight, just as proud, and even more stubborn, if that were possible. In 1950, she noticed a Belgian-owned lumber company preparing to chop down the pine trees above the town of Oka. She confronted the loggers and read part of the Royal Proclamation of 1763, which said that Indian land was not to be "molested or disturbed" without Indian consent. She told the loggers to get lost—this was Mohawk land.

They didn't leave, so she marched down to confront the manager. "The next thing I knew," grandma wrote, "we were striking each other and I fell to the ground three or four times. Each time I fell to the ground he hit me. I got right up and hit him back." The much younger and larger man stunned her with a blow to the side of her head. He pulled her head up by her hair with one hand and struck her again with the other. Then he went over and picked up a large chain and was about to use it when grandma got up and glared at him. He took off and called the cops.

A police officer soon showed up at grandma's door. He told her there was a proper way to do things. "That's what I'm trying to do," she yelled back. He wanted her to go to the police station with him. "No," she said. The next day, the officer returned with a warrant for her arrest. She again refused to go with him. He called in three more policemen. One drew his pistol. "Shoot me if you're man enough." I can just see her standing on her porch saying that, with her hands on her hips, that look on her face that made little kids and dogs scurry for cover.

The police didn't give up. They circled around her. She picked up a piece of lumber, swung it, and kept two officers at bay while her brother, Charlie, wrestled with the other. They finally jumped her, dragged her down, subdued her brother, beat her, and then dragged her off to jail in St. Jerome. She spent two days in a cell until her husband and brother managed to raise $950 for bail, a fortune in those days.

A few months later at her trial, grandma refused to swear on the Bible. She wasn't Christian, she said. She was Longhouse, the traditional religion of the Mohawk. The judge just shook his head. The trial was conducted in French, a language she told the judge she couldn't understand. The judge let the trial go on anyway. Grandma was found guilty of assault and fined $250. She was fifty-four years old, a grandmother several times over, and a "criminal" just like her father.

| | | | | | |

WE'RE IN ONE OF THOSE RUNDOWN NEIGHBOURHOOD BARS in North Syracuse that has small reception rooms off to the side. My sisters, nieces, and their husbands are here with me for a surprise party for Aunt Helen's eightieth birthday. She's my mom's aunt, but everyone calls her Aunt Helen. Even my niece's husband in Kahnawake, on the other side of Montreal, calls her Aunt Helen.

She turns the corner and is nearly knocked over by shouts of "Happy Birthday!" I swear she hasn't changed a bit in the forty years since I first remember seeing her: a thin woman with a slim, kind face and sparkling eyes surrounded by silvery-white hair. There are bits of both mom and grandma here. She's engulfed by family—eight children, a dozen or so grandchildren, maybe a dozen more great-grandchildren.

Later, at her apartment, I pull out a book and spread it between the coffee cups on her kitchen table. I point to a black-and-white photograph. It's a picture of her father. Aunt Helen doesn't say a word. She just stares at the picture for a moment. Then she reaches out and gently traces the man in the photo with her right hand. She takes a deep breath and sits back.

"What's the book for?" she wants to know.

"It's a history book for the kids in Kanehsatake," I say.

"Uh-hmm. That's good. They should know where they come from."

We stare at the photograph. The man in the picture is handsome, with a strong, certain face. He has dark, piercing, deep-set eyes. There's a slight smile above a firm chin. He wears a double-breasted, English-cut suit, typical of the style at the turn of the century, with a tie tucked into his vest. A handkerchief is folded into his breast pocket. He looks proud, confident, almost haughty. He's a farmer, a faithkeeper, and a fugitive. Aunt Helen is Kanawatiron's last surviving daughter.

"He was about six feet tall. He had a medium build. He was stubborn, very stubborn, very firm. . . . I don't remember his voice at all," she says.

> But I can remember everyone considered him an honest man. He took care of the community's farm equipment. Not everyone could afford their own tractors or ploughs. Some could afford to chip in to share equipment, but most couldn't. So my father kept the equipment, and people came to borrow it, or he'd take it to plough their fields, or whatever. He helped people. Like when someone was in jail, he'd help take care of their animals. But not too much, because he was always on the run, you know. He was always gone, always running from the police.

HE'S A GHOST, PEOPLE SAY, ALWAYS ONE SMALL STEP AHEAD of the police. A mysterious figure who appears from time to time; draws the people around him; reminds them of their duties to the faces still in the earth, the generations yet unborn; shames them out of resignation and into action by his example. He makes things interesting, all right. When the men with guns come for him, they find only a half-empty coffee cup or a chair still warm. A ghost, they say.

Kanawatiron is already a fugitive at an early age for the crime of cutting firewood. He slips away for eight years, surfacing in Akwesasne, near Cornwall, Ontario. There he studies the laws and ceremonies of the Longhouse and of the government of the Iroquois Confederacy, a participatory democracy in which everyone has a voice, a system of checks and balances in which women hold the reins of power. They are its foundation. Six nation-states bound by one central law—the Iroquois constitution, called the Great Law. George Washington, Thomas Jefferson, and Benjamin Franklin admired it and, according to some, even tried to emulate it in the U.S. Declaration of Independence and Constitution.

The Mohawk are keepers of the eastern door. Their little brothers, the Oneida, come next. The Onondaga are keepers of the council fire, the large fire at the centre of the Longhouse. The Cayuga are brothers of the Seneca, who keep watch over the western door. It's a longhouse with five fires under one roof. Its realm of influence at one time stretches from James Bay south along the Atlantic seaboard to the Carolinas and west to the Mississippi. Later, the house is extended to include the Tuscarora, making it the Six Nations Iroquois Confederacy.

Kanawatiron disappears again. He shows up riding with Buffalo Bill's Wild West Show. There's a photograph back home of a young man wearing a large, floppy cowboy hat and the fringed buckskins of a cavalry Indian scout. It's taken from an advertising billboard. New York. Philadelphia. Boston. I can only wonder what the young man thinks, but he's smiling, a bit player in the "greatest Indian Scout's" nightly vanquishing of the noble red man to the whoops of joy of an audience. Sitting Bull reduced to a cigar store Indian.

Kanawatiron meets and marries the former Hattie Smith of Springfield, Massachusetts. She's the daughter of immigrants from Scotland who have settled around the Boston area. Highland people, from what I've been able to gather. Clan people. People who know the English all too well. She's blessed with flaming red hair and a gentle face. She's short of stature but strong of character. And very, very stubborn. She'll have to be, because they're going back to Kanehsatake.

Wash your eyes so you may see clearly. Wash your ears so you may hear again. Wash your head so you may think clear thoughts. Wash your heart to rid yourself of anger, doubt, and fear. Wash your body so you may know who you are and be certain, proud, and strong. Give thanks to the Creator for all who have come before and all those yet to come. Ask for guidance in your actions—not for yourself but so you may keep in mind your children's children's children. All my relations.

| | | | | | |

49

IN 1899, KANAWATIRON RETURNS TO FIND HIS PEOPLE walking with their heads bowed, eyes scanning the ground instead of the sky. They've been warned that this day would come, but they're blinded by doubt and fear. The blackrobes, priests of the St. Sulpician order, are determined to drive them off the land by making their lives at Kanehsatake unliveable. Every family has a story of relatives arrested for cutting wood on their own land for fuel to heat their homes, for lumber to build and repair with, for materials to earn money by making lacrosse sticks, snowshoes, and baskets.

Every family has buried children too young. Every family has relatives whose land was taken by the priests and sold to French Canadian settlers while the relatives were hunting or gone for work to support their families. By the time Kanawatiron returns, less than one percent of the original land granted to them 180 years before remains in Mohawk hands.

Kanawatiron has no doubts, no fears. He's just returned from that great altar of learning, the travelling change rooms of the Wild West Show. His teachers have been medicine men such as Sitting Bull. His classmates have been Osage, Cherokee, and Passamaquoddy. He understands that the danger doesn't come in the form of minor laws, such as those prohibiting the harvest of wood, but in the grander schemes of the two most powerful forces in Quebec at the time—the Catholic Church and the federal government.

The Seminary of St. Sulpice and the federal Department of Indian Affairs have found a common goal in the Mohawks of Kanehsatake. For the seminary to have clear title to the land, the Mohawks must go. It's as simple as that. This suits the department just fine because it has embarked on an inflexible policy of assimilation. In the words of a silver-tongued bureaucrat, a Canadian cultural icon, Deputy Superintendent of Indian Affairs Duncan Campbell Scott, the aim is to "remove every vestige of Indianness" from the Indian until there are "no more Indians and no more Indian problem."

To do this at Kanehsatake, they have to destroy the Longhouse. Stamp out the fire that burns there. Take that which Washington, Jefferson, and Franklin admired and forever remove it from the collective memory of the people and replace it with the Indian Act. The act is an abomination that rips out the vocal chords of the people, reduces women to chattel, and places all power over the lives of people, from birth to death, into the hands of those more accustomed to managing rocks, trees, and fish.

For many years already, the songs and ceremonies of the people have been driven underground, forced into hiding by some among them who regard the old ways as "witchcraft" and "voodoo." They want to accept the trappings of "civilized" society and to assimilate. Many have abandoned their ceremonies and even their language. Life is hard. Maybe things will be easier this way. A choice. A fork in the road. Kanawatiron has no intention of walking down the path chosen for him by the priests and the Indian agents, because he knows it leads only one way—to oblivion.

He also knows that replacing the Great Law and all it represents with the Indian Act is a cheap bit of legal legerdemain, a clumsy magician's attempt to distract the audience's attention while he palms the five-dollar bill and replaces it with worthless scrip. It doesn't fool Kanawatiron, nor does it fool clan mothers in Akwesasne who, in 1898, write: "We have considered the elective system as not being intended by us Indians and we would therefore return to our old methods of selecting our life chiefs, according to our Constitution Iroquois government."

Kanawatiron finds the Longhouse at Kanehsatake weak, its adherents few and timid. They've been cowed into submission by constant arrests, fines, and the threats of other Mohawks who condemn them for the increasing wrath of the authorities. Kanawatiron retells the prophecies. He gets the ceremonies going again. Soon he has drawn people in by the sound of social songs and drums. Little kids hang about the Longhouse, soaking in the words of their elders, learning of terrible things in the past and being warned of things yet to come. They hear stories about the Osage, the Cherokee, and the Passamaquoddy. Sitting Bull and his visions. Tobacco burns once more in the council fire, and there is talk of rebuilding the Confederacy and of throwing out the priests and the Indian Act. Kanawatiron has dangerous ideas, and this makes him a dangerous man.

He writes letters and petitions to governments, newspapers, and foreign potentates. He chooses his words carefully. He draws them from acts of Parliament and treaties, from kings and prime ministers, from promises and commitments. He throws their own words back at them. Honour the agreements, he demands, or there will be trouble.

In 1902, the police and the Indian agent surround his home. He watches from behind nearby bushes as the police wave a pistol in his pregnant wife's face. Where is he? they demand. She swears at them, quite fluently at that, in Mohawk. Get off our land, she tells them, quite forcefully, in English. This isn't the first time they've busted into her home in the early morning, rushing from room to room, waving their guns about, shoving her children out of the way, threatening her. The police say they want to arrest her husband for cutting firewood without the priests' permission. If that's so, she asks, why have they been given "shoot-to-kill" orders? Kanawatiron decides it's time he spoke to the king.

The police show up again a few days later, but Kanawatiron and Hattie are gone. They're on a steamship bound for England. He's drawn up a petition. He wants to deliver it—in person—to King Edward VII at Buckingham Palace. When he arrives in London, he is informed about the ruckus he's raised back home in Canada. The dominion secret police are rustling every bush, searching every barn, patrolling every road to arrest him.

He shows up, unannounced, at the gates of Buckingham Palace. He holds a petition in his hand. He wears his best English-cut, double-breasted suit with the handkerchief folded neatly into his breast pocket. A guard arrives to ask his business. Kanawatiron hands him a letter of introduction with his signature, Joseph K. Gabriel, in a long, flowing hand above the X's and the names of the other chiefs of the Longhouse of Kanehsatake.

But the king sends word he will not see my great-grandfather. The royal guard tells him he is not a British subject. He instructs my great-grandfather to go to the American embassy instead.

"What good can the king do?" inquires a reporter.

"Is he not the king?" asks Kanawatiron. "It is to him that I come, to the king of all of us, the great King Edward VII. He can do everything."

But the great King Edward VII does nothing.

The Times of London notes Kanawatiron's visit with a few lines:

There is a dusky Redskin in London endeavouring to obtain an audience of the King, and to lay before the "Great White Father" a grievance of the Iroquois Indians of Canada, which has for generations owned a great tract of land that is being taken from them by the San Joseph Seminary of Montreal.

Chief Joseph said he attempted to obtain admittance to the "King's Palace" but was refused. He says he will now go to the Colonial Secretary and try to arrange through him an audience with his Majesty.

But nothing works. The king still refuses to see him. Kanawatiron and Hattie board a steamer bound for home knowing the police will be waiting. The dominion police and the Quebec provincial police have combined their forces in the manhunt, watching the ports and stepping up patrols around Kanehsatake, more determined than ever to arrest my great-grandfather.

They never catch him. He slips back into the country and goes straight into hiding. He meets a *Montreal Daily Star* reporter who interviews him at a secret rendezvous. Kanawatiron says he'll never give up, never leave his land, "excepting over my dead body." He tells the reporter:

> I remember how my father was sent to gaol for three months for cutting three small logs in the woods to repair his house. I remember how others of my relations, including the father of Beauvais, when they went out in the winter time to cut wood to keep their wives and children warm, were arrested in the bush and carried off to gaol, while their shivering wives and children, not knowing what caused the prolonged absence of their husbands and fathers, vainly waited for the fuel to warm their half-frozen bodies.

The police conduct raid after raid on Kanehsatake, but they never capture him. He's a ghost, occasionally showing up in neighbouring Mohawk territories under assumed names. Sometimes he barely escapes into the woods before the police, the Indian agent, or the priests' hired hands bust down the door to his home. They try to confiscate his personal belongings and farming equipment but arrive to discover that it has all disappeared. Even the head of the band council, Kanawatiron's brother, Angus Corinthe, helps out and is charged with obstruction. Everyone in the territory knows where Kanawatiron hides out, leaves food for him, takes him in at night, warns him when the police approach.

"Kanawatiron used to sleep over there, away from the highway," says Muriel Nicholas. She's eighty-five-years old and one of those "aunts" of mine sprinkled around the territory. From her home about six kilometres west of the Pines in the area known as The Bay, she points to the place near the Ottawa River where she grew up on her father's farm. "That's where we lived—over there. Kanawatiron came in about ten o'clock at night. I don't know if he was walking or he was riding a horse. Anyway, he was running away. They kept him. He was sleeping there until light, then they took him across the river and put him on a train. I don't know where he went. They took him away from Oka so he don't get arrested. Just because he cut the wood."

Headlines from newspapers reflect the mood: "Chief Kennatosse's Wife Hints that There Will Be Bloodshed" and "Detectives Hot on Trail of Chief Kennatosse: Indians Purchase Arms." The Mohawk, weary from police raids, fed up with arrests and detentions, stock up on food and buy every pistol they can find on the shelves of stores in nearby towns. The Department of Indian Affairs sends in police to protect the lives of the French Canadian residents of the neighbouring town of Oka. It is a scene eerily like the events that lead up to the police raids and the Oka Crisis eighty-eight years later.

Kanawatiron stays in hiding, coming out only occasionally to stop a railway or to confront surveyors planting stakes on another piece of land that once belonged to a Mohawk family. Then he slips back into hiding, swallowed up by the forests around Kanehsatake. Eventually, tired of running, increasingly isolated as his own people turn against him and toward the Indian Act band council, he surrenders himself to the police on the advice of his lawyer. It's been seven years since he went to England and fifteen years since he first went into hiding. He wants his day in court. The only charge the police have against him is for cutting wood without the priests' permission. After four years of court battles, the charges are dropped. He's exonerated.

| | | | | | |

BUT NOT IN THE EYES OF THE DEPARTMENT OF INDIAN Affairs and the police. For the rest of his life, they continue to hound Kanawatiron. In 1923, the Indian agent goes to his farm to ask him why his children aren't in residential school. He's hiding his children from Indian Affairs truant officers, believing, correctly, that residential schools are less about education than about assimilation. They get into a shouting match. The Indian agent leaves but later returns with a police officer, charging my great-grandfather with assault. It costs $200 for bail. He walks sixty kilometres home. He's arrested again. He raises bail again, walks home again. And so it goes.

A lawyer and friend of Kanawatiron writes to complain about the police harassment to the minister of Indian Affairs. He says the courts have thrown out the assault charges on the ground that the Indian agent lied. The court finds all the charges to be trumped up, "pretended," in the jargon of the time. Kanawatiron also sets a precedent, arguing that provincial authorities have no right to take Indian children away from their families and place them in residential schools. The lawyer wants the minister to reimburse Kanawatiron for his legal fees, which total the princely sum of $1,239.90. He writes that Kanawatiron and Hattie "have been treated outrageously and wrongfully":

> For his trial Chief Gabriel was obliged to go four times with his seven witnesses to St. Jerome and St. Scholastic where they had to remain several days each time . . . thus causing him heavy expense and loss of time which he could not afford. After keeping poor Gabriel on a hot griddle, so to speak, for a period of two years during which time he was held as a prisoner several times, put in jail, called upon to give bail many times, dragged to court many miles from home many times, put to expense which he is not able to bear, harassed and annoyed beyond human endurance, the Jury returned a verdict of "Not Guilty." Shortly after this, under another section of the Criminal Law, the same charge for the same pretended offense was laid against him and he was again arrested and put through the same humiliating procedure and ruinous expense for one more year, to wit, until the 5th of February 1926 when the charge was again dismissed.

The minister replies that he is "convinced that some powerful influence has been used against the Oka Indians and that they and Gabriel have been 'agrivated' for years regularly and constantly" and that there appears to be "sufficient ground to warrant the Government in reimbursing Gabriel what it has cost him, in time and money, to carry his defense."

But the minister doesn't run Indian Affairs. His deputy does, and Duncan Campbell Scott's reply is short and to the point: "I have nothing to add to the letter which was addressed to you by the [minister] . . . further than that the Indians of Oka have always been treated most generously by the Department, and you are quite at liberty to take any action in the courts that you may consider necessary on Gabriel's behalf."

| | | | | | |

THE NEXT YEAR, 1927, HATTIE KATSITSENHAWI GABRIEL leaves her husband. She moves in with her daughter, my grandmother Lena TewateronhiaKotha Nicholas, taking half of their twelve children with her. "It was hard on my mom," says Helen Adams, Hattie's last surviving daughter,

> because she'd have to take care of all of us kids by herself. She'd have to feed us, clothe us, take care of the farm, take care of the animals and the garden all by herself most of the time. The police or the Indian agent would just bust into the house like they owned it. They had no warrant or anything. They'd just come in, push my mom around, wave their guns around, look upstairs in the bedrooms and everything. They were always doing that, trying to catch my father to arrest him for one thing or another. My mother didn't have much money, so we didn't have much food. Sometimes people would come and share food with us so we could have enough to eat. But they didn't have much either. The police were always arresting them too. They had a hard time feeding their own families.

Aunt Helen says that despite the hardship her mom stuck by her father and left him only when she'd had enough of the beatings. She remembers him coming home occasionally from hiding to find the farm in disrepair or the animals and garden untended. "And he would beat her and us kids as well. It was hard. It was very hard." But she also remembers him as a man who never gave up and was "always fighting the church, the government, and the police. This made them mad, and they made life hard for everyone. In the end, a lot of people blamed my father for making life difficult. After a while, my father and a few of his friends, Longhouse people, were all alone in the fight. They never gave up."

Hattie remains in Kanehsatake for a year. She speaks Mohawk better than a lot of Mohawks. She's adopted into the Longhouse and knows its laws and ceremonies better than most people in the territory. She's written many of the letters and petitions on her husband's behalf. She dies in 1938 in Syracuse surrounded by two sons and two daughters.

Kanawatiron continues to fight after his wife leaves him. The same year, he helps to win another precedent-setting court case. Paul Diabo, a Mohawk from Kahnawake, is arrested by American immigration authorities for working in the United States without a visa. Kanawatiron and other Longhouse chiefs argue that Diabo's arrest is a violation of the Jay Treaty of 1794; the treaty allows Indians to live and work across the international border. The judge rules: "The Indian is a member of an Indian nation and while it is not reckoned as one of the United States, he is, nevertheless, a ward of this country and no matter where he lives, the law considers his home to be the territory of the United States."

In 1935, Kanawatiron dies penniless and alone in Kanehsatake. Police and government officials harass him until the end. His farm and animals are auctioned off to pay his legal bills. He is buried in the Mohawk cemetery under the Pines at the top of the hill overlooking the town of Oka. It's the same cemetery a mayor of Oka will try to bulldoze fifty-five years later—leading to the Mohawk rebellion of 1990.

> We must care for the spirits of our ancestors, for they do not leave us—they are around us everywhere, always. They sit on our shoulders guiding us. We must burn tobacco to strengthen them and to carry our thoughts to them. We must feed them so they may be strong and healthy. We must welcome them when they visit us in our dreams. We must honour them and respect them, or else we wound them, causing them harm and harming ourselves as well. All my relations.

| | | | | | |

IN LONDON, TWO DAYS BEFORE OUR AUDIENCE WITH THE queen, I'm ushered into an office. I'm told the Commonwealth has a problem with me. The Canadian government has decided I'm not Canadian after all, will not see the queen, won't go to the South

Pacific, will have to return to Canada. I ask to be left alone for a while to think about what I'll do.

"You don't have much choice," I'm told.

"There's always a choice," I reply. A fork in the road.

I go to my apartment and burn tobacco. All I want is to get away, to forget the nightmares that flood over me night after night. I'm tired of fighting. I just want peace. All along, though, I've known that I'm not here for myself—I've come here for others: the people back home who made my moccasins, breechcloth, and leggings; who spent long hours over a sewing table stitching my scarlet ribbon shirt; who fashioned, cleansed, and blessed my medicine bundle; and who made my *kastowah*. But I also feel others looking over my shoulder, nudging me in a certain direction, whispering in my ear.

That night I type a letter. I do the same thing my great-grand-father would have done. I take the words of powerful people, promises and commitments, and hurl them back. I explain that I've been told by a senior official at the Department of External Affairs to "Get the American passport. Fly to London. We'll straighten things out when you get there." I fax the letter to Canada House.

The next day, an official calls on me and says that my situation is causing some problems and embarrassment in Ottawa. "Good," I say. He wants me to forget the whole thing and return to Canada. I say I'll drop off my American passport at the American embassy, become stateless, a refugee if you will. Then I'll march on down to the *Times* of London, just as my great-grandfather did nearly ninety years before. I'll tell the whole story. I add: "After 1990, you don't think I'd really trust anybody from the Canadian government, do you? I tape all of my phone conversations—especially when I know there's somebody from the government on the other end of the line. I'm sure the *Times* would be very interested in hearing a tape recording of that official in Ottawa for themselves. You know as well as I do that this is bullshit. You guys got me here. You work it out."

That night I can almost hear the telephone and fax lines buzzing between Ottawa and London. I can imagine the names the govern-ment officials must be calling me. But for the first time in a long while, I feel good about myself. Whatever happens, I am my great-grandfather's granddaughter's son. I'm walking in his footsteps. I know he wants—finally—to be welcomed into Buckingham Palace.

In the morning: "I've got good news," an official of the Commonwealth tells me. "You can complete your fellowship. You'll accompany us to our audience with the queen tomorrow." So we celebrate, James, Peter, and I.

The next morning, I slip my breechcloth over my leggings. I put on my ribbon shirt. I smooth the feathers of my *kastowah* and adjust my medicine bundle so it hangs from my braided belt. Then I put on my moccasins and go out to be with my friends, who have come from every corner of the world.

We pile into a van and drive through the crowds at the gates in front of the palace. Suddenly, we're standing in alphabetical order in an anteroom, making last-minute adjustments to our various forms of national dress, waiting to be summoned. I'm first in line. I feel strangely calm and not at all alone. On the other side of the doors in front of us, Her Royal Majesty awaits.

The doors swing open. I stroll down the length of this huge room toward a little, grey-haired woman in a summer dress. She looks surprisingly like my mother. I stop and nod.

"Are you some kind of an Indian?" she asks in that familiar voice.

"Yes, I am, Your Majesty," I reply, slightly confused but pulling myself up to my full height. "I'm from Canada."

"Oh," she continues. "What kind of an Indian are you?"

"A Mohawk," I say.

"A Mohawk." She pauses slightly. "You're not one of those naughty Mohawks, are you?"

I wait for a second before answering "Yes, ma'am, I am."

All my relations.

1997

| | | | | | |

Fiddle and Bow
A Fugue Essay

| | | | | | |

Kim Echlin

| | | | | | |

A Little of Both

I SEE JOHN DODD, A VIOLIN BOW MAKER, TRIPPING ALONG in frayed coat and broad-brimmed hat toward the Richmond public house as he does four times a day to drink "purl," his personal mixture of gin and beer. The bows he makes command exorbitant prices for their trueness and beauty. He will die impoverished in a workhouse, but he refuses to take on an apprentice or even an offer of a thousand silver coins to reveal the secrets of his bow making. He will be asked on his deathbed in 1839 if he is a Catholic or a Protestant, and he will answer, "A little of both."

A century and a half later, a young bow maker stands in a sunny Canadian workshop holding an original Dodd bow. She does not know about his drinking habits or what he said on his deathbed. She knows only that his secrets disappeared with him, except for what she can glean from the bow itself. She fingers it wistfully and thinks, "How do I make something as beautiful as this?" Her question is both humble and elusive. It is merely one aesthetic question, yet one that includes the whole art.

The Way without a Map

THE FIRST KNOWN PAINTING OF A VIOLIN AND BOW IS *The Madonna of the Orange Trees* (1529–30) by Gaudenzio Ferrari. Sitting at the feet of the madonna and her baby is a chubby, winged cherub holding the instrument. The cherub has just finished playing, his chin lifting, his bow elbow opening up to let the bow fall. He plays the music of the spheres for the arrival of the Christ, the holy chorus on the fallen Earth.

But it is not this decorous, heavenly music that intrigues me as much as other, more disorderly and searching noises. I am drawn to the Greek idea of *aporia,* the necessary confusion that leads to clarity. I am interested in all the voices inside a fiddle and how to hear them.

No one knows how old the bow and violin are, or where the instrument's two names, violin and fiddle, come from. Their predecessors are bow-and-string instruments such as the *crewth,* the *viol da Gamba,* the Arabian *rebab,* the *vielle,* the *organistrum,* the *chyphonie,* and the *rebec.* These earlier instruments were sometimes three-stringed, sometimes four or five, sometimes tuned in fifths, sometimes not, shaped like triangles, pears, and eights. The most immediate predecessors of today's violin appeared in the sixteenth century, viols with such tempting names as *viola da braccio* and *viola d'amour.*

The violin enjoyed great popular favour in brothels and taverns. Then in France, in 1628, it was banned from cabarets and "places of ill repute" by ordinance of the Civil Lieutenant of Paris. Censorship asks us (perversely) to value something, and, if the violin was to be reserved for places such as the court, then what was to play all that sunny music from the brothels?

Fiddlesticks!

THE WORD *FIDDLE* HAS OBSCURE ORIGINS IN THE OLD English *fipele/vedel* and the Latin *vitulari,* meaning "to celebrate a festival," "to be joyful." Fiddling has the feeling of breaking rules. Traditional fiddlers will often say they don't hold the bow "right." What they mean is they don't use the classical hand position. Nigel Kennedy, a virtuoso violinist known for his work in jazz, punk, and popular music, says, "We may play dead composers' works, but we don't have to look as if we're still at the funeral." Cheekily, he calls his Stradivarius and his Guarneri violins his fiddles and refers to his music as fiddling.

62

The word *fiddle* is trickier than *violin,* happy to stray into extra-musical realms. A fiddler was once simply a trifler, a mirth maker who talked fiddle-faddle. *Fiddling* can still mean "to be busy with trifles." To fiddle a contract is to alter it in unorthodox ways. Fiddle is a word that embraces celebration, idleness, frivolity. It has about it a certain trickiness and a whiff of the Fall.

The World of Tiny Precision

WHETHER ONE CALLS THE INSTRUMENT A VIOLIN OR A fiddle, the bow is always the bow. Some have called the fiddle the body and the bow the soul. I wanted to know how a soul is strung, so I went to the workshop of Philip Davis, luthier.

If I were to imagine what it is like to be inside a young monk's head—flesh and bone and blood, but clearly preoccupied with higher things—I'd say that it resembles the feeling in the Davis workshop. His room has a large window at its far end, two work benches, walls mounted with fine woodworking tools, and violins and bows hanging and lying in various states of disrepair. In this atmosphere of pleasing serenity, fiddles and bows are contemplated, caressed, repaired, created.

"The best bow hair probably comes from Mongolia," says Philip, "followed by Canada. The horse must be all white, and it takes about six years to grow out to the right length, thirty to thirty-two inches. They say male hair is smoother, female rougher, I wouldn't know about that. After pollarding, gathering it from around the outside of the tail, it has to be dressed, combed out, and cleaned. Sometimes it is bleached."

He takes a round hank of the horsehair out of a plastic bag to let me see. As I reach my index finger toward it, he says, "It can cost anywhere from four to eleven hundred dollars a pound. Horsehair isn't used generally as much as it used to be, for stuffed furniture and that sort of thing. Did you know that in World War I, five million people died? Three times that number of horses died."

Philip leads me to his tidy workbench. "The hair of the bow is very strong, equal to high-tensile steel, and the wood of the bow needs the right balance of strength and density. You think of the violinist bouncing along at some incredible pace. When we're working with it, we're controlling two- or three-tenths of a millimetre in the timbring of the stick."

He points to the fine tip of a bow that had cracked. He repaired it by "splicing" in a sliver of wood, sanding and finishing the mend to near invisibility.

"There are big stresses on the bow and the hair," he says. "It's possible to play right through the hair." He runs his fingers over the delicate tip of the bow. "I only tackle the bow tip when my nerves feel good." He chuckles amiably and leads me over to meet his apprentice, Christina.

She began her apprenticeship after seeing a violin and bow in a store window one day. She walked in, bought them, and took lessons. But she discovered that she didn't want to play as much as she wanted to hold, touch, and look at the instrument, so she decided to learn how to make them.

She takes some hair out of a flat bag, places it in a vice, and starts to comb it out. "I wet the hair and comb it using a series of smaller and smaller combs. I like doing this part, it's sort of Zen-like."

When it is perfectly even, she pinches together the end and deftly ties it with a piece of linen thread. The knot is made ten millimetres from the end; then the hair is whipped with a series of knots, top and bottom, and the end is singed to the very edge of the linen thread. The burning creates microscopic mushroom caps on the hair that keep it from slipping. Christina flicks a lighter and brings the flame close to her exquisite knot. I watch the flame burning closer and closer through the hair. Christina drops the fire away just as the light illuminates the linen thread. She looks up and smiles. "That's nerve wracking the first few times."

The frog is a tiny insert that slips into a depression in the bottom of the bow called the mortise. Christina shows me how the hair is held by the frog in the mortise. Edges of forty-five degrees must be cut in tiny wedges to prevent slippage. The wedge is soft enough to take the imprint of the hair. There is also a tiny cut made on the mortise. She manipulates fine woodworking tools with deft gestures spanning tenths of millimetres. "It is a world of tiny precision," she says, finally straightening up with a critical glance at her work.

Christina has a platonic image of the ideal frog in the ideal mortise in the ideal bow clearly measured and cut in her head. She is ready to slip the frog into the mortise to anchor the hair. It slides in beautifully, but she's not satisfied, pries it out, and gently shaves and reshapes. "There is so much premeasuring."

"But you can't measure for the weather," says Philip from across the workshop. "The wood is very humidity sensitive. Sometimes we have to adjust by as much as a whole millimetre."

Under a microscope, the horsehair looks like a rod encrusted with fish scales. The scales take the rosin, giving the hair its grip on the strings of the violin. Insufficient grip makes the note hard and strident. Soft grip creates a more mellow tone.

I ask Philip how it feels to watch someone playing with a bow he's strung. He smiles.

> I don't play at all well, and it is as close as I can get to being on stage. Sometimes in a concert I hold my breath when a violinist is using a bow I've strung, especially when they're going at a pace and really bouncing off the strings. It's like watching a mast bend in the wind. I always wonder if it's going to hold. I am probably the only person in the audience, listening, watching, and worrying if the bow will crack. Sometimes I get this terrible feeling of vertigo.

He takes an exquisite old bow out of a glass case on the wall and runs his fingers down the stick. "Bows sell from sixty dollars for little fibreglass ones to sixty thousand. The bows of certain masters, François Tourte, John Dodd, can go up around a hundred thousand."

Christina is already bent over her second bow of the day, tying a strong and tiny knot, a quiet apprentice maker of souls. She has learned to duplicate the traditional knots, and she is experimenting with different knots, looking for something a little better. She has created one of her own.

Philip pauses a moment in the serenity of the workshop, then carefully puts the bow back. "Such a price for a stick of wood."

The Sound of the World

THE VIOLIN AND THE BOW ARE MADE OF CREATURES AND plants from the farthest reaches of the Earth. The back, neck, ribs, and bridge of the body of the violin are made of maple or plane wood.

The belly, moulds, linings, and sound post are made of spruce. The finger board, nuts, pegs, tailpiece, and button are made of ebony or rosewood. The strings of the violin are fashioned with the intestinal membranes extracted from the carcass of a sheep while it is still warm, preferably a sheep raised on dry pastures in a hilly country. Good bows are made of campeachy wood, iron wood, Brazil wood, and Pernambuco. The exotic frog can be ebony, tortoise shell, horn, and ivory. I hear the screams of hunted elephants, the groans of men slaving for pennies a day cutting wood, the astonished gasp of a sheep whose neck is being slit. I see the frightened eyes of a great sea turtle trying to swim into darkness. A violin sings too from the exquisite torture of the world.

But it is the varnishes that I love. Like a thick, wet kiss, varnish alters the sonority of the instrument. There are legends of varnishes made from the blood of dead lovers. I revel in dictionaries of varnishes as others revel in the sounds of the violin itself. Listen to the following descriptions.

Amber: A fossil gum or resin found along the shores of the Baltic and North Seas, especially on the promontory of Smaland, cast up by the sea, and collected at ebb tide with nets.

Cinnabar (vermilion): An ore of mercury, cochineal-red to lead-grey.

Copaiba: An oleoresin from trees of the copaifera species found in the West Indies and the valley of the Amazon.

Dragon's blood: The best gum dragon or dragon's blood is obtained from the Calamus draco, a rotang or mattan palm of the eastern Archipelago and India.

Turmeric: Terra merita or curcum (*safran d'Inde:* Indian saffron), made of the old roots of the Curcuma longa, a plant of the ginger family.

Vermilion: see cinnabar. Lesser-used gums include frankincense from the silver fir, Bombay aloes from Socotra, myrrh, the resin of the Arabian *Baesynnian Balsamodendron* myrrha, exuded in thick yellow drops found in commerce in the shape of tears.

What an animate instrument is this fiddle with its bow, transformed from trees and sheep gut and blood rinsed away, from frankincense and myrrh, gifts of a magi. How alive it is with the Earth and the extravagant invention of its first makers.

Which Makes the Music, the Fiddle or the Bow?

EVERY VIOLINIST OR FIDDLER SAYS BOTH. SOME SAY, "THE colour comes from the bowing." And others, "The tension is in the fingering." "Without good bow technique, the left hand's in a mess." "But if the fingering's off, you're out of tune!"

The only thing everyone reluctantly agrees on is that the rhythm is (mostly) in the bow.

Strathspey and Reel

IN NASHVILLE, THEY REFER TO NATALIE MACMASTER'S FIDDLE and step-dancing finale as "the best seven minutes in show business." Stepping and playing, the stage lights bouncing off her flying hair, MacMaster turns her gaze inward, and she bows as if her bow were the axis of the world. Once, opening for Carlos Santana in front of 80,000 people, she broke a string and continued dancing and playing on her bottom two strings to an entranced crowd. When she plays like that, it is impossible to say whether she is possessed by angels or devils. Her performances are ecstatic.

She is a young fiddler from Cape Breton. She is part of a current vogue for traditional music "jazzed up," as performed by Ashley MacIsaac, a former neighbour, Mary Jane Lamond, and Cookie Rankin. MacMaster was brought up in a musical family, and she began playing at the age of nine, when she was given her first small fiddle. Her uncle, Buddy MacMaster, is a master of Cape Breton fiddle, and she has listened to traditional Cape Breton music all her life. The delicacy of her heart-shaped face and her soft-spoken manner belie a determined quest for technical and expressive excellence and a fierce devotion to the tradition of her music.

I telephoned MacMaster down east to ask her what she thinks about tradition and the music she is recording.

"I really want to sound Cape Breton most times," she said. "I find myself listening to the old Cape Breton fiddlers to enhance my own Cape Breton sound. When you're performing a lot, your style can get all glitzy, but I always bring myself back to the Cape Breton style. This is the real meat and potatoes."

"But what makes you individual in your tradition?" I insisted.

"The reason why I am individual is that everybody is individual. Everybody has their own style, the way their fingers are made up, the way their fiddle sounds, the way they hold their bow. How many different personalities are there? Well, there's that many different fiddle sounds. I don't want to sound like anyone else. But I want to be a Cape Breton fiddler."

For generations, the fiddle has had a folk presence in Cape Breton, around kitchen tables, at weddings and dances. Fiddlers learn tunes from each other, credit each other, and then improvise on the music they learn. Tradition dictates that they be adaptable. One traditional Cape Breton fiddler, Hugh Angus Jobes, born in 1906 and much in demand as an entertainer in earlier decades, would play four or five nights a week after he'd worked all day at a neighbour's farm. He played solo at weddings and community dances from 8 p.m. to 1 a.m. Unsentimental, he welcomed microphones. "I find it a lot easier," he said. "And anyway, when you turn it up, you don't have to work so hard or play so hard."[1] That makes a difference to someone who is expected to fiddle for five or more hours at a stretch.

The techniques specific to Cape Breton fiddling are left-hand fingering patterns with grace notes and embellishments (reminiscent of those played by a Highland bagpiper), doubling (playing two strings in unison), and unique fourth-finger placement to avoid playing on an open string. Cape Breton bowing is distinguished by its "cuts," *spiccato* bowing (up-and-down strokes), and *saltando* bowing (single-direction strokes). Such "bouncing" bow techniques require a loose wrist and the hand position two centimetres or more above the frog, which is different from the "proper" classical grip. Cape Breton fiddlers often use special tunings, open-fifth drone pitches, and foot tapping, step dancing, or clogging to make complementary rhythms. The overall effect is full of life.

"Catharsis," MacMaster's favourite piece on her newest recording, is an arrangement that both draws on the tradition and embellishes it with electronic sounds and a driving rhythm. It is a reel by Amy Cann, a Vermont-based fiddler, popular in contra dance circles in New England. Natalie learned it in a pub session in Edinburgh, Scotland, and has Cape Bretonized it with her bowing. The guitar and keyboards are electric, the beat rock and roll. "Catharsis" is far from a strictly traditional sound.

Yet MacMaster insists, "I don't try to make my style individual. I don't think like that at all. I'm the opposite. I want to sound Cape Breton. That's my tradition." She tells the kind of lie that provokes us toward clarity. She keeps alive traditional music by playing it and adding something to it. Like Nigel Kennedy with his classical violin, she is passionate about the old music, but she's not about to play as if she were at a funeral.

MacMaster feels valued in her tradition, but she's no longer playing with her relatives around the kitchen table. Ten thousand people are at an outside stage waiting for her. The evening is warm and the lights are shining and the smoke machine's going. She's a tiny figure with a little fiddle on a big stage, and—as she says—she has to pump out the goods.

Incidentally, MacMaster uses a bow strung by Philip Davis. When he watches her up on stage stepping and bowing through the smoke, he holds his breath.

The Great Mother

TRADITION IS INESCAPABLE. "NO POET, NO ARTIST OF ANY sort, has his complete meaning alone," wrote T.S. Eliot; ". . . you must set him, for contrast and comparison, among the dead."

And then there is *aporia,* the way without a map, the search for clarity by entering obscurity. Creativity has a little of both.

We do not know where the first violin came from. There are two marble figurines from the Cyclades dating from 2500 BC that are shaped in the astonishingly precise form of the violin. They are thought to be idols of the primordial goddess. It is not so surprising, then, that Gaudenzio Ferrari's cherub should be holding a violin at the madonna's feet. The shape of the violin is the shape of the Great Mother herself, before she was the mother of Christ, when she was the unfettered Mother of All.

Left Hand and Right

GLASS HOUSES #5
Playing Plan   Ann Southam.

The tunes on the "tune sheet" are to be played in the
following order. All tunes are to be played 4 times
each time around except for tune no. 2 which is
to be played twice each time around and no. 15
which is to be played only once.

1, 2, 3, 4
1, 2, 3, 4
1, 2, 3, 4, 5
1, 2, 3, 4, 5, 6, 5
1, 2, 3, 4, 5, 6, 7, 6, 5
1, 2, 3, 4, 5, 6, 7, 8, 7, 6, 5
1, 2, 3, 4, 5, 6, 7, 8, 9, 10, 5, 6, 5
1, 2, 3, 4, 5, 6, 7, 8, 9, 10, 9, 11,
  12, 13, 11, 12, 13
1, 2, 3, 4, 5, 6, 7, 8, 9, 10, 11, 12, 13
1, 14, 15.

                Dur. Approx 8'46"

Left Hand and Right

THESE ARE THE FIRST THREE BARS OF ANN SOUTHAM'S COMPO-
sition for piano, *Glass Houses No. 5*. The "Playing Plan" shows how
the repeating seven-note phrase of the left hand and the "tunes" of
the right hand are put together. When I try to play the first bar, I am
struck not by the unusually fast tempo or the consonant, delightful
sound of the simple C major key but by how cursedly difficult it is to
play seven notes with the left hand and six with the right hand. In this
piece, Southam is asking me to think differently on my right side and
on my left side, and this makes me attend to melody in a new way.
She is asking me to consider how mutable rhythm can be. The piece,
meant to be played extraordinarily fast, has a mad, dancelike quality,
like a child spinning in faster and faster circles or rolling down a hill.
After working on the first bar, I understand, with mind, ears and
hands, that beyond the calm order implied by the apparently simple
patterns of numbers, Southam works from a rebellious heart.

This is called process music, a form that has thrown out the
traditional narrative line. Southam claims that she does not work out
of *any* musical tradition, that she hates Beethoven and rejects the
secrets of Mozart and Haydn. I ask her what she does like.

"I like the *process*," says Southam, sixty. We are sitting in her
kitchen in Toronto looking out on an elegantly leafy back patio. Her
bird book and binoculars are on the table, and she has just sighted a
migrating redstart. She is the great-granddaughter of the founder of
the Southam publishing empire, and—although she prefers to talk
more about ideas and music than herself—she mentions that during
a period of illness as a girl she loved to listen to music in her bedroom
on her small Northern Electric radio, especially the "happy half-hour
with Don Messer and his Islanders." The small girl who found
pleasure in this immensely popular radio show with its folk music and
"dancey" rhythms became the quietly defiant woman who studied
with Gustav Ciamaga in his new electronic music studio at the
University of Toronto in the 1960s. She was the first composer-in-
residence for the fledgling Toronto Dance Theatre, where she was able
to hear her work performed with a frequency most young composers
only dream of. Working much against the grain, she rejected all classical music and resolutely worked out of a plain passion to discover
her own ideas and sound. Her story reminds me of the young Martha

Graham, who put aside her dance training to work alone in a bare studio searching with her body for a new way of moving.

"I *can* listen to Bach," Southam says. "To my ear, his music and East Coast fiddle music have the same shapes and rhythms. But he's a man, too, isn't he? That pisses me off."

"So you work out of a tradition of being pissed off?" I ask.

She laughs, then says, "That is the tradition. You're quite right. Consciously enraged. Consciously resisting. It's the notion of men taking up so much room and having a lot of power. The men in my family carried a lot of weight and then there was this God who was a man, and he had this *son*. Where was I to go in this universe? There was no place to go. I've been struggling with this impression of the world since I was small. I was left with this very small space in which I could work and not much material left over to work with."

But there was a place to go, to a brand new field of music: electroacoustics. "There wasn't a hell of a lot of tradition there to come bearing down on me," Southam says, "and nobody really knew how things were supposed to be done, so I could set my own course, choose my own material. It didn't have to be written down. That was very freeing."

Later, when she heard Terry Riley's minimalist piece "A Rainbow in Curved Air" and loved its "sunny" quality, she returned to notes. She began to listen to Steve Reich, who was experimenting with repetition. She liked the new vocabulary of minimalist music, "cells" of material forming a flow of sound, which in effect replaced the traditional line of melody.

How to describe the sound of a piece such as "Glass Houses No. 5"? It is the sound of a single piano, the left hand playing the same pattern of seven notes over and over. Against that, the right hand plays fifteen "tunes" in different time signatures. The tempo is startlingly quick, rhythmic, and bright. It sounds like a clean brook purling straight over the rugged face of a bare mountain. At first, the patterns are elusive, in a way that the harmonies of familiar classical music are not. Then, after repeated listening, little lyrical "tunes" emerge. I feel in this music the intense energy that leads to serenity.

Southam's preoccupations and thought are wide ranging. A more recent musical interest is how to catch the anonymous dailiness of life—repetitive tasks, repetitive possibilities—in sound. This is the idea Southam explores in a piano piece called "Given Time," in which she tries to express the repetitious labour and patience that frame so many lives. She says, "You don't ever just wash the dishes once and that's it, and now you can get on to the next thing. There has to be a willingness to keep doing this unheroic, life-sustaining work." She leans back in her chair, lifts a large hand in front of her face, and adds wryly, "Not that I ever had to do any of that sort of work, but that's the idea."

"I remember reading a Sandra Birdsell story in which a woman hanging out the laundry day after day amuses herself by hanging it according to different colour combinations," I said.

"There you have it. The continuing process of domestic work, but the woman varies it," said Southam.

> I like that. I wrote "Given Time" as a performance piece for *Dancing the Goddess,* a celebration of the sacred feminine in dance. It was for solo piano, and I had a B flat chord—I love the warmth of that chord—and a row (of single notes) was presented one note at a time against the B flat. Sitting in the curve of the piano was a visual artist, Aiko Suzuki. She was wearing the funny outfit that she always wears no matter what, and she was working with three pieces of yarn. In the end, there was nothing to show for any of it, just the work. I thought it worked. It was so understated. I wouldn't mind exploring things like that a bit more. It is about the quiet going on.

The two components of composition, according to Southam, are idea and sound. She wants both to be sensual and pleasing. She says, "I hope that the audience likes the feel of the ideas on their brains, the *feel* of the sound on their brains."

The sound most deeply buried in Southam's acoustic memory is that of Don Messer's fiddle. The same sophisticated, feminist sensibility that chooses to reject Beethoven returns over and over to the fiddle, the ancient instrument shaped like the great mother, the folk instrument whose bow hold and fingering cheekily defy classical conventions, the brothel instrument once banned by the courts. Southam is interested in things that have suffered censorship—the four neglected notes of the twelve-tone scale, the female composer.

Although she asserts her rage at a world of music in which there are so many male voices, she has listened through those voices for what she likes, for what gave her pleasure as a child, for the shapes and "dancey" rhythms of fiddle music.

Southam says, "I think the fiddle looks wonderful. I identify with whoever's playing. I like it when they dance around and make their bows fly through the air. When I compose, I sometimes have the look of it in mind."

Transparent Things

ROSIN IS THE SMALLEST ELEMENT OF BOW MAKING. ROSIN rubbed on the bow hair is what creates sound on the strings. Without it, there is not enough friction to create a sound. Good rosin should be the colour of citron and transparent. When the bow rubs against the strings, the residue should fall to the foot of the bridge in a white powder. The finest rosin is made by distilling Venetian terebinth.

I see Ann Southam's music as a sunny-coloured, transparent rosin, creating enough friction to make a sound, a transparent agent between bow hair and violin strings. But rosin won't keep the bow hair from breaking. You can't push too hard. If you beat on the soul too hard, it snaps, no matter how much rosin is there. Snapped horsehair is a thrilling, dangerous, marvellous sight, bow flying, two or three broken horsehairs waving through the air like lost notes, shimmering in the light of the concert hall. But remember, once the tension is broken and the friction lost, all that is left is silence.

A Brief Manifesto on Process

1. There is a rhythm between past (collective and traditional) and present (individual and innovative).
2. The present reacts against or builds out of the collective creativity of the past.
3. The past is transformed by the present.
4. Process requires beauty and an idea.
5. Process is creating a pattern (whether ordered or chaotic) and adding a note.
6. We cannot appreciate the new note without a thoroughgoing contemplation of tradition.

Invention Is Art's Main Business

CREATIVITY IS A CONTINUOUS PROCESS OF INVENTION, OF RE-peating—or not repeating—the patterns, of adding a new note.

Why did John Dodd not wish to teach an apprentice the secrets of his exquisite bow making? Perhaps an apprentice would have got in the way of his drinking; perhaps, after the travail that led him to his own great innovations, he did not think he could teach what he knew. Perhaps he believed that tradition is not inherited but obtained by great labour.

What a business the invention of a fiddle and bow. Whoever thought to make strings from sheep gut, rosin from boiled sap, a new knot for tying the bow hair? And playing. Who invents a *saltando* stroke or a new fingering? And composing. Where do the ideas of tone rows and purling rhythms come from? The fiddle is cheeky, earthy, and elegant, at ease in the necessary confusion, inspiration to the hands and minds of those, named and nameless, who ask how to make something as beautiful as that which has gone before.

1997

| | | | | | |

[1] I am indebted for information on Cape Breton bow style and this interview excerpt to the PhD dissertation of Virginia Hope Garrison, "Traditional and Non-Traditional Teaching and Learning Practices in Folk Music: An Ethnographic Field Study of Cape Breton Fiddling," University of Wisconsin, Madison, 1985.

Lise Meitner's
Walking Shoes

| | | | | | |

Rebecca Solnit

| | | | | | |

A SENTENCE, OR A STORY, IS A KIND OF PATH. IN APRIL 1851, five years after his night in jail and a century before the nuclear explosions in Nevada, Henry David Thoreau gave a talk in which he took his audience down a path that few had trod before. The talk was called "Walking," as was the rambling essay published eleven years later, in the midst of the Civil War and just after its author's death. It still stands as a kind of manifesto for wilderness and as Thoreau's most quoted piece—in which he says, "In wildness is the preservation of the world," among other things.

"Walking" really had three subjects: walking, wildness, and the West. "I wish to speak a word for Nature, for absolute freedom and wildness," Thoreau began, but somewhere along the way his words ran away with him, and he lost sight of his original destination, or lack of destination. In the beginning, he says both a word for wildness, and many more in praise of walking, not as a way of getting anywhere but as a way of being somewhere—in the wild. Every walk is a sort of pilgrimage, he says, and suggests that in nature one has already reached a holy land, that the landscape is not an obstacle course one must pass through on the way to some built-up shrine or other. The landscape, any landscape, is itself holy land enough, and so Paradise is here on earth ("one world at a time," he said on his deathbed). And if Paradise is nothing more elusive than countryside, then one need go no farther than the nearest field or forest to have arrived.

Thoreau praises what walking can do for thinking. Walking is nearly alone among all our human activities in its poise between doing something and doing nothing; it is not idleness, and yet, as the legs move and the eyes gaze, the mind can roam with a kind of discipline and scope hardly possible in an armchair. As the rhythm of the walk is interrupted by the surprises and irregularities of the landscape, so ideas arise from lengthy concentration interrupted by epiphanies. That is, new ideas often arrive as though from outside, seeming more like discoveries than creations, but it is only long work that takes one to them, as the walk takes one to the landscape. And in walking in the woods, one is, as Thoreau says, "an inhabitant of nature, rather than a member of society," part of a world of larger scope. And so he speaks, a few pages later, against "all man's improvements," which "simply deform the landscape." He tells a fable of a miser who digs a posthole in the midst of Paradise as the angels move around him, and whose land surveyor is the Prince of Darkness.

The miser's drama takes place on the unsettled prairie of the American midwest in the 1850s. And thus Thoreau takes up the subject of the West, the direction he himself always chooses to walk. "The future lies that way to me," says the tour guide of "Walking," "and the earth seems more unexhausted and richer on that side. . . . Eastward I go only by force; but westward I go free. Thither no business leads me. It is hard for me to believe that I shall find fair landscapes or sufficient wildness and freedom behind the eastern horizon. I am not excited by the prospect of a walk thither; but I believe that the forest which I see in the western horizon stretches uninterruptedly toward the setting sun, and there are no towns nor cities in it of enough consequence to disturb me. I should not lay so much stress on this fact, if I did not believe that something like this is the prevailing tendency of my countrymen. I must walk toward Oregon, and not toward Europe. And that way the nation is moving, and I may say that mankind progress from east to west. . . ."

As one may reach the crest of a mountain in what looks to be wilderness and see a city on the other side, so Thoreau in his rhapsody about the wild and free suddenly joins forces with the march of progress that will spread cities, railroads, mines, and military bases across his vision of the West. It may demonstrate the power of the jingoism of the time that even so obstinately independent a citizen as

Thoreau falls under its sway. Halfway through the essay, the guide who has set out to show us the glory that is absolute wildness is taking us on a tour of the marvels of progress, cultural and geographical. In fact, in the spirit of his time, he conflates the two in one tide of advancing civilization, one celebration of the westerly ascent of Europeans in America.

The citizens of the United States laboured under a mighty inferiority complex when they looked back at Europe. The European landscape was given meaning by the long history that could be read in its names and ruins and monuments. The American landscape lacked all that to its newcomers. Over the decades, a new Yankee credo arose, in which the landmarks of Europe were evidence that the place was weary, spent, used, soiled almost; the supposed newness of the United States demonstrated that it was fresh, young, pure, a child of promise with its history all laid out before it, a tabula rasa on which a heroic history would be inscribed. (Thoreau proclaims that his is the heroic age itself.) In 1835, the godfather of American landscape painting, Thomas Cole, laid out the thesis. "I will now venture a few remarks on what has been considered a grand defect in American scenery," he began as disarmingly as Thoreau began, "the want of associations such as arise amid the scenes of the old world. . . . But American scenes are not so much of the past as of the present and the future. And in looking over the yet uncultivated scene, the mind's eye may see far into futurity. Where the wolf roams, the plough shall glisten; on the gray crag shall rise temple and tower—mighty deeds shall be done in the now pathless wilderness; and poets yet unborn shall sanctify the soil."

Thoreau chimed in from his podium in 1851. He even suggested that the sky was higher and the stars brighter in the Americas, and that the Mississippi was preferable to the Rhine, for its heroic age had just begun, whereas Europe's was exhausted, as was its mythology. "As a true patriot, I should be ashamed to think that Adam in paradise was more favorably situated on the whole than the backwoodsman in this country." The Old World mythology of Adam didn't trip up Thoreau, and Adam was the key figure in this new American credo. Not the Indian but the backwoodsman clearing the forests of Paradise is his hero, his Adam, in this swampy midsection of "Walking"—the New World wasn't new enough to its Natives. He doesn't note that with the backwoodsman swinging his axe and the nation heading toward Oregon the forests might not long stretch toward the setting sun. Nineteenth-century Americans had a hard time thinking of the continent as less than boundless. In this world that was just beginning, in which the pioneer was a new Adam, memory was of no use, the past was a burden to be dumped (Thoreau calls the Atlantic a river of Lethe—forgetfulness—to be crossed in this march toward a higher civilization under a higher sky). He proposes a Society for the Diffusion of Useful Ignorance. And he proposes a Gospel According to This Moment, and gives us the credo of this religion that supplants that of the Bible: "I believe in the forest, and in the meadow, and in the night in which the corn grows." And then Thoreau seems to forget his strange detour and finds his way again, against the American grain and the war with Mexico and in favour of undeveloped landscapes.

The United States of America has, ever since this strange upwelling of nationalistic optimism, been distinguished by its amnesias, its sense of prodigious destiny (its looking ever forward and never back), and its frenzied transformation of landscape into real estate. Not Thoreau but Cole traced the impetus braided of these three strands to its logical conclusion. In 1836, he created a five-painting cycle called *The Course of Empire,* which traces a single landscape through aeons of human history. The first big panel is titled *Savage State,* and in it half-nude figures rush across a tumultuous, misty landscape. This savagery is succeeded by *Pastoral State,* in which the deer hunters and spear chuckers have become contemplative shepherds. It is this panel, rather than the next one, *Consummation,* that seems to represent Cole's ideal, for in *Consummation* the landscape—but for a mountaintop—has been obscured by a fairyland version of imperial Rome, whose splendour is a little repellent. *Consummation* leads to *Destruction,* and the dubious figures of the previous scene begin to lay waste to the fairy city and to each other. *Desolation* concludes *The Course of Empire:* the landscape has returned, and a few ruins grace it. The people seem to have succeeded in extinguishing themselves, for the landscape that has emerged from the buildings is uninhabited.

THREE YEARS AFTER THE END OF WORLD WAR II, THE POET
W. H. Auden wrote an essay titled "Arcadia and Utopia" in which he
proposed the two places as categories of belief. Arcadians believe
that Paradise existed in the past; propose that we return to a simpler
state, a lost state of grace; and distrust government, technology,
progress, and anything that tends to uproot, to supplant the country
with the city, the simple with the complex. Utopians reach for their
shimmering vision of a perfectible future with all the authority and
technology within their grasp. In "Walking," Thoreau is an Arcadian
who briefly lapses into the Utopianism of his time. In *The Course of
Empire*, Cole interrupts his Utopian visions for the American landscape with a little pessimistic Arcadianism. Probably the most perfect
example of the two philosophies in conflict today is in the confronta-
tions between antinuclear activists and nuclear physicists.

ARCADIA IS A PLACE, A MOUNTAINOUS REGION ON THE PELO-
ponnesus peninsula of Greece. It was old when Theocritus set the first
pastoral poems there before Christ was born, and its inhabitants
claimed to be of a lineage older than the moon. When Roman Virgil
took up Theocritus's pastoral mode, Arcady was no longer a rough
backward part of Greece renowned for its singing but an ideal. Virgil's
Arcadian world was a refuge from the strife and intrigue of Rome, and
he established the pastoral as a celebration of the simple over the
complex and the rural over the urban. Another pastoral poet, Sir
Philip Sidney, summed up the setting of the pastoral as "a civil wilderness, and a companionable solitude," a paradoxical ideal. Pastoral
comes from *pastor*—shepherd—and the pastoral is a poem or painting in which pensive shepherds converse of love and loss; the pastoral's
principal themes are time and nature. Shepherding served the pastoral
poets as walking serves Thoreau.

The nature writer and Sierra Club founder John Muir—who took
the thousand-mile walks Thoreau only talked of—spent his first
summer in the Sierra among shepherds, and he was appalled by the
brutish minds of his companions and their indifference to the glories
around them. Still, one can't imagine Marie Antoinette playing at
being a turnip-gatherer or a goose-girl rather than the shepherdess role
she favoured. The aristocracy of Europe kept up this involvement

with the pastoral, and Virgil's pastoral poems were widely taught until sometime in the twentieth century. His shepherds are less true images of rural labour than counterimages to the city: ideals of an uncorrupted, natural intelligence. So in some sense the pastoral is not about the country but about what the country means to the city, and what the past means to the present. The pastoral celebrates a paradise lost, less that of Eden than the secular paradises of the Golden Age, on which a later age overlaid the classical past, the world from Plato to Virgil or so, and to which the Romantics, who were adamant Arcadians, added childhood, the last paradise lost for all of us. Arcadia is the land of a universal childhood in which the Earth brings forth fruit without toil, a generous mother to her blameless children. Although pastoral poetry has been out of vogue for half a century, its themes were taken up by children's literature—*The Wind in the Willows* is a superb example—and by landscape novels, from the exotics of W. H. Hudson's *Green Mansions* to the bucolics of Thomas Hardy's Wessex countryside.

Utopianism is of a more recent genesis than Arcadianism. Until the seventeenth century, the New Jerusalem stood at the end of history as Eden stood at its beginning (though humanity was still moving from a garden to a city). Only divine intervention could undo the Fall, and all the time between these paradisal landmarks was essentially static, or in mild decline. The seventeenth century was the century of René Descartes, Francis Bacon, and Isaac Newton, who brought us scientific method and a vision of secular progress through technological achievement—that is, through the control of nature. Earlier visions of improvement emphasized social rather than technological change, but the two gradually ran together in the Utopian vision of a rationally ordered society. (The word *utopia* was coined earlier, by Thomas More, who cobbled it together out of Greek— *ou topos:* no place—and had mixed feelings about Utopias.) Most contemporary historians of science declare that the modern era began with one of those three men, and the scientist rather than the capitalist or the land developer serves them as the very type of the manipulative Utopian.

For example, Bacon proposed that the purpose of knowledge was utilitarian—the domination of nature—as it still is to us, but to his predecessors knowledge was primarily for spiritual improvement.

Bacon audaciously suggested that "man by his fall fell at the same time from his state of innocency and domination over creation. Both of these losses however can even in this life be in some part repaired . . . the latter by the arts and sciences." In his model of knowledge, what had been considered a sacrilegious prying into the mysteries of creation was reconfigured as a morally neutral, even an innocent, act. The sciences he described were those of empirical knowledge and scientific experiment, the idea of containing and manipulating something to discover its secrets. Bacon is often credited with establishing the scientific method, as well as the pattern for scientific purpose. And he wrote a Utopian novel about a technocratic society.

Descartes, who was as much younger than Bacon—about forty years—as Newton was younger than him, was equally radical. He abandoned the whole edifice of classical knowledge to begin again, and he established as a new foundation for knowledge reason and mathematics. Descartes tore a whole cosmos apart with his Discourse on Method. And by asserting that such eternal verities as mathematics governed the universe, he displaced God as an active participant. The Earth was no longer the way it was because of providence— divine intervention—but because of the laws of nature. "God sets up mathematical laws in nature as a king sets up laws in his kingdom," he wrote, but it was the laws, not the king, he found, and the universe he described resembled the great wonder of his age, clockwork. The universe was a clock wound up by a God who was no longer involved. And having driven away God and the ancients, he proceeded to drive the mind out of the body: the body becomes another machine, and machines are controlled from without. Thus a cosmos in which the divine and the creation are separate, as are the mind and the body; because mind is a quality of human beings alone, the mind and nature are also separate; and nature—this distinct, soulless thing—is the subject of the new science. The nuclear physicist Werner Heisenberg commented that Descartes differed fundamentally from the ancients in that they endeavoured to understand things through connections and affinities, Descartes through isolations and divisions.

Newton is significant here as the man who realized much of what Bacon and Descartes proposed. He laid down the principles of classical physics, describing the laws of the universe—the design of clockwork—with a mathematical certainty that had never before been attained and has hardly since been exceeded. Like them, he asked a fundamentally different kind of question of the universe than theologians and alchemists had: not why but how things were. And with such questions asked and others unspoken, Bacon's vision of the moral neutrality of science was established. In the work of these three men, the vision of progress was born—a vision in which knowledge allowed rational man to exert increasing control over the Earth.

As means, the scientific methods they established are of unquestionable value; as an end, they are more dubious. The desire to know is as often motivated by love as by hate. Lovers and interrogators have curiosity in common, and they have differences: the desire to understand the universe is not the same as the desire to control it. But the definition of progress came to mean not understanding but control, and not spiritual or social improvement but the advancement of power—which meant geographical manifest destiny in the United States of Thoreau's age, and means technological manifest destiny in our own.

Those antiseptic scenarios of optimistic science fiction—rational men and women dressed in rational uniforms, living in highly artificial circumstances, and probing farther into the cosmos—are the logical outcome of this vision. Like Bacon's and More's Utopias, they seem to be cultures in which children, dreams, poetry, idleness, and mystery have no place, and even the intricacy of the landscape itself has disappeared in a more efficiently human-oriented life-support system. It is Cole's *Course of Empire* painting *Consummation,* without the capstone of *Destruction,* a destruction wrought by the urges that fester unacknowledged in a Utopian regime. For Arcadians, nature is good enough, and Paradise is at least a memory; for Utopians, Paradise is a supernatural ideal waiting to be realized on Earth by men. Nature and the past are problems to be overcome.

Thus, Arcadians and Utopians.

PICTURE A CONFRONTATION BETWEEN NUCLEAR PHYSICISTS and antinuclear activists and you get the most vehement and extreme advocates of Utopianism and Arcadianism, staring each other down across an abyss of incomprehension. They don't often meet at the Nevada Test Site, for the physicists only fly in for bomb tests, but they have often run into each other during protests at the nuclear weapons laboratories—Livermore Labs near San Francisco, and Los Alamos near Santa Fe. The blockaders are a motley group, ranging from adolescents to elderly clergy and old leftists, perhaps including a Buddhist monk in saffron robes (Japanese Buddhists have been persistently involved in antinuclear activity), some antinuclear lawyers, a doctor from Physicians for Social Responsibility, but professionals are the exception in the US direct-action movement (though not abroad). Most of them are poor—not born to poverty but middle-class people who choose to live modestly and devote themselves to general welfare rather than personal security. Many of them look countercultural—during the 1980s, a lot of punks were involved, and there's still a sizeable number of hippie diehards out there for TV cameras to zoom in on. *Everything should be as simple as possible, but not simpler,* Einstein once said, and one of the besetting sins of these Arcadians is oversimplification. With their platitudes of love, they can represent the nadir of Arcadianism. I often find it embarrassing to be associated with them, but I agree with their general principles if not with their style. They are liable to be singing, carrying banners and signs they've made, and trying to strike up conversations with the sheriffs and security guards. At some point, one of the arresting officers will ask who the leader is, and the activists will say they don't have leaders, though they may offer up a spokesperson to negotiate.

The spokesperson may offer to halt the demonstration if the development or testing of nuclear weapons is halted. The activists seem unrealistic, for the adjustment they are asking for is enormous. It affects economics, foreign policy, and the very definition of national security, as well as the continuing employment of physicists by the defence industry. They might say they are realistic on a larger scale, for they are concerning themselves with disasters that the bomb-making institutions downplay or deny: disasters whose chances are slim—accidental detonations; disasters whose impacts are a long way away—disposal of waste that will be radioactive for tens of thousands of years; and disasters in which the people who can deploy nuclear weapons are not adequate to the decision to do so—no one is.

The physicists are more homogeneous. They are government employees with security clearances, in their middle years between acquiring PhDs and retiring, mostly white and male; they are extremely well paid for their work, and most of them seem to believe in the rightness of weapons design and deployment. They may refuse to discuss the issue on the ground that nonscientists are unqualified to assess the dangers of the highly technical weapons (I have been told this myself). They may say instead that the weapons guarantee peace, that only the vast array of missiles has prevented a third world war, and that they need to continue building safer weapons—less likely to detonate accidentally, for example. (Although they say they need to continue nuclear testing for safety purposes, the tests—at about $160 million apiece—are needed only for developing new, more destructive weapons.) They may refuse to believe that nuclear weapons are out of control or must be controlled, for to them they—the designers—are the ones who control them. As engineers, they may consider the worst-case scenarios as allowable risks: in the 1950s, Livermore Lab's founder, Edward Teller, argued that a nuclear war was winnable: "perhaps twenty million might be killed . . . yet within about three years' time we should be back on our feet." They may argue that arms reduction is a political, not a scientific, responsibility.

Olav Suleymenov, the Kazakh poet and founder of the Nevada-Semipalatinsk Antinuclear Movement that shut down the main Soviet test site, once met with Livermore Lab officials. Many questions were asked and answered, and then Suleymenov asked what they were going to do about the waste. It took several reiterations of his question for them to be sure that the translator was not missing the point, and then the physicists said that nuclear waste was not their department but that of geologists, and so they didn't think about it. This is as fundamental a distinction as any between Arcadians, the amateurs at the gate, and Utopians, the professionals in the control room. The former believe that the bomb is everybody's responsibility, and that plans need to be laid not for the next decade's national security but for all time and the whole Earth. The latter accept a division of labour, and a compartmentalization of moral responsibility.

Or the fundamental distinction between them could be summarized with a kind of symbolic geometry. Arcadians believe in cyclical time, in the eternal return of nature; Utopians in the linear progress of culture, and these forms emerge in many ways. The most common formation of the activists—for discussions or celebrations—is a circle, with everyone equidistant from the centre and equal. The formation of the scientists could be envisioned as a pyramidal grid, with respon-sibilities divided and delegated according to a chain of command and a compartmentalization of expertise. And though the physicists may hardly touch ground as they are shuttled from their airplane to the windowless control room for nuclear tests, the activists will be out of doors for the duration of their time at the test site, living literally on Earth, exposed to the elements (and radioactive isotopes thereof), and sheltered only by the tents of good pastoralists.

The physicists I have been discussing are in many ways tech-nicians, applying the principles of physics to bomb-building, not pure theorists. They seem to represent most of the values of the Utopians of the scientific revolution, and that moment of progress worship that Thoreau fell into in the course of his meandering talk on walking. It wasn't always that way.

IN 1900, THE PHYSICIST MAX PLANCK AND HIS SON TOOK A long walk through the Grunewald, the forest surrounding Berlin. He confided to his son that he had made a discovery of the first rank, perhaps as significant as a discovery of Newton's. The conservative Planck was reluctant to unleash a revolution upon the world, but after a summer of calculations he found no way out of his conclusions. So, late in the first year of the twentieth century, he presented his findings to the German Physical Society—findings that, says a later physicist, "were so unusual and so grotesque that he himself could hardly believe them, even though they caused intense excitement in the audience and in the entire world of physics." Energy was emitted by vibrating particles in discrete quantities, or *quanta,* Planck demon-strated, rather than in the continuous flow described in classical, Newtonian physics. Not only did Planck change the picture of energy, but he also supplied the mathematical formula with which to measure this basic unit of energy, a number that became known as Planck's constant. The physicist Arnold Sommerfeld sent to Planck a delicate compliment to his originality: "*You* cultivate the virgin soil / Where plucking flowers was *my* only toil."

Planck had gone into physics, he wrote later, because "it is of paramount importance that the outside world is something inde-pendent from man, something absolute, and the quest for laws which apply to this absolute appeared to me as the most sublime scientific pursuit in life." But Planck's constant was the tool that took physics in another direction, toward quantum physics and a more complex picture of the universe. In 1905, the year Einstein also published his Theory of Relativity, he also interpreted Planck's constant in relation to light and heat, with revolutionary results: light behaved as though it were particles—quanta of light—as well as though it were waves, an apparent contradiction Einstein left for posterity to resolve. In 1913, Niels Bohr used Planck's constant to remap the atom, describing the specific orbits and energies of electrons in terms of it. In Bohr's new theory, energy at the atomic scale was also no longer a continuous flow but an accretion of discrete packages, of quanta. In contemporary terms, the universe, which had been so long assumed to be analogue, was turning out to be digital. In terms of early-twentieth-century science, it was the beginning of quantum physics. A big, athletic man, a terrible writer and a famous mumbler, Bohr was, after Einstein, the greatest physicist of the era, remarkable not only for his intuitive brilliance but for a kindness that extended equally to his friends and to humanity.

IT WAS THE SUMMER OF 1922, AND BOHR WAS TAKING A WALK on the Hain Mountain above Göttingen in north-central Germany with Heisenberg, a student who had just won his admiration by contradicting him in public, on their first meeting. Heisenberg had been the most promising student of Sommerfeld, who wrote that couplet to Planck and who brought his protégé to the University of Göttingen to hear Bohr speak. "My real scientific career only began that afternoon," Heisenberg declared.

The historian Richard Rhodes recounts that Heisenberg was a member of Germany's youth movement, whose members went on "hiking tours, built campfires, sang folk songs, talked of knighthood and the Holy Grail and of service to the fatherland. Many were idealists, but authoritarianism and anti-Semitism already bloomed poisonously among them. When Heisenberg finally got to Copenhagen at Eastertime in 1924, Bohr took him off on a hike through north Zealand and asked him about it all." Heisenberg laid Bohr's fears to rest during their several-days walk, and the two began their great work together.

Between them, they established a basis for quantum physics that undid classical physics and alienated even Einstein (who refused to accept the tenets of quantum physics for the rest of his life). Heisenberg's greatest contribution came in about 1926; he writes of it, "I remember discussions with Bohr which went through many hours till very late at night and ended almost in despair; and when at the end of one discussion I went for a walk in a neighboring park I repeated to myself again and again the question: Can nature possibly be absurd as it seemed to us in these atomic experiments?" Thus far atoms had been looked at as though they were tiny planets, and if the location and velocity of a planet are known, then its motion can be predicted, as Newton first demonstrated with eclipse predictions. It could not be done with the atom: the same apparent cause could produce different effects, violating the principle of causality.

Heisenberg came back from his walk in Copenhagen's Faelledpark convinced that the results they were looking for could never be found: the atom was so small that the attempt to look at it via instruments disturbed it and thus dictated its behaviour. To identify its velocity changed its location, to identify its location changed its velocity: measuring one aspect made the other uncertain. His conclusion came to be called the uncertainty principle, and its implications reached far beyond the experiments it explained; it subverted the entire scientific model of observation and set a barrier to one progression of discovery. There was no distinction between looking at something and affecting it on this scale. From the uncertainty principle, Heisenberg arrived at a redefinition of science and of knowledge. "Natural science does not simply describe and explain nature; it is part of the interplay between nature and ourselves; it describes nature as exposed to our method of questioning. This was a possibility of which Descartes could not have thought, but it makes the sharp separation between the world and the I impossible." Bohr added later, "After all, we are both onlookers and actors in the great drama of existence." And thus they undermined the absolute Planck sought in physics.

While Heisenberg had been pacing through Copenhagen, Bohr had gone off skiing in Norway to ponder a different conundrum: Heisenberg and another atomic physicist, Erwin Schrodinger, had each explained properties of the atom with beautiful mathematical formulae that began from different premises and used different methods but arrived at identical results. Schrodinger had abandoned Bohr's model of the atom altogether, and calculated as though it consisted of waves of energy rather than of matter; Heisenberg had stuck with matter. Bohr stood up at a conference of physicists in Como in 1927 and announced that one could best proceed on the assumption that they were both true, even though they contradicted each other. The truth available from both descriptions was more complete than the truth either offered, and so they were complementary, rather than contradictory. Bohr's principle of complementarity, as he called it, and Heisenberg's uncertainty principle described a universe more complex and less easily knowable than the world of classical physics in which they had begun.

Bohr's theory seemed, too, to bear traces of the generosity and justness of its creator. Long afterward, J. Robert Oppenheimer wrote, "It was a heroic time. It was not the doing of any one man; it involved the collaboration of scores of scientists from many different lands, though from first to last the deeply creative and critical spirit of Niels Bohr guided, restrained, deepened, and finally transmuted the enterprise."

| | | | | | |

IT WAS 1927 AND THE YOUNG PHYSICISTS ROBERT ATKINSON and Fritz Houtermans were on a walking tour near Göttingen. As they strolled together through the German countryside, they began to speculate on the nearly inexhaustible energy of the stars, and of the sun that shone on them. "Such was the origin of the labors of Atkinson and Houtermans on their theory of thermonuclear reactions in the sun, which later achieved such fame," wrote the physicist Robert Jungk, in his history of atomic physics, *Brighter than a Thousand Suns*. "The theory for the first time put forward the conjecture that solar energy might be attributed, not to the demolition, but to the fusion, of lightweight atoms. The development of this idea led straight to the H-bombs that threaten humanity today."

All the European physicists of this era were people of enormous cultivation, classically educated and concerned with politics, poetry and music, as well as science. Their walks evinced a taste for landscape, for the Romantic and Goethean tradition of nature worship, and for the informal and unhierarchical Socratic tradition of thinking and talking while walking, rather than doing so in offices and classrooms. In the university town of Heidelberg, there is still a famous path where several German philosophers did their thinking, and by taking such walks the physicists positioned themselves as philosophers of matter, not as technicians, however much time they also spent in laboratories.

It seems that walking maintained their sense of human scale and thus of humanity even while they speculated on the activities of stars and subatomic particles. Their epiphanies and confidences in the landscape suggest that they thought of themselves as innocents involved in a beautiful and morally neutral practice. They had shattered other worldviews, though, and their own was about to be shattered. The Soviets often considered the breakthroughs of Einstein and of quantum physics to be subversively bourgeois, and the Nazis and a few German physicists denounced them as Jewish physics.

A decade after his speculative walk near Göttingen, Houtermans, who was Jewish, emigrated to the Soviet Union from the Germany of the Third Reich, but the Soviets were also in the middle of an era of terror. He was tortured and interrogated by the secret police and then handed back to the Gestapo. And thus the Soviets missed their chance to have an atom bomb first. Houtermans spent the war working in the private laboratory of Baron Manfred von Ardenne and obscuring the details of how to make a bomb as far as he dared.

IT WAS CHRISTMAS EVE OF 1938, AND OTTO FRISCH AND HIS aunt Lise Meitner were taking a walk in the Swedish countryside near Göteborg. Both of them were Austrians, physicists, and Jews. Frisch worked at Bohr's physics institute in Copenhagen, a sanctuary for many Jewish and dissident physicists before Denmark was invaded. Meitner had stayed in Berlin until Hitler annexed Austria and made her subject to the German racial laws. Then she fled to the position her colleagues found her in Sweden, a bitter exile for her. Frisch and Meitner had spent the holidays together for many years, and their reunion in the midst of the turmoil of the time was a triumph. But Meitner was excited about something else.

Frisch had wanted to go skiing, Meitner had wanted to talk. She had asserted that she could keep up with him on level ground, and so he skied while she strode across the snowy ground. Her curiosity had been set aflame by an experiment her longtime collaborator, the chemist Otto Hahn, had just written to her about, in which the element barium had appeared in uranium bombarded by neutrons. (A gentile, he had stayed in Berlin, but defied the Nazis in continuing to work with her.) Hahn was the preeminent chemist of his day, and so there was no possibility that the new element came from impure samples. As Frisch and Meitner went past the river and in among the trees, they became more and more excited. Finally they sat down on a fallen tree, and she began to calculate on scraps of paper. They used Bohr's model of the atomic nucleus as resembling a drop of water held together by surface tension—the binding energy of the atom. The formula Meitner used to calculate the amount of energy released had already become famous, Einstein's $E = mc^2$, energy equals mass times the speed of light, and with it they explained the odd events in Hahn's laboratory. When one atom burst into two, it released a quantity of energy enormous for a single atom—enough to visibly move a single grain of sand, Frisch later wrote.

They concluded something that immediately afterward became obvious to their peers: Hahn had split the atom. Atoms were not so stable and strong as Newton had envisioned them when he wrote, "God in the beginning formed matter in solid, massy, hard, impenetrable moveable particles . . . even so very hard as never to wear or break in pieces; no ordinary power being able to divide what God himself made one in the first creation. . . ." Atomic elements with very large and very small neutrons—hydrogen isotopes at one end of the periodic table, uranium at the other—were unstable, and more readily split, unleashing their tremendous binding energy. This is why no element heavier than uranium exists in nature—plutonium would first be created by Glenn Seaborg in the cyclatron at Berkeley in 1940 and in nuclear reactors thereafter.

Frisch wrote to his mother, "Feel as if I had caught an elephant by its tail, without meaning to, while walking through a jungle. And now I don't know what to do with it." And he asked a biologist what the word was for the way a cell divides into two as its means of reproduction, and the biologist said, *fission.* They named what had happened to Hahn's atoms fission, and the news that the atom could be split stirred physicists as few possibilities had stirred them before.

| | | | | | |

IT WAS A HOT DAY SIX MONTHS LATER, JULY 1939, AND LEO Szilard was in too much of a hurry to walk. He seems out of step with his peers in all the histories and reminiscences—while they walked musingly forward, he scurried around them, fearful they were approaching a precipice. Amnesia made belief in progress possible for Thoreau, memory made it terrible to Szilard. He says in his recollections, "Apart from my mother's tales the most serious influence on my life came from a book which I read when I was ten years old. It was a Hungarian classic, taught in the schools, *The Tragedy of Man*. . . . In that book the devil shows Adam the history of mankind, with the sun dying down. Only Eskimos are left and they worry chiefly because there are too many Eskimos and too few seals."

Szilard had foreseen the destructive possibilities of splitting the atom many years before—suddenly as he was about to cross a street in Bloomsbury, London, in 1933, and he had tried hard to prevent it then. When Eugen Wigner (like Szilard, a Hungarian, and a Jew—and therefore a refugee) had told Szilard the news of Hahn's experiment and Meitner's conclusion in January 1939, his fears about fission came to life again. "I immediately saw that these fragments . . . must emit neutrons, and if enough neutrons are emitted . . . then it should be, of course, possible to sustain a chain reaction," he declared. That is, if neutrons could split an atom, and a split atom emitted further neutrons, then the splitting would continue. This is the chain reaction that makes the energy increase from the scale on which a grain of sand visibly jumps to the scale of a small exploding star that can make an island vanish from the face of the Earth (as did the South Pacific island of Elugelab when the United States set off a fission-triggered fusion bomb there in 1952). Most of the physicists saw fission in a scientific light, and some imagined nuclear reactors, but few seem to have foreseen bombs: in the months after Meitner's and Frisch's Christmas walk, even Bohr offered reasons why bombs would be impossible.

That hot day in July 1939, Wigner and Szilard went looking for Einstein. The two physicists set off for the town of Patchogue on the south coast of Long Island in a car and, after searching fruitlessly for two hours, decided they must have been given the wrong address. Perhaps it was Peconic that Einstein vacationed in, and so to nearby

Peconic they went, but there too they failed to find their friend. Finally, as an ironic aside, the perspiring Szilard asked a boy of seven or eight busy adjusting his fishing rod if he knew where Einstein lived—he had become famous by that time—and the child gave them directions.

Szilard wanted to use Einstein's prestige and his friendship with the Queen Mother of Belgium to try to prevent the bomb from being built. "The possibility of a chain reaction had not occurred to Einstein," he said later. But Einstein agreed to use his influence to see that a letter reached the Belgian government, warning it about the potential uses of its stockpiles of Congo uranium. Szilard's letter grew through many stages, from a letter trying only to prevent a Nazi bomb to a letter encouraging President Roosevelt to pursue a US bomb. "Through a paradox of fate," Jungk writes of the great pacifist Einstein, "he had decided to give the starting signal for the most horrible of all weapons of destruction." After he signed it, Einstein mused that for the first time humanity would use energy that did not come from the sun.

| | | | | | |

IT WAS LATE IN OCTOBER 1941. BOHR AND HIS FORMER protégé and collaborator Heisenberg were taking a walk together again, although everything around them and between them had changed. Bohr, whose mother was Jewish and who would soon flee Denmark himself, had taken the lead in the Danish effort to rescue Jews. Heisenberg had stayed in Germany and apparently in the good graces of the Nazi party. He was, in fact, working with Meitner's former collaborator Hahn and a few others on the bomb Szilard had feared, though the ranks of German physicists had been reduced by the ethnic cleansings of the new Reich. Officially he had come to Copenhagen to attend a scientific meeting.

They were walking near the house that Bohr had lived in since 1932, the House of Honour. It had been built by the builder of the Carlsberg Breweries and modelled after a classical Pompeiian villa, and then its builder had established it as a place for Denmark's most eminent citizen to live in. The house stood among tall trees, and a beautiful garden covered the expansive grounds. Heisenberg had come not to admire the gardens, however, or to philosophize. Out of doors and in motion, they could speak with less fear of being overheard. What Heisenberg said on that night will never be certain, nor will his intentions. He himself said that he intended to reassure Bohr and through him the world of physics that the German physicists would never succeed in building an atom bomb during the war. The English physicist and writer C. P. Snow considered Heisenberg an outright Nazi. But Houtermans, the carefree youth who speculated on the energy of the sun and later lost all his teeth in a Soviet torture session, said he helped Heisenberg to smuggle out a note to a friend in the United States in 1941, in which Heisenberg declared that he was delaying the program "as much as possible, fearing the catastrophic results of success." The preponderance of evidence is in Heisenberg's favour.

Bohr was a famous murmerer and mumbler, but it is strange that Heisenberg should have been so unclear on so crucial an issue. Perhaps he was ambivalent about so definitively treasonous an act amid his long campaign of equivocal loyalty and mild sabotage. But the Danish physicist came back from the walk convinced that his former collaborator had told him the Nazis were successfully pursuing an atomic bomb, and he warned the Allies. His warning gave additional impetus to the US bomb program, which succeeded where the Germans—perhaps misled by Heisenberg—failed.

IT WAS AUGUST 7, 1945, AND HEISENBERG WAS WALKING IN a rose garden with the physicist Carl Friedrick. They walked up and down it for hours, talking about the horrific news they had just heard. The rose garden was in an English country estate called Farm Hall, where the two walkers were kept captive with Hahn and several other physicists. They had been captured as the Third Reich collapsed that summer, but few prisoners can have been housed in more pleasant circumstances. Heisenberg read the complete works of the Victorian novelist Anthony Trollope while he was interned, and Trollope's portrayals of the small crises of rural gentry must have offered an interesting foil to the forced tranquillity of the "guests," as their warden referred to them. Every bedroom and living room had been bugged, and for six months the British recorded their every conversation indoors, even the noises they made alone. In 1992, the transcripts were declassified. Rather as Bacon described nature taken captive and spied upon as the basis for experimentation, so these physicists themselves had become the specimens to be examined for information on the German bomb effort in the glass jar of Farm Hall.

On August 6, their warden told them that the United States had used a nuclear weapon against the Japanese. He reported, "Shortly before dinner . . . I informed Professor Hahn that an announcement had been made by the BBC that an atomic bomb had been dropped. Hahn was completely shattered by the news and said he felt personally responsible for the deaths of hundreds of thousands of people. He told me that he had originally contemplated suicide when he realized the terrible potentialities of the discovery and he felt that now these had been realized and he was to blame. With the help of considerable alcoholic stimulant he was calmed down and we went down to dinner where he announced the news to the assembled guests. . . . The guests were completely staggered by the news. At first they refused to believe it and felt that it was bluff on our part. . . . After hearing the official announcement they realized it was a fact. Their first reaction, which I believe was genuine, was an expression of horror that we should have used this invention for destruction. . . ."

Later, in a private conversation with Hahn, Heisenberg made some astute guesses. He conjectured that the Allies must have used much of their $2 billion budget on uranium isotope separation and estimated the amount needed to produce a critical mass—that is, the amount sufficient for a self-sustaining chain reaction—at about sixty kilograms. And then he told Hahn that he had never pursued that avenue, "as I never believed one could get pure 235." (Most naturally occurring uranium is uranium 238; only the rarer U-235, with three fewer neutrons, is readily fissionable.) Heisenberg was beginning to imagine the extraordinary effort expended at Los Alamos, where Oppenheimer had orchestrated the making of the atom bomb, and at Hanford, Washington, and Oakridge, Tennessee, where the U-235 and plutonium were refined. The conversation recorded by concealed microphones concluded with political speculation. "They must prevent the Russians from doing it," Hahn said. Heisenberg replied, "I would like to know what Stalin is thinking this evening. Of course they have got good men . . . and these people can do it too."

The report on the German physicists in Farm Hall on that epochal day concludes, "Although the guests retired to bed about 1:30, most of them appear to have spent a somewhat disturbed night judging by the deep sighs and occasional shouts which were heard during the night."

| | | | | | |

IT WAS 1959, THE SOVIETS HAD HAD THE BOMB FOR TEN
years, and both sides had developed and tested hydrogen, or fusion,
bombs. Teller had just succeeded in designing a nuclear reactor for
General Atomic, and Bohr had been persuaded to officiate at the
dedication in San Diego. The physicist Freeman Dyson, who worked
on the reactor, writes in his memoir *Disturbing the Universe*, ". . .
Bohr became restless. It was his habit to walk and talk. All his life he
had been walking and talking, usually with a single listener who
could concentrate his full attention on Bohr's convoluted sentences.
That evening he wanted to talk about the history of atomic energy.
He signaled to me to come with him, and we walked together up and
down the beach. I was delighted to be so honored. . . . Bohr told me
that we now had another great opportunity to gain the confidence of
the Russians by talking with them openly about all aspects of nuclear
energy. The first opportunity to do this had been missed in 1944,
when Bohr spoke with both Churchill and Roosevelt and failed to
persuade them that the only way to avoid a disastrous nuclear arms
race was to deal with the Russians openly before the war ended.
Bohr talked on and on about his conversations with Churchill and
Roosevelt, conversations of the highest historical importance which
were, alas, never recorded. I clutched at every word as best I could.
But Bohr's voice was at the best of times barely audible. There on the
beach, each time he came to a particularly crucial point of his conversations with Churchill and Roosevelt, his voice seemed to sink lower
and lower until it was utterly lost in the ebb and flow of the waves."

THERE ARE TWO REASONS TO GO WALKING. ONE IS TO GET SOME-
where. The other is to walk. Thoreau displays for us both ways of
walking, and the kind of thinking behind each one, the ways I have
been calling Utopian and Arcadian. Like Thoreau, the physicists had
set out to take one kind of walk and taken another. On their strolls
through the stately forests of Europe, they had begun, slowly, imper-
ceptibly, inexorably, to march toward the Nevada Test Site. Szilard
knew it first, as he stepped off the curb in London in 1933, and he
spent most of the rest of his life trying to wake his colleagues to the

peril they were approaching. After the war, he abandoned physics and became a biologist and a peace activist.

Until I read their stories, I believed that the scientists who had made the bomb were ruthless Utopians. The contemporary Department of Energy scientists I had heard and read had such a mind-set, and it seemed safe to project it backward onto their founding fathers. I had often heard the story of their calculation of the chances that the first atomic bomb would cause a runaway chain reaction that would ignite the atmosphere and destroy all life, and I believed that they were such Faustian arrogants, taking it upon themselves to decide the fate of the Earth. I believed that their scientific work was undertaken with the desire to control nature, and through it to control culture. They often serve as symbols of such desire in contemporary writing, but only Oppenheimer in his immense ambition and Teller in his reck- lessness and dishonesty—the father of the atom bomb and the father of the H-bomb, as they were called—seem to deserve it. Oppenheimer thought that the bomb would make war so terrible humanity would advance beyond war, a strange Utopian belief that technological progress could so neatly bring about social transformation.

It was the gentleness of the other key physicists that struck me in their biographies, and their cultivation, and their penchant for thinking while walking. They seemed to be the utter incarnation of Arcadian shepherds in their long musing walks together, in the sublime beauty they found in speculating on the fundamental principles of the universe. The chessplayers' offensive of the arms race could not be further from the wonder and leaps of imagination that built up atomic physics before the bomb, and until Hahn's fission experiments took on practical possibilities their accelerating knowledge of the basic structures of nature seemed to have no practical use. Afterward, Oppenheimer explicitly compared the physicists' situation to Paradise before the Fall: "Science has known sin," he said, standing in the dust of the Jornada del Muerte immediately after the first atomic explosion had taken place there on July 15, 1945. And another physicist, Mark Oliphant, said, "This has been the death of a beautiful subject." It all changed at Los Alamos.

LOS ALAMOS IS BEAUTIFUL. IT IS A MESA SEVEN THOUSAND feet above sea level, even now accessible only through narrow roads that wind along steep slopes and precipices, a fortress of rock thrust up into the deep blue ever-changing New Mexico sky. The mesa is part of the rim of a gigantic extinct volcano, one of the biggest in the world, and from it the Sangre de Cristo (blood of Christ) mountains dominate the eastern view. One reason Los Alamos was chosen was that the laboratory had to be isolated, to keep the world from the scientists and the scientists from the world. The place had to be remote, but not near a border or coast, and it had to be defensible. Originally the army looked for a canyon whose surrounding rim could be guarded, but it settled on this mesa, which also had abrupt edges that could be secured. And perhaps there was another reason. Oppenheimer played a part in the final choice, and he chose it as a theatrical space, one whose austere magnificence and sweeping views would confer nobility on the work to be done there. He seems to have been trying to match the loftiness of his ambitions to a landscape, and in Los Alamos he found an ideal site. And, with this site, physics turned from philosophy to war technology, left the gracious European forests in which so many of its crucial ideas had been realized, and moved into the desert expanse that has been its terrain ever since. The desert is no place to meander and fatal to innocents: you must know what you are capable of and what lies ahead.

It was a strange instinct that took the bomb to the desert. It is possible to read the flight of the physicists to this remote setting as a kind of Exodus, as the Mormons read their own flight from persecution to the Utah desert a century before. It is like the westward march Thoreau describes in his detour through Utopianism, a mingling of geographical migration with technological manipulation of nature, a double forward step of progress. There are many echoes in this gathering up of the physicists in the wilderness of 1942. In 1492, the year that Columbus landed in the Americas, his patrons Isabella and Ferdinand also began to expel the Jews from Spain. They had to leave, convert, or die, but many of them chose to dissemble. For more than a century, the Spanish Inquisition attempted to root out secret Jews, and many of them went to the New World to escape discovery. The first European settlement of New Mexico was in large part by a mix of Christians of Jewish descent and secret, or crypto-,

Jews, and it was they who established Santa Fe. They had invaded Pueblo Indian territory, and in 1680 the Pueblos rebelled and expelled the Spanish. Reconquering the territory distracted the Spanish from their campaign of rooting out Jews in the region, and many Hispanic families have practised Judaism clandestinely to the present day.

Los Alamos was also an invasion into Pueblo territory, one that the Pueblos have recently begun to fight back with lawsuits for radioactive and toxic contamination of the land and water still in Pueblo hands. And, as with the settlement of Nuevo Mexico, many of the physicists were also Jewish refugees. Some, like Oppenheimer's family, came from earlier waves of anti-Semitism; Einstein was the first of the current wave to emigrate to the United States; Szilard, Wigner, and Teller came; Bohr came briefly with one of his five sons; Enrico Fermi came from Italy with his wife, who was a Jew and in danger; Otto Frisch, the mathematical genius John von Neumann, and Hans Bethe all came. . . . C. P. Snow commented that the refugees made the United States, "in a very short time, the world's dominant force in pure science." So it is possible to see these two epochal events for New Mexico—the first European incursions and the first atom bomb— not only as manifest destinies but also as effects of the same smouldering intolerance in a distant land. And it is thus possible to see the bomb and its quick and slow armageddons as one of the byproducts of Hitler's "final solution."

Bacon had thought that science could redeem humanity's fall from grace, but that science culminated in the atom bomb, which Oppenheimer saw as the fall itself when he said, "Science has known sin." He never clarified what sin it—or rather the physicists of the Manhattan Project—had known, whether it was the sin of believing that they were on an Arcadian excursion when they were in fact part of a Utopian project or whether their sin had been that of turning it from an excursion into a project, changing a disinterested international pursuit of truth into a race for national advantage. Only Bohr and Szilard saw ahead to the impending arms race they tried to warn the Allied leaders of, but their warnings went unheeded. "Any temporary advantage, however great, may be outweighed by a perpetual menace to human society," Bohr told Roosevelt, but Roosevelt died soon afterward.

It is said that the Chinese had gunpowder for many centuries but
chose not to use it for war, and that the Maya put wheels on the toys
of their children but chose not to build wheeled vehicles for practical use. It seems that they attempted to preserve their cultures in a
state of equilibrium, rather than to push them down a road of progress
toward an unknown destination, that they valued stability more than
the unknowns that come with improvement. It is conceivable that if
the physicists had been Chinese or Mayan, they could have realized
the possibility of the bomb without ever building it. But theirs was a
Utopian culture overall, and it took less than seven years, from
Christmas 1938—the day Meitner and Frisch went walking—to July
15, 1945, to fulfil the possibilities they realized in atomic fission. The
bomb was made to fight the Nazis, but only one scientist dropped out
of the Manhattan Project when Germany collapsed in late 1944. There
was no way the military was going to spend $2 billion and have
nothing to show for it, and so Oppenheimer's bombs at Hiroshima
and Nagasaki were meant to justify a budget as well as to fight a war.
They were dropped for scientific reasons too: even the Department
of Energy's own handbook of nuclear tests lists those two explosions
as tests. To call such an act a test clarifies how far the mind-set of scientific control had warped the vision of those who would call all future
bomb explosions tests, no matter what their effects on the world
around them.

Perhaps the bomb was inevitable, but the arms race was born
of the suspicion between Germany and its enemies and then between
the Soviet Union and its former allies in the war against Germany. It
is a great irony that for much of the Cold War, the United States and
the Soviet Union stationed nuclear missiles in the divided Germany
and planned limited nuclear wars on its soil; another great irony is that
some of the greatest resistance to nuclear weapons arose in Germany.
But those who suffered most from the nuclear tests of the Cold War
have been elsewhere, in Kazakhstan and the Uigur province of China
(China, not the China of fireworks but the China of Mao, has had the
bomb since 1964), in the Aboriginal lands of Australia and in Algeria,
in the Marshall Islands and French Polynesia, and in the Great Basin
lands downwind of the Nevada Test Site.

The anthropologist Hugh Gusterson studied nuclear physicists
and antinuclear activists for several years and came to some inter-

esting conclusions about the cultures generated by nuclear weapons. At the end of the Cold War, as Iraq began to replace the disintegrating Soviet Union in bomb makers' justifications, Gusterson wrote about the beliefs about nuclear weapons and their uses as a kind of story the nation had been told: "The cold-war narrative is simultaneously utopian and despairing about human nature, and it mixes a faith in the redemptive power of technology with an American sense of manifest destiny that is paradoxically reinforced by our government's crimes and failures. By adhering firmly to the belief that America, both morally and technologically, is a chosen nation, the cold-war narrative extends the myth of American exceptionalism—the conviction that America is a country apart, blessed with vast territories and tremendous wealth as part of its historical mission to redeem the fallen nations of the earth. The myth of American exceptionalism runs throughout the country's history, from the Puritan settlement of New England, to the settlement of the frontier, to the nation's rise to global empire. . . . We will not see deep cuts in military spending and a fundamental restructuring of the American warfare state as long as this narrative and the institutions that sponsor it remain powerful. . . . Displacing the narrative will require political organizing against the military-industrial coalition, of course, but it will also require the construction of a new peace narrative that is as compelling and authentically American as the cold-war narrative."

THE PHYSICS THAT LED UP TO THE BOMB, LIKE THE WALKS that preceded the march toward the bomb, seemed to be a path to a different world, a richer, more complex story. Einstein's relativity, Heisenberg's uncertainty principle, and Bohr's complementarity suggested a subtler model of truth than classical physics and Cartesian philosophy put forward. The scientific method had been premised on the clear separation of the true and the false, the observer and the observed: in these newer concepts, they began to blur. They suggested a model of the world in which what is seen is contingent upon where you look from, the objectivity of the spectator is undermined, observation becomes a form of involvement, and no position is detached (something the Nuremberg principles would affirm in a vastly different arena). In recent years, many writers have attempted to interpret quantum physics in terms of Buddhism, Taoism, and other mystic traditions (and when Bohr was initiated into the Danish Order of the Elephant and given a coat of arms, he chose the Chinese yin/yang symbol as his emblem). Heisenberg wrote, "It has been pointed out before that in the Copenhagen interpretation of quantum theory we can indeed proceed without mentioning ourselves as individuals, but we cannot disregard the fact that natural science is formed by men." He went on to say that science is a description not of nature but of the interaction between scientists and nature, "nature as exposed to our method of questioning." In other words, science is a conversation in which the answers depend on the questions, and the narrative, the account of the conversation, has to include the questioner. The pigeonholes that had been so central to the ideals of scientific method could not encompass such a narrative.

Bohr had hoped that the implications of complementarity would be far-reaching. In a lecture to anthropologists and ethnologists in 1938, he used complementarity to undermine the intolerance of the Nazis: "Using the word much as it is used in atomic physics to characterize the relationship between experiences obtained by different experimental arrangements and visualizable only by mutually exclusive terms, we may truly say that different human cultures are complementary to each other. Indeed such culture represents a harmonious balance of traditional conventions by means of which latent potentialities of human life can unfold themselves in a way which reveals to us new aspects of its unlimited richness and variety." Bohr also extended the lessons of the uncertainty principle into a lifelong emphasis on the nonobjective involvement of the observer in what is observed, in the way that what we see is conditioned by what we believe and what symbols we use to describe it. A friend of his recounts, "When one said to him that it cannot be language which is fundamental, but that it must be reality which, so to say, lies beneath language and of which language is a picture, he would reply, 'We are suspended in language in such a way that we cannot say what is up and what is down. The word "reality" is also a word, a word which we must learn to use correctly.'" Like Heisenberg, he believed there was no story without a teller, no fact beyond the influence of its context.

It seems as though quantum physics should have left as its legacy an understanding in which the absolutes and pigeonholes of classical physics and objectivist philosophies became something more rich and strange. Perhaps the principle of complementarity could have reconciled the communist and capitalist worlds to each other. Perhaps the fantasies of control over the political future and the weapons themselves might have been dispelled. Perhaps. But the governments and their strategists took from the physicists not their ideas but their invention.

| | | | | | |

I WANT TO TALK ABOUT THE PASTORAL ONE MORE TIME. THE physicists saw themselves as being on a pastoral excursion. In a pastoral, nothing happens; Arcadia is a refuge from happenings, from history. But something happened, and they, and we, can never go back. Perhaps when they moved from the forests to the desert, or perhaps when they moved from ideas to inventions, they left their pastoral and entered a genesis, a time of creation that in their case included a fall into history—the sin that science knew in New Mexico. A story in which nothing happened—a pastoral—became a story in which an epochal change happened—a genesis—became a story of a stalemate with an apocalypse hovering behind it—the Cold War narrative. Or perhaps they mistook Arcadia for a sanctuary, rather than just an ideal—a peace narrative—with which to gird themselves against utopia's seductions.

The bomb served the function it was intended for in the wake of World War II. It girded the superpowers against each other and gave each side an argument for trampling and terrifying and sometimes killing its own citizens. But it inadvertently served other functions as well, and in doing so it may have fulfilled the promise of quantum physics. The Bible describes a few occasions when the cosmology of the world changed: the expulsion from Paradise, the Deluge, the Resurrection. At these times, the covenant between human beings and their environment was profoundly altered. The bomb was such an epochal event, both the consummation of utopian fantasies of control of nature and their end—Bacon's redemption and Oppenheimer's fall—and it is easy to imagine its story becoming in

1,000 years a second creation story tacked onto the Bible after the Book of Revelation. It changed everything: the notion of human scale— physicists had manipulated the subatomic to generate destructive power on an unimagined scale, brighter than the sun and deadly for half a million years; the possibility of morally neutral science; the nature of nature itself, with radiation's insidious effects on genes and health. Most significantly, the bomb seemed to close a lot of the divides that had organized the Western worldview: between observer and observed, between matter and energy, between science and politics, between war and peace—after the bomb, any place could be annihilated without warning, and the nuclear powers were permanently prepared for war. Finally, the potential effects of the bomb were so pervasive over time and space that notions of containment and separation collapsed.

The radiations of the bomb, along with the herbicides and pesticides developed from chemical warfare research, were the first quiet messengers that the Earth could no longer be regarded as a collection of inanimate objects but must be seen as a network of intricately balanced systems—that is, the substances themselves first spoke out against the inadequacy of the Cartesian worldview, and Rachel Carson first gave them a voice: "In this now universal contamination of the environment, chemicals are the sinister and little-recognized partners of radiation in changing the very nature of the world—the very nature of its life. Strontium 90, released through nuclear explosions into the air, comes to earth in rain or drifts down as fallout, lodges in soil, enters into the grass or corn or wheat grown there, and in time takes up its abode in the bones of a human being. . . ."

Carson echoes the credo with which Thoreau returned to his senses: "I believe in the forest, and in the meadow, and in the night in which the corn grows." The understanding that everything is connected, which should have come as a vision of harmony, came as a nightmare of contamination instead, but it came, and it came from the bomb. And from this fear of contamination and of armageddon and this distrust of nuclear authorities came the vast resistance movements of Britain, Germany, Russia, Kazakhstan, and the United States, came the voices of opposition from Szilard to Carson to Sakharov to Suleymenov to Caldecott. From it came an antiauthoritarianism that would challenge the governments and their judgement and their legitimacy, that would put into practice the Nuremberg Principles that were likewise a legacy of the Third Reich, and that would bring the Arcadians to the gates of the Test Site again and again. And so, if the great early physicists of the bomb were walking toward the Test Site without realizing it, perhaps a few of them were marching across the cattle guard before us, not landing in the government jets.

1993

Hoovering to Byzantium

| | | | | | |

David Carpenter

| | | | | | |

F OR A LONG TIME, I'VE BEEN LOOKING FOR AN ALL-
purpose verb that describes what writers do when they use (lift?
recycle? borrow? deconstruct? steal? rework? draw from?) someone
else's story to tell their own. Take the case of Herodotus. He is very
popular these days. More than twenty-four centuries have passed
since he recounted the story of Gyges and Candaules, but this story
still beckons modern writers to the keyhole of a certain ill-fated
bedroom. Candaules, king of Lydia, has conceived an immoderate
heat for his queen. She is never named, but she is the most powerful character in the story. The irrepressible king doesn't seem to realize
this. He brags to his friend Gyges (bodyguard and confidant) that the
queen's beauty is unsurpassed. He insists that Gyges hide in their
bedroom and see for himself. Gyges declines the offer. It is improper,
he argues, but the king insists. Under orders, Gyges hides in the royal
boudoir. He spies the queen naked, then steals from the room. The
next day he is summoned by the queen, who spotted him slinking
out of the boudoir. She is outraged by her husband's indecency. She
gives Gyges an ultimatum: either die for this act of voyeurism or kill
the author of it and marry her. Once again, Gyges protests against any
involvement, and once again to no avail. He agrees to serve the
queen, murders Candaules, and rules by her side in Lydia.

Modern writers as different from one another as Mario Vargas
Llosa and Michael Ondaatje have revived (revived?) the Gyges and

Candaules story in various ways. Here is an interesting example from another contemporary novelist. The story is about a middle-aged man of reasonable affluence who has yet to learn the fundamentals of love. He is a historian of sorts, but at this difficult time in his life he discovers he would rather read myths than history. One of his favourite stories is that of Gyges and Candaules. In fact, it turns into a real-life scenario when he is given the opportunity to play Gyges, destroy the king, and leap into bed with the queen.

Our man meets a fascinating, learned, intuitive woman whom he considers to be ugly and obnoxious. She has an irritating habit of lecturing him. He believes her to be interfering with his private concerns, and in some mysterious sense he sees her as a devil, perhaps even *the* Devil. They argue and eventually have a fight. A physical fight. He wins by beating her in the face, but for both of them this brawl is the beginning of love.

His ordeal is far from over. He has to confront his best friend, the Candaules figure, and humiliate him so severely that the two can never be friends again. This revenge (described as "eating up" the other fellow) involves forcing him to see his own duplicity.

By now some of you will have guessed which novel I am summarizing. In case not, I can provide a final clue. The symbol that draws together the separate threads of this story is a severed head believed to utter prophecies that lead to strange and forbidden knowledge. Its voice is that of the demonic woman, who has an uncanny grasp of our hero's deeper self.

Many readers of contemporary British fiction will have guessed that this novel is *A Severed Head* (1961) by Iris Murdoch, the story of Martin Lynch-Gibbon and his bewildering love for Honor Klein. Well done, except my summary is also of the plot of *Fifth Business* (1970) by the Canadian novelist Robertson Davies. Virtually every detail of my summary fits both novels. More than a decade ago, I was jolted by my discovery of these similarities. Hmm, said the young scholar, eyebrows raised, moral judgements in their silos at the ready. Hmm. This bears looking into.

I was living in Toronto, finishing my first book of fiction (*Jokes for the Apocalypse*). It was late in the winter of 1983, and I was on a very long leave from university teaching. I thought I could take a brief rest from the rigours of fiction writing to do an essay on the

similarities between the two novels. *A Severed Head* was present in
Fifth Business like a palimpsest. You just had to scrape a bit and there
it was. I would first approach Davies and give him a chance to defend
himself by phrasing my key question as diplomatically as possible: is
Fifth Business your response to *A Severed Head?* Fifteen years ago, such
a question might have been considered part of the new critical
discourse. Among certain university writers, *all* novels were responses
or reactions to previous novels.

Early in 1984, I called Davies's secretary at Massey College and
made an appointment to see Davies. He greeted me with warmth
and consideration, and he answered my first few questions without
difficulty.

"Is *Fifth Business* your response to Iris Murdoch's *A Severed
Head?*" I said boldly.

"What do you mean?" he said.

I rattled off my list of similarities, which was not short, conclud-
ing with the way Davies uses the story of Gyges and Candaules, and
he grew quiet. The temperature in the room seemed to drop.

"Well," he said at last, "you must realize, Mr. Carpenter, that
many writers of the twentieth century like to use myths."

Until that moment, his answers had been direct and thoughtful.
This response seemed preposterously inadequate. Aha, I said to
myself. Bull's-eye. I pushed my thesis further, but to no avail. Our
conversation wandered into innocuous territory.

The more I thought about my interview with Davies, however,
the less enthused I became over my planned essay. What was I going
to say? That Davies the master novelist was a closet literary lifter? And
what business did I, a young neophyte with more ego than reputation, have meddling with the reputation of a man I respect? I dropped
the project, and it died right there.

But I never forgot Davies's discomfort at my question—that it
had been an invasion of some kind. To this day, I'm convinced that
Robertson Davies read Iris Murdoch's *A Severed Head* before he wrote
Fifth Business and found things in Murdoch's novel he could use in
his own. (Readers will note that I have not used the *p* word.)

To be fair, we also need to look at the differences between
these two novels. Murdoch's is a modern comedy of manners for a
sophisticated 1960s audience with at least some familiarity with D. H.

Lawrence and his "dark gods." Her story begins when Martin Lynch-Gibbon's marriage breaks down. His lovely wife, Antonia, is a fashionable society beauty five years Martin's senior. She tells Martin one day that she has fallen in love with her psychoanalyst, a charismatic American named Palmer Anderson who is Martin's best friend and our King Candaules figure. Until this moment, Martin has been drifting along in a complacent wooze of pleasure and comfort. He loves his mistress, Georgie, sort of, but keeps her a secret from everyone. He also loves his wife, sort of. He is a wine merchant, and he finds the business prosperous and fulfilling, sort of. But when wife Antonia tells him that she wants to leave him for Palmer, Martin promptly falls, however shallowly, in love with her. These three characters attempt to be civil about things. Martin outdoes himself as the good loser. "There was nothing I could do," he says, "except act out with dignity my appointed task of being rational and charitable." His wife tries to mother him through his agonies and maintains an almost daily connection with him. She persuades him to go and see her new lover. Martin does, and the two men try to revitalize their friendship.

Enter Honor Klein, half-sister of Palmer, a Cambridge professor of anthropology and custodian of the dark gods of the Aboriginal people she lectures about. It is dislike at first sight, but Honor and Martin are thrown together on a number of awkward occasions because Honor's half-brother and Martin's wife are now living together. They fight, and soon after Martin acquires a fascination for the repellent and devilish woman. He is falling violently in love. Things have become very complicated indeed. Martin pursues the woman all the way back to her home in Cambridge and, under the influence of drink and eros, breaks into her boudoir when she is in bed with— are we ready for this? —her half-brother, the psychoanalyst, who is supposed to be with Martin's wife, Antonia.

The charismatic king has been exposed, so to speak. From this moment on, Palmer loses his power over Martin, Antonia, and even Honor, Palmer's half-sister and longtime lover. Martin repels Palmer from his wife, regains her for a brief, quiet, boring reunion, but soon yearns to be with Honor. No longer does she seem to be ugly. He tells the woman of his hopeless passion for her. She tells him, "Because of what I am and because of what you saw I am a terrible object of fascination for you. I am a severed head such as primitive tribes and old alchemists used to use, anointing it with oil and putting a morsel of gold upon its tongue to make it utter prophesies. And who knows but that long acquaintance with a severed head might not lead to strange knowledge." She discourages his advances, and he backs away.

Just when Martin feels as though the two halves of his life might be coming together (the feeling and the thinking halves), Antonia delivers her second little surprise: she has always loved his brother, Alexander, and wants a divorce so that she can marry *him*. Once again, Martin prepares himself for the loneliness and confusion of living alone, but this time without his mistress, Georgie, who is undergoing therapy with (you guessed it) Palmer Anderson. Re-enter Honor Klein. She has decided not to turn her back on Martin. By the end of the novel, they are about to embark on an adventure with one another that just might have something to do with love.

In summary, this novel might sound like a soap opera for people with a BA in psychology, but it's wittier and more challenging than my summary has allowed. All six characters have gone through the convulsions of love and separation, and all six emerge from their chaos and futility with a new partner. Georgie flies off with Palmer to New York, the place Martin has never managed to take her. Antonia settles in with Alexander, whom she has always adored. And Martin and Honor bring the novel to a close with a relationship that "has nothing to do with happiness, nothing whatever." Martin says to Honor, "I wonder if I shall survive it." She says with a smile, "You must take your chance!" And here are the last words of the novel: "I gave her back the bright light of the smile, now softening at last out of irony. 'So must you, my dear!'"

"Irony" is the operative word here. Much more than a diversion for the jejune at heart, Murdoch's novel is an ironic look at the breakdown of familiar patterns in the life of a middle-class man and the world he walks through without ever quite getting the goods on. Martin's world is filled with self-assured, articulate, well-educated people who dispense a great deal of advice, but almost always the advice is wrong or leads to chaos. Murdoch's characters live amid the plenty of the British postwar boom, but the one commodity they cannot seem to lay by is certainty. *A Severed Head* is a manual on how to survive without certainty. The novel enjoyed popular success and an afterlife when it was made into a film in 1970, the year *Fifth Business* was published.

Davies's novel was one of the first serious works of Canadian fiction to reach an international audience. Writers as different and eminent as John Fowles, Anthony Burgess, Saul Bellow, and John Irving have sung its praises in print. An impressive stack of scholarly articles has been published on The Deptford Trilogy, of which *Fifth Business* is the first and most illustrious instalment. It seems to draw heavily on *A Severed Head* for some of its characters and subplots and for some of its themes and mythic structures, but the novel has a life of its own.

Fifth Business is the story of Dunstable Ramsay, perhaps the most famous curmudgeon in Canadian literature. His story begins when he is ten years old and has a disagreement with his friend, Percy Boyd Staunton. Dunstable refuses to fight Percy and instead tries to ignore his bad-tempered taunts and snowballs. To avoid Percy's last salvo, he steps in front of a couple going for a walk. One is Reverend Amasa Dempster, the other his young pregnant wife, Mary. Percy's snowball (which has a stone inside) strikes Mary on the head with great force, and she falls to the ground. She is taken to the doctor and gives birth prematurely to a grotesque and unnaturally small child. For the rest of her life, Mary will be confined in one way or another. She will be stigmatized as the "simple" woman of Deptford.

Her assailant, Percy Boyd Staunton, is our Candaules figure here. He's the son of the richest man in Deptford. He manages to silence young Dunstable (a reluctant Gyges figure) with a threat, and Dunstable takes on the guilt of the entire tragedy. He devotes a good part of the next sixty years of his life to the care and maintenance of Mary Dempster, whom he comes to see as a saint.

Paul Dempster, the tiny grotesque child of Mary, grows up to be a strange, inverted Christ figure. While still a boy, he is seduced by the circus and runs away from home to become a performer and a master conjuror who creates miracles of illusion on stage. He changes his name to Magnus Eisengrim. Percy Boyd Staunton grows from a young son of a bitch to a very rich bastard, but he still maintains a connection, even perhaps a friendship, with Dunstable Ramsay. He is so proud of his queen Leola's beauty that he insists upon showing nude photographs of her to Dunny/Gyges. (Just as Dunstable is a

reluctant Gyges figure, Leola is a reluctant queen of Lydia figure.)
Percy changes his name to Boy Staunton, which is consistent with his
self-image as an eternally young and fatally handsome swordsman
among the ladies. Dunstable grows up to be a schoolmaster of history,
a hagiographer of world renown, and changes his name to Dunstan
Ramsay, after St. Dunstan, who in saintly lore is said to have grabbed
the Devil by the nose with a pair of tongs. He resists the role of Gyges
or any other heroic role thrust upon him to become instead a sort of
moral historian. Dunstan Ramsay is Fifth Business. He is

> the odd man out, the person who has no opposite of the other
> sex. And you must have Fifth Business because he is the one
> [in an opera] who knows the secret of the hero's birth, or comes
> to the assistance of the heroine when she thinks all is lost, or
> keeps the hermitess in her cell, or may even be the cause of
> somebody's death if that is part of the plot. The prima donna
> and the tenor, the contralto and the basso, get all the best music
> and do all the spectacular things, but you cannot manage the
> plot without Fifth Business.

The woman who tells Dunstan this is Lieselotte Vitzlipützli (Liesl for
short), a Swiss gargoyle and personal devil for Dunny. Very much
like Honor Klein in *A Severed Head,* Liesl becomes less loathsome to
Dunny. Indeed, after she and Dunny fight, they make love. Liesl is
the brains behind Magnus Eisengrim's magic show, the *Soirée of
Illusions.* One of her functions with the magic show is to be the voice
for the Brazen Head, a severed head that speaks prophecies and tells
fortunes to the audience.

I have mentioned that *A Severed Head* is a comedy of manners
about a society in disarray. Appearances are deceptive in the extreme.
The gurus in Murdoch's novel are frequently wrong. Circumstances
in Martin's world dictate a disengagement from anything resembling
a traditional morality. Martin can try to do good, he can try to acknowledge his own guilt or judge others as guilty, he can try to see the
many ways in which he too is culpable in this conspiracy of infidelity
and counterinfidelity, but he must eventually pursue a quest for identity that leads away from the comforts of middle-class morality or any
recognizable code of decency and move into the darkness of Honor's
neoprimitive vision of things. Whatever Martin gains, it will be at the
cost of stability in his life.

By contrast, Dunstan comes from a family and a small town that have none of the grace, affluence, and sophistication of Martin's world. Dunstan grows up under the shadow of Calvinism; if he can't feel enough guilt, he will manufacture some more. When his gurus (such as Liesl) teach him at last that his Calvinistic beliefs are more destructive than they are redeeming, he comes to espouse a Jungian vision of life, with its timeless cycles and archetypal world of wonders, and this vision lends stability and a sort of poetry to his life. In *Fifth Business,* the gurus are usually wise and almost always right, and like Dunstan Ramsay, who is frequently lectured to by priests, philosophers, and learned women, we the readers are enticed toward this Jungian vision of things. Utterly unlike *A Severed Head, Fifth Business* is a masterpiece of didactic fiction, a learned polemic on the eternal verities by a devout Jungian. Indeed, there is enough theoretical discussion in Davies's novel to constitute a sort of Jungian gloss on Murdoch's. The difference is that Dunstan and Davies remain relentlessly moral in their outlook.

It starts with an accident. Or is it syncronicity? A small missile strikes a saintly, sensual, and allegedly simple woman on the head. The missile mysteriously disappears throughout most of the novel and then reappears. Our narrator spends the rest of his life trying to come to terms with this life-altering event, and from boyhood to manhood he sees miracles that could belong in a history of the saints (for example, the miraculous appearance of a statue of Mary). From the favourite hangouts of his small town to the musty rooms of the private school where he teaches, haunted by religious miracles, he carries with him the secrets of the past. Perhaps the greatest secret has to do with the grotesque and tiny child whose parents are a sad parody of Mary and Joseph. But their child's life is a sort of miraculous epic. Our narrator remains a bachelor in Toronto and courts the company of priests and theologues. He is inflexibly moral to the end.

I know, I'm repeating myself. But I'm also summarizing for you the plot of a more recent American novel, John Irving's *A Prayer for Owen Meany* (1989). All of these bizarre details fit Irving's novel. This time the saintly/sensual Mary figure dies in the accident, and she's more of a Magdalene than a Madonna. So is the mysterious statue that seems to preside over her memory. The missile is no longer a snowball with a piece of granite inside; it is now a baseball. (Irving's story is, after all, primarily an American novel.) But all in all, these and many other plot details are remarkably similar.

John Irving has made no secret of his admiration for Robertson Davies's *Fifth Business*. And he goes one step further. His schoolmaster narrator, John Wheelwright, reminds us that he has taught *Fifth Business* "with the greatest pleasure" to his literature class in a Toronto private school. "I consider Mr. Davies," Wheelwright tells one of his colleagues, "an author of such universal importance that I choose not to teach what is 'Canadian' about his books, but what is wonderful about them."

Perhaps something "wonderful" from Davies's novel survives in Irving's, something to do with the narration of miracles to an audience in need of them. But my speculation scarcely does justice to Irving, for *A Prayer for Owen Meany* is utterly and unmistakably irvingated with his own concerns and obsessions, such as the war in Vietnam, and with the memory, the smell, the mythology of his New England setting. Speaking of New England mythology, note Irving's debt to Nathaniel Hawthorne. Both novels deal with saintly/sensual New England women who have a child out of wedlock because of a liaison with a minister whose cowardly lips are sealed. And both women are pretty fond of red and handy with the needle, as I recall.

I wonder if Davies could have prevented himself from smiling at the above passage from *A Prayer for Owen Meany*; no doubt it is Irving's acknowledgement to Davies. I wonder if Davies could have prevented himself from smiling at the entire novel. Surely imitation is the sincerest form of flattery. (And if so, perhaps Iris Murdoch and Herodotus are also smiling.)

I MUST ADMIT, THIS ESSAY IS A BIT MORE PERSONAL IN ITS origins than I have so far admitted. I have a little confession to make. A few years after my meeting with Davies and after the publication of my first book of fiction, I attended a literature conference. A colleague of mine, David Williams, approached me. He had just read my book, *Jokes for the Apocalypse*.

"What's this Robertson Davies connection?" he said.

"What do you mean?" I asked.

He quoted a phrase to me: "the revenge of the unlived life."

I must have lost the same amount of colour as Davies had some years earlier. The phrase, spoken by my narrator, Ham Walmsley, originally came from the mouth of—you guessed it—Liesl in *Fifth Business.*

Williams offered to extend his list of similarities, but I derailed him. I couldn't bear to hear it. I, David Carpenter, a "good lad" the neighbourhood mothers had said, a former boy scout, a regular attender at the local Sunday school, a man who had grown up believing that honesty is the best policy, I had taken . . . lifted . . . stolen . . . appropriated . . . I had . . . I had gone and p-p-p. . . .

My embarrassment was the beginning of this essay. Why was I embarrassed? Why did Davies become so diffident? Were we both getting protective of our lair, or were we wondering whether we held full title to it? Or, better still, where do writers' notions of ownership of literary commodities come from? Where do our notions of originality and literary theft come from? I can begin to confront these questions by looking first at my own sense of culpability at having been discovered with my net in Davies's goldfish bowl.

What interests me here are the ways in which we writers deploy our reading in order to write our books. I have to approach this phenomenon not as a theorist or an academic sleuth but as a writer. So many theorists and academics from Eliot to Foucault have made pronouncements on the ways in which literary discourse arises from a whole galaxy of literary discourse that the long shadow of an orthodoxy has been cast over the subject. One is apt to forget the utterly personal, sometimes turbulent, even neurotic process by which a writer's words find their way onto the page. If we listen to theorists only, we might be tempted to think of the creative process as a self-possessed act of scholarship or an exercise in cleverness, or that the best literature is like a rising corporate executive, the literature with the best connections.

I want to begin with the state of mind that led up to my work on "Jokes for the Apocalypse," the title novella of my book. I began writing it in the summer of 1980 at a Canadian writers' colony in Fort San, Saskatchewan. We writers lived and worked in a huge, spooky old chalet in the Qu'Appelle Valley. This residence was filled (it seemed to all of us) with the ghosts of hundreds, perhaps thousands, of mustard gas victims from the First World War and many more victims of tuberculosis. Our chalet bore a physical resemblance to the one in Thomas Mann's *The Magic Mountain*, with its rows of screened-in porches for sitting in the cool dry air. Strange and memorable things happened to me in that chalet and to other writers who went there, year after year.

The place was frequented by ghostly memories, and so was I. I was not thinking a great deal about literature or about Robertson Davies. As always, the words of my favourite books were hovering somewhere in my brain and even lodging in my tongue, but my mind at the time of composition was unusually feverish with the story I was about to write, peopled by characters who already had their own voices, which in turn emerged to some extent from some personal details in my life. I was hungrily sucking up all sorts of things from life and memory. For one thing, I was uneasy over an affair I had had with a young woman. I couldn't be sure that I had acted responsibly. I was beginning to wonder whether I had ever acted responsibly. A sentence from Adele Wiseman, a writer and friend of mine, kept circling around in my head: *How can men ever begin to understand the delicate ecology of those adoring young women? The men just haul on their woodsmen's boots and stomp around on the flowers.*

I began my story with an accurate memory of once picking up a hitchhiker. Soon the memory passed into fiction, and my main narrator lurched into his own identity, oozing alcohol from every pore. Ham Walmsley is long on charm and short on compassion, and his life is about to collapse. Just as I was on my way to Fort San when I picked up my entirely real hitchhiker, he too is on his way there. He is going to a job, teaching band to teenagers.

Walmsley is a charming man haunted by an emotionally desolate past. He has a curious relationship with guilt: he repels it and courts it with impressive ease. He has long, carefree lapses from the ordinary rules of consideration for others and then sudden attacks of guilt. The guilt is part of a cycle; it is so overwhelming that it guarantees and renews Ham's need for another binge. He has sex with his lovely young hitchhiker and then drops her off the next morning so that she can hitch back to the city they both came from. A terrible fate befalls her, and Ham begins to feel responsible. Then he blocks her out so that he can no longer even remember what she looks like. But still he suffers terribly. Part of his atonement is to unburden himself to a colleague down at Fort San, an artist who is older than he, a woman named Lena Rotzoll with an adventurous past who has done her share of suffering. They exchange anguished accounts and for a while form a bond of fellow sufferers. When his atonement is in full swing, Ham is at last visited by Lola, his mysterious hitchhiker, who is either a ghostly memory or a memorable ghost. I could never be sure about the ghosts of Fort San (which is a book in itself); Ham Walmsley can never be sure if this last visitation from Lola is anything more than a desperate eruption from his own suppressed imagination.

His imagination has begun to turn on him and clamour for expression. Here is a rumination from near the beginning of "Jokes for the Apocalypse" in which Ham is thinking back to the dog he loved when he was a boy. His mother finally had the dog put down. "I blew up. . . . I yelled at her and she told me she knew I slept with that dog. The only reason she'd ever let it go on was that she felt sorry for me. It occurred to me years later what she was really accusing me of. Not that there would have been anything wrong with it. In the absence of love you start to wonder if any kind of love isn't perhaps its own justification . . . such thoughts for a man who teaches band. *Revenge of the unlived life.*" (italics added)

Compare the above with the following passage from *Fifth Business*. Liesl, that beautiful gargoyle, is lecturing Dunny about the stupidity of his Calvinistic background. "But even Calvinism can be endured," she says, "if you will make some compromise with yourself. But you—there is a whole great piece of your life that is unlived, denied, set aside. That is why at fifty you can't bear it any longer and fly all to pieces and pour out your heart to the first really intelligent woman you have met—me, that's to say—and get into a schoolboy yearning for a girl who is as far from you as if she lived on the moon. This is the *revenge of the unlived life.*" (italics added)

I am now quite sure that Liesl's last sentence above is my source for Ham's words in my own book. I am also sure that the Lena-Ham relationship draws heavily on the Dunny-Liesl relationship. I have always loved that part of *Fifth Business*. I must have carried this construct and these words somewhere inside, and when Ham begins his furtive ruminations on love and the desolation of his own life— there they were, these words. This concise wisdom. The writer in me chose them. A few years later, the author in me was embarrassed by them.

This distinction between writer and author is an important one, and perhaps more important now than ever before, because never before in literary history has the split between author and writer been wider. The writer is still the person who sits in a musty little room and scribbles things down. The writer is a dull fellow or gal but does the real work of writing. The author is the one who *has written* it. He wears the ascot, or she dresses all in black and signs copies of her books, says provocative things at readings, and lives in the world we call society. She is a public perception of the writer, sometimes even a public icon. She is just as often a fake, or he a dandy, a self-important bohemian who sits in cafés and flirts with waitresses and bemoans his state of misunderstood genius to all who will listen. Authors hold court. Only when they hold pens are they writers once again.

When Chaucer translated the poets of the Italian Renaissance and borrowed from Boccaccio to write *Troilus and Criseyde,* it was the writer who did it. And thank God he did. Who would argue that Chaucer's poem about Troy isn't also a very English poem? Again, when Shakespeare absorbed all those materials by Geoffrey of Monmouth, John Higgins, Edmund Spenser, and others for *King Lear,* the writer in him did it. To worry about literary lifting at the time of composition—to the writer then or now—would amount to so much fussiness. Such worries would interfere with the delicate process of a story or a poem unfolding. Such worries might well have inhibited the flowering of the English Renaissance. (Let us remember that Shakespeare *the author* has all but vanished from sight. We don't know who the hell he was. The more we speculate about it, the more we become suspect as scholars. Shakespeare *the writer,* now there's another case entirely.)

When it comes to the work of contemporary writers, I sometimes detect a bad smell hovering over conversations about the ways in which writers deploy their reading for their own purposes. How many times have I heard the phrase that so and so's work is too derivative? Perhaps so and so's work *is too derivative,* but sometimes I can't escape the pervasive assumption that influence is a problem rather than a normal state of affairs. This assumption has evolved slowly over the last four centuries.

Thomas Mallon, the American English scholar and critic, gives a lively account of the evolution of literary borrowing of all kinds in his book *Stolen Words* (1989). He begins with the Aristotelian notion of literature born of imitation. Imitative writing was seen as a virtue. "The great critical cry of classical literature was not an Emersonian call to 'trust thyself' but a Horatian exhortation to follow others." Around the time of Shakespeare's rise in the theatre world, however, the virtues of imitation must have been wearing a bit thin. Elizabethan writers such as Robert Greene grumbled about Shakespeare's habit of borrowing plots. As writers began more and more to live by their pens instead of through the good graces of their patrons, they began to do more than grumble about borrowing. They began to make some unmistakably territorial sounds. Robert Burton (whose *Anatomy of Melancholy* [1621] was to be looted by Laurence Sterne) emerged to set the standard for acknowledged borrowing in the early seventeenth century. Mallon tells us that at this time "the word was getting around that words could be owned by their first writers" because literary property was now being thought of as "both imaginative and financial capital." We can trace this emerging attitude toward literary property by looking at the evolution of the word *plagiarism*. In classical times, a "plagiary" (from the Latin *plagium*) was a kidnapper. Not until Ben Jonson readapted the term was it associated with literary theft. And it wasn't until the eighteenth century that we had an authoritative (albeit spare) definition of plagiarism, Samuel Johnson's: "Theft; literary adoption of the thoughts or works of another." This definition came about (mid-eighteenth century) when the notion of originality was beginning to spread. What oft was thought but ne'er so well expressed—the words themselves—had at last become a commodity. The fear in the mind of a seventeenth-century writer, that he might be vilified as a word-for-word plagiarist, became an official crime in the eighteenth century. In the nineteenth century, again in England, originality finally became an orthodoxy, and the copyright statute was amended so that a writer's publication was protected for forty-two years after publication. If plagiarism and copyright piracy in the England of Dickens were still concerns, in America they were a veritable plague. Not until the end of the nineteenth century did Americans begin to honour the spirit of English copyright laws. Mallon tells us that "only in 1988 did the Senate vote to allow American participation in the Berne Convention on international copyright that was drawn up in 1886." The world and all of literature have always been the storehouse of the writer. But what is a storehouse to the writer is now a loans department to the author.

It's fair to assume that with the growth of our notions about originality and literary theft came a more intense awareness of shame and infamy at being accused of plagiarism. Indeed, for most of the authors surveyed in Mallon's book, the greatest fear was not of lawsuits but of the moral stigma of getting caught in a furtive act: using the materials and especially the words of other writers without proper acknowledgement. The more readers and writers revered "original-ity" as an absolute artistic virtue, the more the spectre of guilt floated over the "influenced" writer's horizon.

The influenced writer. Does that sound like a euphemism? Alert readers of the world, merlin-eyed scholars, I beg you to think otherwise.

EVEN WITH THE PROLIFERATION OF ELECTRONIC TECHNOLOGY, the world of the writer hasn't changed much. Writers are still at their best alone with a story in a private little room. But the world of the author has changed drastically. Authors must learn how to project a public image. To sell their books, they must become *good copy*. It helps if they look good on television. Once they have become well enough known to make a living by their words, they need good agents and lawyers. Now that film and television contracts constitute a large chunk of the successful author's income, the money stakes are much higher. The author is more like a sports hero or a corporate star than ever before, and because authors live very much in the world their ethics must conform even more to the rules of corporate law. As busi-nesspeople, they are disengaged from the thing they do best: pecking away in their studies or garrets, where imagination is the only legis-lator and where conscience has more to do with getting it right than with trying not to offend other writers. Little wonder that dullard pecking away in the garret is so much happier. The writer can forget for a little while that he or she is compelled to be an author.

WHEN MY BROTHER AND I WERE SMALL BOYS, IN WINTER-time we would play on the living room floor with our box of metal cowboys and Indians, engaging them in a perpetual battle that rang throughout the house. On certain days, my mother would come along to hoover the floor. In our house, one did not vacuum, one hoovered. We had scarcely acquired this machine when it became a verb.

"Out of my way, you varmints," she would say. "When I'm hoovering rugs, nothing escapes this machine."

The Hoover sucked up dirt, nails, toys, lint, fuzzy candies, and coins with an impressive lack of discrimination. With a little imagination, our Hoover could become a science fiction nightmare. Sometimes my brother, being an older brother, would object to this invasion.

My mother's reply was usually something like this: "You can do without cowboys and Indians for a few minutes, but you can't do without a clean house. Vamoose!"

Thus the birth of authoritarian morality.

David Williams, wherever you are, I was hoovering for art's sake. At the first time of composition at Fort San, I may have been aware that the phrase "revenge of the unlived life" had come from the pen of Robertson Davies. The more I think about it, my character Lena Rotzoll from "Jokes for the Apocalypse" shares a great deal with Liesl. I may have been aware that I was using a phrase from Davies's book, but if I was I brushed this awareness aside, because in the fever of composing a first draft these were the right words. In the subsequent drafts, I paid no attention to these words—unless it was to congratulate myself on them.

Some readers might well wonder if there is any such thing as plagiarism. I believe there is. If I copy down someone else's words or ideas and pass them off holus-bolus as my own, I am plagiarizing. If I copy down someone else's poem—even if I've just translated it— and say to my reading audience, "See how clever and wise and sensitive I am," I am a plagiarist plain and simple. Again, Thomas Mallon is helpful here. The writer, he claims, "need not blush about stealing if he makes what he takes completely his, if he alchemizes it into something that is . . . thoroughly new." But this form of enlightened lifting "is not put unchanged onto the dinner table by someone who pretends he's been cooking all day."

How much is too much? To make judgements on this question, the literary sleuth looks for an entire pattern of stolen words and ideas done with unmistakable cunning. But hoovering up a plot (or an idea, a maxim, a character, a technique, a moral dilemma, a phrase) for one's own use is as common for the writer as breathing. Tracing the process of lifting or any other legitimate kind of influence leads us into labyrinths as byzantine as the human mind. At best, this is a fascinating exercise in the impossible. But this much I can say with a degree of certainty. Murdoch lifts from Herodotus enough so that her own characters can become modern, ironic reflections of the original story. Davies tries both Herodotus and Murdoch on for size. He isn't drawn much to Murdoch's comedy of manners in which intelligent characters seethe with futility, but he seems to love Honor Klein every bit as much as I love Liesl. John Irving leaves Herodotus alone, and he demonstrates little patience with Davies's many monologues and his bowing toward the superior wisdom of Europe, but he seems drawn to Davies's full rendering of grotesques, his intellectual vigour, and his skill in recounting a spiritual journey full of miracles. Murdoch, and then Davies, make fascinating use of heads without torsos. Irving leaves the head and arms and takes the torso.

The supreme lifter would seem to be Davies. His debt to Murdoch probably goes beyond what my summary has revealed, but he has written such a fascinating novel, such an *original* novel, that he easily escapes my earliest suspicions of excessive borrowing. In fact, *Fifth Business* is a livelier novel than *A Severed Head*. For all its wit and sophistication, Murdoch's early novel never gets out of the drawing room and into the dark gods, the *ékstasis* of Martin's awakening. Davies's not only promises a world of wonders for his improbable grump of a hero; he delivers on these wonders.

I have a writer's memory, not a scholar's. Perhaps I have very little to teach the scholars who make their living from close reading. Perhaps only this: that when the words or ideas of another writer find their way unacknowledged into a lively and original tale, well, sometimes a good Hoover doesn't discriminate too well when it's sucking things up. It is too busy going about its work, moving forward in a fine frenzy rolling. It has been doing this from before Genesis 1.1. And sometimes it still does this in a sacred cause.

1994

Race to the Future

| | | | | | |

Kyo Maclear

| | | | | | |

O N THE TWENTY-MINUTE CAB RIDE FROM LA GUARDIA into Brooklyn, I watch the city's architecture scroll by my window. Steel girders crisscross my view of an old industrial neighbourhood whose boarded-up houses and warehouses await either urban "rejuvenation" or demolition crews. I notice a sandblasted advertisement for Timothy Tailor's still faintly visible on the brick exterior of a building that now sports a giant Coca-Cola billboard. Leaning back in my seat, I feel the trance of the highway. It strikes me that the road is one of the few places in American life where myths of social mobility and advancement can be played out seamlessly: all cars fusing into one colourful stream, going at equal speed in the same direction with ease and efficiency.

The particular throughway I'm travelling is leading me into New York's downtown sprawl. It may also be taking me closer to the future. I'm here to meet with members of a young cyborg generation, an outpost of expatriate Japanese artists who are making a mark on the North American mainstream through the interconnected worlds of animation, fashion, music, and digital culture. I'm interested in what they have to say about their reception in America. More specifically, I'm interested in the vibrant place Japanese popular culture is beginning to occupy in visions of the technological future. Does this new transnational presence signal the advent of the borderless world we have all been hearing about? Does it mark the end of old social and cultural divisions, which, among other blights, have fettered U.S.-Japanese relations for 100 years? I'm not so sure.

On the eve of the last century, W. E. B. Du Bois, the prescient African American intellectual, predicted that this would be the century of race: that the colour line would be the most pressing barrier facing us. Nowadays, commentary tends to paint a more ambiguous forecast for the advancing era. On the one hand, we have grim evidence of an increasingly stratified world, in which ethnic and class-based differences seem to become more rather than less entrenched. On the other hand, we have blithe celebrations of technology and popular culture that foresee a wired world of universal equality. The latter vision is broadly reflected in magazines such as *Wired* and *Mondo 2000* and by corporations such as IBM and Benetton. In fact, the dream of technological transcendence, promoted largely by white male Net enthusiasts, seems to become more focused and intensified as the millennium approaches. The prospect of leaving body, time, and place for a virtual future is becoming more seductive as the wreckage of history piles at our feet.

Japan has a special place in the virtual future. In its embrace of technology as passion and lifeblood and its extensive association with science fiction imagery in which humans fuse with machines, it is taken to foreshadow the coming age. Will the future have the shiny, streamlined quality of Japanese comic books? Like the star of the Japanese-influenced film *Johnny Mnemonic,* will we proceed to dump memories of the past to free space in our Net-wired brains?

The real and virtual highway I am travelling cuts across North America's many subdivisions. As the cab speeds over a bridge, I experience the dizzying sensation of headlong movement. Colours whipping by, streams of traffic merging, plunging me into a narrow urban corridor—the exit ramp is just ahead.

THE NEXT MORNING, I MEET KEN. WE'RE BOTH WANDERING aimlessly around SoHo. After a brief chat in front of an animation gallery ("Closed Sundays"), he offers to show me around town. At twenty-seven, he is the image of the émigré artist, lank and Bohemian with his hand-me-down corduroy jacket, crumpled jeans, and mussed hair. I'd say his appearance is studied, but he looks as if he's spent prolonged periods laundryless. Basically broke but well fed on culture, coffee, and a Cooper Union arts education, he is hoping to join the New York media scene.

Ken leads me to an Irish sports pub around the corner from the Chelsea Hotel. The bar feels very Old World with its solid-oak finishing, plush-velvet armchairs, and nicotine-stained maps of Ireland. A shelf groans beneath a welter of books by Chaucer, Joyce, and Dickens. We order two pints of Guinness from a jocular bartender, and Ken unzips the portfolio he has placed on the small table between us. He pulls out a stack of his latest animation drawings. Over the next hour, I flip through several dozen staple images of girlish women sporting metallic bustiers and prosthetic limbs that double as weapons. They are vampishly cute, drenched in male libidinal fantasy, despite their dangerous accessories. The sci-fi aesthetic, Ken eagerly assures me (as if reading my doubtful mind), is finding a broader audience.

His work is, in fact, almost severe in its simplicity. Vacant, inexpressive blue eyes liquidate the identities of the women. They are androids ready to be switched on and off. Human personality has been flattened to degree zero. He has made hundreds of these drawings.

Ken is confident that his work will take off in the next year and find an audience beyond the dank cafés in which he has been hanging out. "I want to create a new Factory of pop artists," he tells me, "and I want it to be welcoming and international." Like the young Andy Warhol, he is perched to make a mark in his new land. He carries— as they say in the movies—a suitcase full of hopes.

Just the same, Ken isn't sure yet whether America will be his final destination. For now, New York City is just one pit stop on a circuit that includes Paris, Sydney, and London. Ken, you see, is really Kenji, and he's coming from, as well as going to, a shrinking world of cars and computers. He's part of a new wave of globe-trotting immigrants from Japan, a growing vanguard, clustered for the most part in New York and Los Angeles. Unlike their late-nineteenth-century counterparts, they're not coming with families, nor are they coming, for the most part, out of duress. Ken is light-years away from early Japanese immigrants who arrived on the shores of America with nothing but a straw satchel in hand. For Ken, material comfort and mobility are givens.

In Japan, Ken's generation is called the *shinjinrui,* or "new breed." The label, conjuring up an alien species, projects a degree of moral panic and xenophobia in a country that has made dissidence and difference taboo. Like media images of Gen-Xers in North America, diverse Japanese youth are uniformly portrayed by journalists as late-capitalist renegades and slackers. Nowadays, Japanese editorials lament, fewer young people are prepared to sacrifice themselves to a corporation or the nation. They regard leisure as central to life, the cult of individuality and instant gratification as preeminent. In North America—thanks to the enduring transpacific visions of Ridley Scott's *Bladerunner* and the best-selling science fiction of William Gibson—young Japanese are more apt to be seen as high-tech global nomads.

Ken/ji has just returned from visiting his family in Tokyo. Following a thirteen-hour Pacific crossover and a few days' jet lag, he is ready to switch the channels of his identity. He has just landed an interview with a new animation company in Jersey City. He is optimistic, his upbeat outlook reflective, perhaps, of the security provided by the cool glow of cybernetic culture and the warm flush of material well-being.

WITH KEN BUNKERED IN HIS APARTMENT PREPARING FOR his interview, I spend Saturday evening in the East Village with my friend Akeo. At twenty-nine, Akeo is a film school graduate. Born of Jewish and Japanese parents, he's lived in the United States all his life. He makes his living preparing fake food for Japanese film productions. "You wouldn't believe," he laughs, "all the things you can sculpt with powdered mashed potatoes."

The East Village is bustling with Japanese youth in search of a good time. I follow Akeo in his shiny silver fireman's coat as we weave in and out of the crowd, catching the relaxed shuffle of Japanese conversation along the street. A young man jovially slaps his friend on the shoulder, pushing him off the corner curb: "Hey! *Omai nani yuteno?"* English and Japanese words loiter together in casual disharmony. We amble past a convenience store, Keys While U Wait, past a jewellery vendor selling silver rings. The picture keeps changing as the voices slide by, often drowned out by the Doppler effect of car stereos streaming music from half-opened windows.

Akeo and I are jaywalking. Ears perked. We both grew up in countries where Japanese communities were dispersed following internment in World War II—"no two families on one block"—so this lively diasporic presence is slightly disorienting. We've long associated *nihongo* with the hushed intimacies of our family homes—with quiet, even shame—not with the boisterous street scene of North America.

Part participant, part voyeur, I enter this pleasure quarter. An endless stream of Japanese stores and exported bric-a-brac recapitulates stages of my life. The night dance of display figures—Godzilla, Ultraman, Power Rangers, Doraemon—in the shop windows reflects a familiar rhythm, a familiar commerce. I am reminded of long-ago summers spent in Tokyo malls.

To a child growing up in Toronto in the 1970s, Japan felt like *no place,* a setting eluding translation. Beyond evocations of Zen gardens and karate dojos, beyond dim images of concrete towers and assembly lines, Japan seemed to recede into the distance as soon as I came home. When September rolled around and classes resumed, I would try to hyphenate my (then "Far East") summer with the summers of friends who had spent their time basking together *some place* more . . . *some place* more . . . descriptive? Touchable? Meaningful?

"What was it *like* in Japan?"

"Hot. Very hot and humid. Oh, and rainy."

When the sushi craze hit North American cities in the early 1980s, and when karaoke bars started cropping up around town, I felt an odd sense of relief. I got a rush of delight when James Clavell's best-seller *Shogun* was adapted for an NBC TV miniseries in 1980. Few may remember Lady Mariko, a protagonist in the series, but I do. Mariko is my mother's name. *Shogun,* a kitschy melodrama with a flimsy historical base, drew a near-cult following and, in so doing, made my mother's name pronounceable and real.

Several years earlier, I had given up speaking Japanese to become more ordinary or, at least, less alien. The cadence of my imagination had told me what blond English sounded like, and I had cupped this dream language in the bowl of my tongue. Now the palpable flavours and sounds of Japanese words began rising from the gutter of memory. *Teriyaki, Sony, hari kiri, tsunami, Fuji, sake, Toyota.* A babble of words and products migrating across the twain of East and West. True, much of this added up to a rehashing of stereotypes about the East and its diverse inhabitants. But the gradual inception of things Japanese into the fold of Western popular culture was something that *seemed,* at least to my young eyes, to be making a difference: Japan was *some place* after all.

Being *no place,* I realize increasingly, is about feeling banished from the warp and woof of a dominant consumer culture. Being *no place* is about searching furtively for familiar road signs: a Coca-Cola billboard, a Nike store, a movie theatre marquee advertising *Speed* (and now *Akira?).* For better or worse, they are progressively becoming the collective markers we use to help locate private experiences on a collective thoroughfare. Popular culture can make my mother's name *real* and pronounceable. Consumer marketing can introduce formerly foreign-sounding nouns such as *futon* into the vernacular and bedrooms of North America.

| | | | | | |

AKEO AND I FINALLY ARRIVE AT THE 9TH STREET RESTAURANT he's been searching for. As we settle in for a *sashimi* dinner, he tells me what I've already gathered—the area we've just walked through is known as J-town, and it's the new hub of hip in New York. Home to an estimated 6,000 recent immigrants from Japan, the East Village has garnered a special identity among world drifters. Expat bands groove in local clubs. Uber-fashionable young folk stray through the night. The area has been the focus of trend spotting in the pages of *Raygun, Spin, New York,* and the *Village Voice.* The Far East Village, as it is described in *Spin,* is a sanctuary for Japanese "cultural castaways flooding New York," but they're not confined to the Big Apple. Rattling around in America without green cards, featured in GAP ads and MTV videos, they represent a new transnationalism.

At a pine table under a delicate frosted lamp suspended from the ceiling, I listen to Akeo rhyme off a list of rock stars who have paid homage to Japan: David Bowie, The Vapours, David Sylvian, Boy George, Kurt Cobain. Akeo loves to talk, and with his Woody Allen gestures he segues easily from the profound to the banal. He's the buddha of urban trash, the guy who aligns himself with the cosmos by asking the hot-dog vendor to "make him one with everything."

Anyway, that's what I'm thinking when we're interrupted by a waiter arriving with hand towels and a black tray arranged with tiny, fragrant cups of green tea.

Japanophilia, Akeo tells me, has been waxing and waning since the 1970s, but lately it has become more constant. Words such as *manga, anime,* and *karaoke* are now ensconced in the pop lexicon of young fans in North America. Japan has become a signifier of cool, with mainstream stars Michael Jackson and Matthew Sweet blending *anime* clips into their videos and twenty-year-olds in Manhattan and Toronto sporting loveable mascots such as Hello Kitty and Sailor Moon on T-shirts and knapsacks.

The sheer force of capital realignments has ushered Japan to the frontlines of global consumerism. With 125 million people watching TV and a growing middle-class population in neighbouring countries, Japan has the market to support its own pop culture industry. And now, with roughly nine studios in Tokyo constantly producing new *anime* (Japanese animation) exports, J-pop, as it is known colloquially, has become a major offshore commodity, proliferating in the converging worlds of international fashion, film, and music.

These days, I notice more and more young Japanese men and women portrayed in North American fashion spreads as the successor species. Linked to cyberculture, modelling high-tech toys and synthetic clothing, they are emissaries from another world, bidding us to enjoy the addictive joys of constant recreation. They project an image of a future full of Utopian sparkle. But the dream always ends in freeze frames. It is as abstract as it is dehumanizing. Flipping through an issue of *Spin,* I'm left with this static snapshot: the strange optical effect of Vaseline-slathered bodies cutting across blue beams of light into an anonymous underground tunnel.

Now, I've spent a good deal of my life living under the spell of fashion (acquiring, I might add, a tattoo and a few piercings along the way). I know how easy it is to become obsessed with the magic of cosmetic change. How quickly we grow enamoured of the swirling shoals of images that allow us to shift personality, that permit us to create art with our bodies. Fashion trends—from mod to alien-chic— give ritual expression to our desires: they come and go like spasms, more or less intense, more or less passing.

Fads sweep through New York at the speed of light; new subcultures and electronic communities take off, thrive for a few months, and then vanish. As Akeo bites into a translucent morsel of hamachi, I wonder aloud: "If this Japanese cyborg culture represents the fast lane to the future, *doko ni ikuno?* [Where are we heading?]" The question hangs like a riddle in the air, open and uncertain.

| | | | | | |

EXITING THE BATHURST SUBWAY STATION IN TORONTO, I notice a poster for an animation festival at the downtown university campus. A Japanese woman in a micro latex dress strikes a martial arts pose against a ruby background. Computer-generated ideograms crawl like graphic spiders along the borders. Silhouetted words such as "BOKA!" "DOTA!" and "GIYEAH!" detonate across the page. They're made-up words, onomatopoeic explosions of punches and screams. I can't imagine a more appropriate cue for my next stop.

I'm on my way to the Suspect Video store. Located in Toronto's Mirvish Village, where bargain basement wares jostle with the fineries of art boutiques, Suspect caters to progressive tastes in video. With its eclectic blend of mainstream blockbusters, B-grade movies, film noir classics, and feminist porn, it draws a loyal clientele despite the Blockbuster megastore just down the street. This is where *otaku*, or "hard-core" Japanimation fans, come to stock up on the latest magazines and serial flicks.

Manager Merrill Shapiro tells me that over the last few years he has seen a burgeoning interest in *anime* primarily among white men. The best-selling items are total fantasy *anime* stripped of cultural references, which nevertheless retain a degree of foreignness. "Viewers," Shapiro says, "are attracted to the way *anime* combines exoticism with a Western sensibility. It seems important that the anglicized characters with their Caucasian features are set in unfamiliar locales. But it doesn't seem to matter if the alien location is Tokyo or outer space."

The idea of cultural and historical transience has, in fact, been an integral component of *anime* marketing since its beginnings. Many North American fans of syndicated TV shows *Robotech* and *Speed Racer* (1980s) probably never realized that their favourite characters were Japanese shorn of context. They probably didn't have an inkling that these shows were originally produced for Japanese tots, because they were edited and dubbed to downplay their Japanese origins. Those who watched *Astro Boy,* imported by NBC and syndicated on American TV in the early 1960s, were likely unaware that Osamu Tezuka had developed this program in response to Japan's nuclear history.

Like *Godzilla, Astro Boy* was a product of the radioactive rubble that ringed the psyches of postwar Japanese citizens. Born in the wake of a U.S. hydrogen bomb test in the Bikini Atoll, *Astro Boy* was originally intended as a protest against nuclear destruction. Today the tiny character—with his punky hairdo and red rocket-engine legs—is more a camp icon than a symbol of Japan's atomic legacy. Sealed in sterile bubble packs, available at Wal-Mart, *Astro Boy* merchandise has become just more fodder for Christmas.

There is, naturally, some sense of loss in all this. Tezuka, who died in 1989, had created fallible characters who wrestled with issues of war guilt and responsibility, doubt and faith, death and rebirth. To have his rich characters gutted of depth and streamlined into a generic joy-quest culture imparts a lamentable lesson in the power of transnational marketing. As context is wiped out with a casual gesture, products can be hurled across oceans like stainless superheroes, coming and going without past or direction.

A film such as *Akira* (1990), billed as the biggest animated release of all time, stands out because it makes no attempt to hide its Japanese references. In *Akira,* the supernatural and the minutiae of Japanese daily life coexist. *Anime* heroes can take a break from intergalactic battles over a steaming bowl of soba noodles. Despite fantastical pretexts, the introduction of the surprisingly ordinary— street signs, convenience stores, motor bikes—helps to make Japan more scrutable and less alien. But *Akira,* with its periodic flashes of Japanese life, is the exception to the rule.

For the most part, *anime* bears no stamp of particularity. The story settings float lightly in a pop culture ether. The atomized characters in *Sailor Moon,* for example, have no family, no discernible cultural ties. Dejapanized with her blonde pigtails and misty saucer eyes, *Sailor Moon* transcends nationality only to end up looking strangely white and Western.

For Professor Tim Craig, *anime* fan and organizer of an annual Japanese pop culture conference at the University of Victoria, this "open humanism" is the essence of Sailor Moon's appeal: "She may morph from tot to teen, from student to avenger, but ultimately she's just every kid, lazy at school, with a lot of not very admirable or heroic characteristics." In other words, her open weaknesses and foibles, not to mention her alleged racelessness, have made her a smash hit internationally. Since 1993, over twenty-three countries, including Brazil, Mexico, and Australia, have been exposed to *Sailor Moon*. In Canada alone, the show draws 200,000 viewers daily. Browsing on the Net one night, I discovered that there are many websites devoted to each character in *Sailor Moon;* they rehash every story line, every word of dialogue.

Plugged into this animated network, where nymphettes cavort in panties and teenage boys happily fetishize disaster, I get a weird sense of displacement. Chaos is the new program. There are no bearings—geographical, historical or social. Silliness runs amok. Frivolous clichés and shallow moral lessons are delivered with strange earnestness. Manga City is envisioned as a world gutted of intellectual enterprise and wit, where we are constantly dashing to escape our bodies, our histories, our everyday lives.

Admittedly, social commentary isn't *anime's* main draw. But there are other *anime* videos, adaptations of Japanese literary classics such as *The Harp of Burma,* that gather dust in the corners of the Suspect Video store. Merrill Shapiro thought he could lure an audience for them, but so far no one is biting. The imaginative chatter of a literate and articulate society doesn't seem to have the same crossover appeal. The hot *anime* items feature hormonally overdriven characters, a large dose of end-time spectacle, and garish graphics. It is precisely *anime*'s cartoon-calibre violence, the overall predictability of the genre, that invites viewer comfort. *Anime* provides an invitingly legible dream of the future. U.S. scholar and critic Susan Napier argues that the popularity of sci-fi *anime* can be attributed to its ability to sum up late-century capitalism in an easy-to-understand way: combining awareness of swift change, ideologies of progress toward some anticipated future, and the omnipresence of technology.

Disaster in films such as *Akira* and *Ghost in the Shell* gives viewers vicarious access to safe horrors. *Anime* films, predicated on transhistorical battles between humans and technology, are oddly reassuring, especially when the locus of conflict can be imagined in some abstract, offshore place. Crowds scurry away from monstrous mutants, atomic bombs tear cities apart, but there is usually a light moral centre despite the ballistic ambience. The positive evaluations of Sailor Moon (who tells us that, "with the help of friends, anything is possible"), and the strange calm that descends after Tetsuo in *Akira* has returned to his human form, mitigate the horror. Social and cosmic order are always restored, the forces of evil vanquished, the traditional boy-girl reunion performed. There is catharsis of a surprisingly predictable sort.

A medium that emphasizes exaggeration, hyperbole, caricature, and pidgin English is hardly the best conductor of social information, let alone values, but it may be the perfect vehicle for domesticating the strange and foreign. Providing a vox pop for fears about the future, technology, and global migration, *anime*'s euphoric nihilism can have a pacifying effect. Once impenetrable, Japan reappears as clichéd and easy to read. This imaginary Japan, with its simple theatrics and seemingly relentless penchant for kitsch and standardized fantasy, is striking a friendly chord among mainstream Americans venturing into the unknown twenty-first century.

Anime characters, flying back and forth across the Pacific Rim, invite us to romp in a cultureless future governed by world capitalism. Most significantly, they represent the heady prospect of leaving behind our bodies and our geographical origins for the hip swoon of cyberspace and the neutered new world. The central conceit here, of course, is the assumption that technology will set us free. (From the perspective of metal orbiting in space, this may well seem true.) The more disturbing implication is that race is a defect to be liberated from, that—to fit in—we must change our very eye shape.

The dominant culture of cybernetics, with its projected image of bright optimism, loudly announces new priorities for the future, a new cultural politics. We now enter into a sense of euphoric timelessness in which retro styles (bouffant hair, Nancy Sinatra boots) and nostalgic textures (a gutted cityscape) provide our only segues into bygone eras. Here we have a new global lifestyle, one predicated on slick surface and temporal amnesia.

Right now such a soulless life is a fiction, but it is a fiction that is finding a growing audience among American whites who profess themselves tired of hearing about "minority suffering" and the growing gap between haves and have-nots. It is a fiction, needless to say, that comes gift-wrapped for those who think that we have grappled with the burden of history long enough.

Of course, it also has its detractors. Cartoonist and *anime* artist Takeshi Tadatsu, for one, remains sceptical—questioning whether we can or, for that matter, should become fused with our celluloid projections. Driven by wanderlust, he arrived in Brooklyn in 1991 from Tokyo. In his thirties, tall, and bespectacled, Takeshi, like other global nomads, was attracted to the mixture of culture in New York. His comic strip, "Tokyo New York," published regularly in *New York* magazine, is full of thoughts on how diasporic Asians are faring in the sprawl. "My comic strip develops from my daily sketchbook. It reflects my daydreams and a stranger's impressions of America."

Cast against the rumblings of technology, Takeshi's characters playfully refract clichés about the Japanese. A Manhattan high-tech ninja battles foes while holding a take-out pizza in front of a local deli. Two prep cooks surrounded by the bubbling alchemy of science develop the tofu burger. A *yakuza* ("gangster") cartoonist sends terror into the life of a white American art director. Takeshi calls these pop impressions "mutant messages."

In one poignant strip, loosely based on an experience Takeshi had last year, a young Japanese man carrying a radio controller goes looking for his old buddy "Gigantor 28." His search through New York's East Village goes awry when he is beaten up by two white thugs. Faced with such everyday hatreds, Takeshi's protagonist is reminded of his fleshiness and human fragility. Even in the global sprawl, even amid the romantic flux of "Tokyo New York," conflict persists. If technology is the elixir, then racism is the hangover. In the final frame, as bitter tears stream from the young man's saucer-sized eyes, the caption reads with mangled irony and pidgin English, "He lost everything, but at last he've got be free!"

| | | | | | | |

KYO MACLEAR

FROM THE ROOF OF AKEO'S BROWNSTONE APARTMENT IN Brooklyn, I have a clear view of the Manhattan skyline—the Statue of Liberty, the Empire State Building, and other fixtures of New York tourism. I can also see the Rockefeller Center. This midtown Manhattan complex is home to the Radio City Music Hall and famous tourist attractions such as the sunken skating rink, the plaza where an enormous Christmas tree stands every year, and sculptures of Prometheus and Atlas. When Mitsubishi Corporation bought the building in the late 1980s, it became a symbol of Japanese infiltration.

It was a time of rising economic status for Japan, but its consumption of American historical landmarks and entertainment institutions—which also included MCA and Columbia Pictures—incited open hostility among many white Americans. Complaints about Japan's "adversarial" trading practices and its predatory role in export economics became regular fare on nightly newscasts. Films such as *Rising Sun* and *Black Rain* reflected this combination of fear and fascination. Gorgeously filmed, they played to a popular xenophobia, conveying images of a Godzilla-like invasion or an economic Pearl Harbor.

When Mitsubishi sold the Rockefeller Center in July 1996, Japan dropped a notch on the sinister scale. With the collapse of the bubble economy, Japan entered a recession. No longer perceived as a menace, it was defanged.

The Park Slope sidestreet where Akeo lives is lined with cars. As we talk, I'm distracted by a red Ford Bronco pulling into a parking space. The sun, gleaming on the hood and roof, blots out the face of the driver. Despite its "American-made" label, it's likely to contain a Japanese fuel pump, a German exhaust system, and Mexican windshield wipers. If I were optimistic, I might take that Bronco, with its hybrid organs, as a welcome sign that we're moving closer to a consumer culture with a single planetary soul. But the mind is a curious vehicle in its own right, and my own mind, as I stand there surveying the street, begins to whir with a commotion of images soaring and dipping through my thoughts like so many Toyota and Honda blue-chip stocks.

The Japanese, it occurs to me, have long been cast as cyborgs in the Western imagination. The plated samurai warrior jeering with sadistic fury. The stooped houseboy with monkey features and glinting buckteeth. The kamikaze showing fanatical disregard for life. The

139

enemy alien travelling by train to an internment camp. The third-rate junk producer sweating on an assembly line. The blue-suited CEO carrying a cell phone. The eager tourist equipped with camera pack. The Japanese have lived where reality and fiction collapse in bouts of paranoia.

"To go from 'japboy' to 'mistersony' inside the timbrels of a lifetime argues a place for mirth in our benumbed lives." So wrote Japanese Canadian poet Roy Kiyooka, wryly capturing the confusion of those trapped in the shifting sands of legend. During his sixty-odd years, before his death in 1994, he witnessed the aura of traitorous flux give way to the presto of invention. For Kiyooka, mirth rested in having been vilified and then saluted by the same engine of thought: the *general motor* of the white imagination. Smoke and mirrors, perhaps, but the image changes us.

Today the Japanese cyborg is more congenial than predatory: a friendly creature bodying forth in a panhistorical flight, drawn like a pencil line, a clean evolutionary ascent. Yellow-bellies and nips are dead, their places taken by amazingly well-adjusted young men and women—almost as alien but smartly dressed, likeable, and wired. A feckless portrait of modern progress, it fills me with a sense of vertigo, made all the more palpable as I stand here in Brooklyn six storeys above the ground.

I tune in to voices rising from the street. A woman walks by with casual, unhurried grace, her attention focused on the potted zinnias lining the brownstone façades. A Chicano boy, who looks about eight, is yelling to his friend across the street: "I'll be Captain Picard!" Their game of *Star Trek* needs a galaxy, which they find amid a forest of street signs, car antennae, weeds, garbage cans, and bus stops. The game heats up. I watch the two boys scramble along the pavement in interplanetary struggle. It's a sophisticated game of hunter and prey, an elaboration of shoot-'em-up cowboys and Indians. Only there's a twist. These kids are looking for signs of extraterrestrial life. They want to root out the aliens in our midst. To greet? To kill?

When I was young, it was a flat insult to be called an alien. It meant that you were foreign, an outsider. You didn't belong. Even an alien as loveable as E.T. *must* go home, my friend Hiromi recently pointed out—it's a "scripted given and an expected and accepted conclusion." It dawns on me that to be both Japanese and an alien is a double bind.

It is the white imagination that invented the Japanese alien, after all. It is the white imagination that has run with the image of Japan as an antiseptic, even paranormal, technocracy as a means of grappling with its own sense of cultural flux and uncertainty about the future. What better backdrop for imaginations bridging a new century than a country where the standard-issue future, in which demolished urban landscapes are re-created phoenixlike, has already been glimpsed? It is the white imagination that is still at the mercy of this image. For North Americans harbouring strange dreams of the millennium—visions of Utopia but also apocalypse—Japan continues to provide a compelling outlet for working out broader fears and obsessions related to the unknown.

| | | | | | |

JAPAN IS TO THE FUTURE WHAT ROME IS TO THE RUINS. The result has been as much anxiety as joy. Nowhere are these contradictions more evident than in Ridley Scott's "Pacific Rim" action film, *Bladerunner.* The 1982 movie—adapted from Philip K. Dick's novel *Do Androids Dream of Electric Sheep?*—has had a remarkably long shelf life.

Set in 2019, *Bladerunner* launches viewers into an end-time Los Angeles where a 200-storey chrome-and-glass metropolis, headquarters of the ruling Tyrell Corporation, towers above an oppressively dark Asiatown. Dirt-infested ghettos, crowded with techno-equipped Asian peasants peddling spices and software, impart an image of a segregated future. But signs of hybridity (or globalization) appear too. The first time we meet Rick Deckard (Harrison Ford), handsome hero and future cop, he is ordering a meal from a Japanese prep cook at an outdoor noodle bar, speaking an Esperanto of Spanish, German, and Japanese.

Thus refreshed, Deckard sets out to destroy six humanoid replicants who have invaded Earth. We follow him on a romantic, and often neurotic, quest as he tries to find and police the boundary between the human and the technological: *which characters are the replicants?* It is a grim depiction of a society skidding toward the last exit on the digital superhighway. A blue-grey electric light is the dominant tone, with rare flashes of pink skin streaking through the gleam of technology. A sense of moral and spiritual decay dogs the plotline. In this, it shares the same twisted, xenophobic, postapocalyptic sensibility of many sci-fi films.

The film's dystopic dimension is linked to overpopulation and the physical presence of *living, breathing, eating* Asians. Its utopic dimension is drawn from glimpses of technology's friendlier, sexier, albeit more "feminine" side. In *Bladerunner,* these two visions are united in the image of a digitalized geisha refracted on a gigantic screen banked right off the expressway. Seen at different points throughout the film, this celluloid Japanese woman—with her serene smile—projects an ambivalent image of the global future. Foreshadowing a dematerialized world, literally rising above a rank-and-file Asian American presence, she can become the object of both colonial love and contempt.

Bladerunner images, so defining of the 1980s, proved that combining a vision of Japan and one of the future is potent. Taking on transnational, transhistorical significance, Japan could be the place of *no place* and *everyplace.* In recent years, however, pairing Japan with the future has led to somewhat brighter forecasts. Although still representing a blankness at the heart of late-millennial culture, Japan has had generous airplay in the sci-fi work of, among others, William Gibson, a writer widely considered the high priest of cyberpunk culture. In his *Neuromancer,* for example, the whole world has become a "Chiba City." The Pacific Ocean has been turned into a sublime cyberspace across which his transnational cowboys leap, eating sushi along the way. Granted, there are grimmer moments, such as the detritus of his shantytowns or his cities rendered uninhabitable by multinational corporations. But, in the main, Gibson provides an antidote to the repressive side of technology, a virtual idol upon which to rivet lusty fantasies, a superhero whose cape doubles as a parachute.

| | | | | | |

THE DAY I VISIT HUSHI ROBOT, THE NEW YORK SKY IS overcast. The city radiates with a soft computer screen glow. It's the kind of light that brings out the grime, making everything that wasn't built yesterday look derelict. Robot co-owns a Japanese pop culture store in the East Village called Sears and Robot. As its name suggests, it sells certain staple wares to eager pilgrims: *Astro Boy* T-shirts, Ultraman robots, Keeropi bags, and Hello Kitty stationery. Entering through a small doorway, I feel as though I've walked onto some pristine Jetsons set, the silver mylar walls, stainless steel floor, and chrome fixtures all screaming "The future has arrived!"

Robot, who is just twenty-five, came to New York City from a cushy neighbourhood in Marin County, California, in the mid-1980s. Today he sees himself as a "happy cyborg" living in a new synthetic moment in a city where more and more people are becoming "transformers" through silicon implants, liposuction, and body piercings. He changed his name to Robot because he liked the outer-space ring. His choppy brown and blond hair, cut in an even line across his forehead, makes him look wide-eyed, doll-like.

Part-time manager, full-time scenester, Robot runs his life on an almost constant adrenaline high. During our initial phone interview, he worked his *sell-sell* routine until burnout set in: "Look, I need a coffee." I had to laugh—mere mortal after all?

The phenomenon of cuteness is nowhere more available to a roving eye than in Robot's store. Sparky morsels of pop culture are neatly arranged on clear plastic shelves. Wading through the merchandise, I pick up a powder-pink gizmo made of thick, shatterproof plastic. The oval-shaped item I'm fingering is called Tamagotchi. It's a pocket-sized, egg-shaped, electronic "pet" that communicates through a chirping speaker and liquid-crystal screen and "lives" on batteries for about two weeks. It's a toy with demands. Lest their pets perish, Tamagotchi owners push buttons every few hours to feed, clean, and care for them. Some five million have been sold in North America. Alarmed teachers have banned them from their classrooms. Parents have been recruited to pet sit.

Still, I don't get it. There's no wiry fur to stroke, no musty-sweet odour. In fact, to the novice, the whole thing seems rather cold and impersonal. I can't imagine joining Tamagotchi by a fireplace, walking through a park, nuzzling close. Apparently, many urban professionals can. These pets seem to have touched some tripwire among an adult generation.

The digital world is okay. Perhaps that's the message. Personalized mouse pads, virtual idols, anthropomorphic toys—all smooth the way for those who, like Harrison Ford in *Bladerunner*—are perturbed by the rapidly dissolving boundary between humans and machines. They provide comfort, tranquillizing the nerves of those unsettled by Deep Blue, those who still root for the victory of flesh.

Hushi Robot has other ideas. He thinks that toys such as Tamagotchi fulfil a longing for prolonged infancy. If you listen carefully, he says, you will hear the "electric crackle" of youth spreading like a "friendly virus" in his store. He talks that way—evangelically. I have to admit it's compelling. So is his merchandise. Childish iconography reigns. *Anime* smiles sprout up everywhere, happiness jangles from the joists of this consumer culture like a charm bracelet. Confusing and mistranslated phrases simply add to the charm. Japanese English malaprops can be collected with glee—making shoppers feel like kindergarten kids. For example, a plastic pencil case patterned with tartan tells me that "Teddy bears are a girl's best friend," and a red lunch box shows a wide-eyed Hello Kitty in her white-picketed yard. The overwrought sentimentality is hard to take seriously. The pairing of "Made in Japan" labels with American suburban nostalgia is also a bit of a throw. Yet Robot's toys seem to be telling me something. Celebrating the gentle, the innocent, they are imparting a modus vivendi for an imperfect and confusing world. Their mangled pop scripture carries a message of reassurance: we can lead simpler, bucolic lives without letting go of the tinsel charm of material culture. We can be ardent and unapologetic consumers, nose-dive into the contradictions of late capitalism, without fear of alienation, because— all together now—commodities are *our friends*. In a dog-eat-dog world, we can have kitty-cat distraction.

Yet this approach, epitomized by Sailor Moon's celestial struggles against the Negaforce, still troubles me. It isn't modern pop living, I think; it's duck-and-cover ideology. Even Robot suggests that the charismatic appeal of techno toys is especially strong in New York because the social order is so uncertain and ambiguous: "Life is gruelling and bleak here. We want an escape route. J-pop and cute culture more generally are helping to create a force field, a protective bubble, that helps cushion the blows of social reality." I think about the Manhattan edict: stop hustling and you sink without a trace; get sick and God help you.

Of course, finding diversion in pop culture isn't a new phenomenon. North American audiences anxious to take extended intermissions from the sobering pressures of politics, eager to flee the high-stress zones of daily life, have been seeking refuge in radio, TV, pulp fiction, and Hollywood blockbusters for a long time. From the special effects of *Star Wars* to the jingle-jangle lyrics of Hanson, pop culture has provided smatterings of joy and hope to those steeped in the blahs.

What feel new to me about Asian pop culture are the peculiar expressions of euphoria and futurism attached to it. Pitched into a world not right, these Utopian emblems of childhood are providing a simple compass for a socially turbulent decade. As signs of the times, the mainstream media seem to have moved away from images of Japanese businessmen and toward images of young (Japanese) sailor-girls stalled in the oral stage. Pop products that might have been dismissed ten years ago for their naïveté, their fluffy chintziness, are now openly embraced by Robot's overwhelmingly adult patrons. Wearing a *Speed Racer* T-shirt at thirty is no longer a sign that one has repressed into childhood. The style of childlike cuteness, packaged in a country that General Douglas MacArthur once described as a "nation of twelve year olds," has become an international force, particularly in Asia and North America. Being at constant play, being aliens from adulthood, encourages us to be in the moment, which these days also means a historyless present.

In a certain light, I am inclined to think that being childlike is a radical act, requiring a mercurial spirit that rails against the dictates and corruption of adult life. But at a time when contemporary culture broadly reflects a sense of cheerful fatuousness, when everything from movies to fashion is lending itself to an ethos of happy nihilism, I'm left to wonder how radical kidding around really is. Is the drift toward extended youth just part of a collective policy of swerve and avoid?

I AM BICYCLING ALONG TORONTO'S QUEEN STREET WEST past a parking lot and a row of drab storefronts when I encounter a full-colour photo billboard featuring a larger-than-life portrait of a young Asian woman. She is decked out in futuristic fashion, with silver bob wig and icy blue inset eyes. Her hands lightly offer up a crystal ball. I stop and stare, cued for a mega-ad. Is this the latest glacial beer promo? Is it another one of those don't-show-the-product jean pitches? I'm stumped.

Several weeks later, I'm surprised to learn that the billboard, commissioned by Toronto's Art Metropole, is the latest cibachrome work of Mariko Mori. Mori is a former fashion model from Japan who exploded on the international art scene in the early 1990s. Born in 1967 in Tokyo, she now lives in New York City. Her signature style involves constructing photographic scenarios in which she is invariably the protagonist, though in diverse guises. Her photographs have been carefully staged in Tokyo subways, red-light districts, and office strips. Each picture has the visual overload and *Bladerunner* dazzle we associate with things futuristic.

Insisting that her perfect plastic world is a product of media conditioning, Mori shape-shifts according to the latest synthetic trends. I have seen her impersonate a schoolgirl, a secretary, a prostitute, a high-tech Madame Butterfly. These prototypes, she suggests, have encased Japanese women in a "synthetic reality," which has been further distorted by technology. In creating caricatures of male-fantasy figures, she wants to refract the desire and make its excesses obvious.

Mori's airless compositions take on cinematic proportions with titles such as *Empty Dream* (1995) or the more apocalyptic *Last Departure* (1996). They have been shot in the early hours of the day, her Japanese androids haloed by the blue light of morning. They appear to dwell at the cold bottom of the digital world, their pale anonymity cancelling out the possibility of human response. While appropriating an advertising idiom and striking seductive poses pulled from soft-porn comic books, they insinuate the hollowness of consumer culture.

In Mori's work, I witness a courageous and creative attempt to think outside the closed horizons of technological society. But this is art, far from the spectacle of the living. If Mori wants us to overdose on fantasy until we abstain from sheer embarrassment and boredom, she will wait a long time. The fusion of fantasy and reality—through advertising, technology, and fashion—has become a fixture of contemporary urban life. Virtual reality has come to stay.

The consummate expression of artificial pleasuring can be found in the pixielike figure of Kyoto Date. Singer-actor Date has attracted a good deal of attention lately even among those who have not yet seen her perform on Japanese TV or CD-ROM. It is not every day, after all, that one hears of a virtual idol (Max Headroom aside). Created through a computer program by software engineers and Japan's top modelling agency, Horipro, Date was introduced in November 1996. Since then, the "eighteen-year-old" singer has enjoyed a busy virtual life, gracing the covers of several Japanese and American mags, even cameoing in a Japanese soap opera. Her on-line bio tells me she's a sassy Scorpio and her hobbies include collecting sneakers.

William Gibson, perhaps reminded of the heroine in his 1996 novel *Idoru,* ranks himself as a Kyoto Date fan and plans to interview her for an upcoming issue of the men's magazine *Details.* Carbon-copy pop stars are a huge industry in Japan, but Date sails above the usual star machinery. Immune from tabloid gossip and melodramatic sagas of deceit and divorce, she is so perfect as to become holy.

In fact, Kyoto Date is eternal. Through digital choreography, her svelte body can wind and dance endlessly without ever becoming taxed. Her microchip-developed face can glow perpetually without ever giving in to the sag of ageing flesh. Her high-pitched melodies, sung in a combination of English and Japanese, can be heard "live" into the next century without fear that her vocal chords will be burnished by time, booze, or cigarettes. Those are mere mortal concerns. With Date, we can vicariously approximate the dream of being forever young.

As a Japanimation character come to life, Kyoto Date exemplifies the sexual valuing of simulated beings through cybertechnology. Make no mistake, the sticky screen-and-joystick crowd is not being hoodwinked. There is an astute awareness that artifice surrounds the drooling dream of an on-line skank. In fact, the prospect of freedom from the real-life pressures involved in human interaction has contributed greatly to the popularity of cybergirls such as Kyoto Date and Lara Croft (star of the video game *Tomb Raider).* They promise that we can be with anyone or anything, that we can enjoy a rush of sexual exhilaration, mystery, violence from a remove.

On-line, we can caress the libido via the optic nerve. In these plague years, when promiscuousness breeds worry and intimacy takes high-wire courage, the Net provides a venue for risk-free sex. Moreover, we're always in control—at least that's the general line. These images can be filled with any need. Enjoying the piquancy of pixels, we can be conductors of desire, programming, upgrading, and discarding our fantasies.

The mainstreaming of soft-core porn through cyberculture is disquieting to Mariko Mori. I share many of her misgivings. She thinks that being fleshless is neither universally simple nor desirable. While websites fetishizing young Asian women are enjoyed by men entertaining a Lolita complex, actual women are being lashed to their flesh in skin flicks. In Tokyo, eleven porn videos are made every day. The chief attraction of these videos, which are consumed throughout Asia and North America, is teenage girls. Mori suggests that the proliferation of synthetic Asian girls—who simultaneously tap into themes of sexual possibility and impossibility—is affecting wider social and sexual attitudes. These are not simply free-floating images. When women have become this empty of personality and history, they are not ciphers any longer but monsters.

In the world of digital media, the common wisdom is that ethnicity and gender become forms of "noise" or "image" with no internal consistency. On-line, we can become tricksters, male one moment, female the next. Equipped with virtual reality visors, we can box with Muhammad Ali and then tango into the night *con un hombre muy lindo* in a Buenos Aires nightclub. The story lines are *potentially* as infinite as the personas we might adopt. Identity is endlessly reprogrammable, which makes the predictable contours of virtual idols, their sheer obviousness, all the more perplexing. I keep wondering why it is that when the body morphs it often ends up mirroring some over-pixelated ideal. Boosted busts, syrupy voices, mile-long legs: why are these women always so faddishly feminine?

I'm still looking for signs of fluid personality—those inimitable tones, turns, tics, and quirks that cut through the celluloid static. Surely the dream of futuristic transcendence has different shapes.

MUSIC TUNNELS THROUGH THE NIGHTCLUB. TONIGHT AT Lee's Palace in Toronto it's Cibo Matto, captivating a packed room for two hours with a surreal looping of 1940s swing, bossa nova, mutated jazz, and trip hop. Yuka Honda navigates the turntable and sampler, steering silky mixes into stormy lo-fi riffs. At one point abandoning her disk-loaded cybership, Honda raises a portable tape recorder up to the mike and plays back a standard rock guitar solo. Singer Miho Hattori wails into Cibo Matto's hit single "Know Your Chicken." I'm swigging a Corona, watching my friend's white shirt beam as strobes of light cross the room. By the second set, I'm dancing to electric covers of "The Candy Man" and Yoko Ono's "Talking to the Universe." I am plugged into a vague but nonetheless exhilarating current. Yuka's floppy Afro and Miho's blonde Marilyn wig are setting the tempo. The place is bouncing.

Yuka Honda and Miho Hattori live in New York City when they aren't touring clubs. In 1994, they signed with Warner Brothers and released their debut CD *Viva! La Woman*. By early 1996, billed as "East Village Rappers" who sing about "betrayal and food," they had made the front page of the *Village Voice*. Since then, their bilingual tunes have attracted fans among notables such as John Zorn, the Beastie Boys, Yoko Ono, Richard Thompson, and the Lounge Lizards. No longer consigned to the import bin at Tower Records, they have joined bands such as Pizzicato Five and Buffalo Daughter in a global grope for celebrity. They are rude and funny, and they have cart-loads of attitude, which means they don't feel compelled to reproduce the charming, copy-cat qualities associated with Asian idol singers. They don't see themselves as novelty acts or gimmick bands. And they certainly don't want to be relished or mocked as naïve musicians. Yet, gauging from their reviews in North American newspapers and music magazines, it's hard to tell if their efforts to be taken seriously are working.

Timo Ellis is a twenty-six-year-old musician who plays with Cibo Matto and Yoko Ono's band IMA. I sit with him at the Lee's Palace bar after the concert crowd has dispersed. He is wearing the same clingy, wide-collared shirt he wore on stage, tapping his fingers to some phantom beat on the edge of the counter. A self-described "Polish-Russian white guy," he offers some sobering thoughts based on his experiences playing with diasporic bands. He says that reviews almost always downplay the edginess of the music. "Yuka and Miho, for example, still get taken up as cute girls who like food. Even when they are challenging people to rethink images of Asian women, they are reduced to camp. The idea of an outspoken Japanese woman is still a threat to most people. If they don't appear to be sweet and passive, they get slagged. Yoko Ono faces this all the time." There is a correlative racism tied to the embrace of camp, he suggests, a history of condescension that turns everything "Made in Japan" into a consumer joke.

Los Angeles-based feature filmmaker Eric Koyanagi thinks that many diasporic bands undercut themselves: "This music is celebrated for being vapid because it's a movement that promotes free abstract thinking about nothing." For example, the air of glacial cool makes it all feel dreamy. We can kick back in a bean bag chair and listen to Miho Honda wail about white pepper ice cream or follow Maki Nomiya of Pizzicato Five as she sings songs that are chock full of consumer brand names. Unlike grunge, punk, hip-hop, or other mass-marketed youth cultures, J-pop does not condemn rampant materialism and hyperconsumption. It revels in it.

Cibo Matto lyrics are riddled with creaky English phrases, made up of clichés and everyday idioms: My weight is 300 pounds / My favourite is beef jerky / I'm a vagabond, I'm a vagabond / My mom says, "You are kinky!" / Who cares? I don't care / A horse's ass is better than yours.

The appropriation of the English language creates strange displacement effects; everything is sent back sounding different. There is something potentially subversive, not to mention humorous, about word riffs that jangle up the meanings traditionally associated with language. Yet those looking for social bite are left with this to chew on by Shonen Knife: "Let's send out for some pizza or something . . . and we'll get, you know, like world peace, you dig?"

No doubt the sense of wide-eyed wonder surrounding these bands, their ingénue status, has contributed to their appeal. It's as if they're a metaphor for Japan itself, a country still imagined as having just joined the modern age. Here they've picked up guitars and keyboards and gone electric—and, lo and behold, they're fairly proficient.

Still, there's nothing radical in the mainstreaming of Japanese pop bands. Intentions aside, they are being heard on a lite register—hardly punchy when it comes to social commentary. Granted, the commercial imperatives of our culture can co-opt anything—from cartoon rappers busting flavour-crystal rhymes in a Kool-Aid commercial to cozy images of Aboriginal celebrities wearing GAP clothing—but on the race dial J-pop is predisposed to easy listening and absorption. It's hard to make fun of rampant consumerism when your words can be taken as ad copy or corporate nu-skool rip-offs. Whether they are inciting chuckles or creating "noise," there's no big message such as "Fight the Power" here.

Little wonder, then, that Eric Koyanagi, looking for a soundtrack for his upcoming feature, *Hundred Percent,* about Asian Americans living in Los Angeles, opted for black hip-hop. In Eric's mind, the countercultural presence of African Americans offers a strong contrast to the endearing and conciliatory images of Asians on offer in the media. Blacks remain America's harshest critics. Like DJ Krush (b. Hideaki Ishi), who is fast becoming one of the hottest hip-hop artists in the United States, Eric sees hip-hop as an enduring symbol of defiance. For DJ Krush, a former Yakuza member, it provides a way of expressing his sense of alienation from Japan. For Eric, it's a means of identifying with the political aspects of his own third-generation Japanese Canadian identity.

Hundred Percent is one of the first commercial features about Asian Americans ever made. It tracks the fictional lives of slackers living around Venice Beach (or Los Angeles's Shangri-la). It isn't "cinema with a cause," but Eric believes that any effort to locate Asians in America, and particularly in Los Angeles, has a political edge. "*Bladerunner* wasn't prophetic if we're talking about a naturalized Asian presence in Los Angeles. That time seems a far way off. The 1992 Los Angeles riots were the big chance for Asians and Latinos to be recognized, but the whole thing was swept under the carpet. We're still perceived as foreigners and offshore imports." Wayne Wang, who directed *Smoke* and *Blue in the Face,* still gets slotted into the foreign film section at the video store. Despite a glut of new martial arts films and anime features, it's proving hard for Asian Americans to carve a niche, let alone make a mark, in Hollywood's studio system.

As for diasporic Asians, it doesn't help them to be exclusively associated with a meaningless commodity culture, says Eric. Quite the opposite. These products atrophy the imagination, preventing mainstream Americans from looking at the lived and historical meanings of race and difference in North America and elsewhere. The common bond of consumerism cannot replace democracy as an ideal. If everything is governed by commerce, surely we'll lose the will and the capacity to sustain a meaningful citizenry.

Themes of cultural neutrality and social transcendence prevail as we enter the future dome of electronic media and cybercommunications. If *Bladerunner* is any indication, then there is reason to be alarmed. In a film that openly uses a vocabulary of slavery and colonization, a film that is set in Los Angeles, of all places, it is shocking to note the absence of African Americans. From all available evidence, few blacks have ever set foot in this futuristic village.

Certain fantasies of racial destiny, it seems, linger on in the digital new world, impervious to the passing of time. Technological advantages belong to the rich and swift. Those still toiling away in the factories, those bound to their labour and the mere meat of their bodies (and this includes much of peasant Asia), are excluded from this virtual geography. In the march of progress, those caught lagging behind the corporate swagger are no place. Caught beyond the present closure of the technological order, caught between an irrecoverable past and a shrinking future, they are being consigned to the forgotten margins of a user bandwidth.

"White nerds and mobile Asians are behind the new culture," Eric Koyanagi says. "They are the new technological class. These people are controlling our vision of the future and the shape it'll take." There are disturbing repercussions in this. The racial hierarchy promoted in books such as *The Bell Curve* has found a more popular and insidious expression: namely, in the view that for every threatening black person there is an enterprising Asian person. It's a crude Cartesian split: blacks = raw physicality, and Asians = mechanistic minds. Yet through such deep-seated stereotypes, we are seeing people locked into future roles. The absence of blacks, Aboriginals, and Latinos in this technological vision of the future contributes to their alienation from the world.

It's a world that remains driven by the desires and politics of a few urban centres—with an increasing number of people being pushed to the periphery of the wired universe, the edge of the "consensual hallucination" that William Gibson describes in *Neuromancer.* Those who don't have access to basic technology (telephones, televisions, computers), those who are finding it difficult to make the journey out of their bodies and histories, are rapidly becoming "virtual" unknowns. It's hard to swallow the optimism of the transnational digeratii when it comes from a privileged minority who possess the means to influence others disproportionately—and abruptly.

| | | | | | |

THIS RACE TO THE FUTURE, WHICH BEGAN IN NEW YORK'S East Village, ends in Los Angeles, headquarters of *Giant Robot* magazine. Twenty years before *Bladerunner*'s replicants are scheduled to invade, *Giant Robot*'s editors, Martin Wong and Eric Nakamura, are hatching their own transpacific vision, their own dream of the future. Their magazine, available at Barnes and Noble and Virgin megastores across the continent, features everything from *anime* film to ambient electronica to skateboarding. Published quarterly, it's like a *Michelin* guide to another galaxy, with an idiom steeped in the grammar of cybernetics and technotrash. Although, at first glance, *Giant Robot* appears to be kin to fanzines and other schlocky teenage fare, upon closer look it's doing a lot more than hyping pop culture.

Eric and Martin spend most of their time dwelling inside computer and video games. They live in a ghostly universe where millions of people are connected without the possibility of "organic" interaction. Even over the phone, Eric and I get off to a bad start. His rapid-fire lingo tells me that we're travelling in different dimensions, and when I ask him to slow down he strikes a fuck-you attitude. He softens, finally, when I start talking to him about a piece in the spring 1997 issue.

In the article, *Giant Robot* goes scavenging for an off-ramp experience, hoping perhaps to expand the conceptual horizons of its primarily twenty-something white and Asian readers. In central California, between Sequoia National Park and Death Valley, near the rugged eastern Sierra, Martin and Eric find a place far removed from the strip malls of Los Angeles. They arrive in a town called Manzanar equipped with skateboards, off-road XT wheels, and backpacks. Here, amid the sundry remains of naked racism, they enter a microworld of displacement.

In 1942, Manzanar was evacuated of its Native American inhabitants and turned into an internment camp for 10,000 Americans of Japanese descent, one of ten such camps scattered throughout the United States. American rage and hysteria over Pearl Harbor and the paranoid suspicion that some vast conspiracy was afoot culminated in mass incarceration. Japanese Americans from California, Oregon, Washington, and Hawaii were rounded up under government orders and brought to Manzanar. Convicted without trial as enemy aliens, they were given a few days to pack two suitcases and bid a final farewell to their homes and businesses. "The citizens of Manzanar were prisoners, pure and simple," writes John Hersey. They lived in the penitentiaries of their bodies.

Back then, Japan was not perceived as the technological dynamo it is today. On the contrary, the aerial attack on Pearl Harbor was all the more surprising because the Japanese were then regarded as technological primitives.

Today, amputated from the rest of the country by a morass of highways and exit ramps, Manzanar feels like a no-man's land. Fifty years ago, it was grimmer still. But you'd never know that from the work of the famous photographer Ansel Adams, who travelled there in 1943 to take pictures of the people and their circumstances. He chose to shoot the brighter aspects of the internment experience: youth singing in a choir, a family gathered in a Christmas celebration. Surveying these photos, I notice how fashionable people look. Sporting wing-tipped shoes, wide lapels, zoot suits, sturdy wool coats with aristocratic fur collars, they are the image of middle-class American life. In one makeshift living room, I notice ironic symbols of patriotism: the stars and stripes, a camping stove, a tea towel from Yosemite National Park. What I don't see, what Adams ignored, were the rows of barracks hedged by barbed wire, the search lights, the guards on eight towers armed with machine guns and orders to shoot to kill anyone who tried to escape.

Eric and Martin feel the desolation, a ghostly spectre hanging over Manzanar. The tar-paper structures are long gone; all that is left is desert wind, a few unremarkable cement foundations, and weeds. It's as if, by deleting the structures, the government thought it might erase all evidence of its shame.

Eric and Martin visit a cemetery, a memorial called the Tower of Memory, and a reservoir built in 1942 by prisoners. They traverse rocks, skate on overgrown paths, and finally pick up speed on the reservoir's dry concrete surface, noting how people in passing cars freak out at "the sight of skateboarders in the middle of hell."

Amid the cold confusion of the former camp, away from the glistening surfaces of the digital superhighway, they have an interzonal experience. The sense of timelessness is different in Manzanar, less euphoric. This is a ghetto of memories. At a time when it is hard to think about yesterday, let alone history, Manzanar forces an encounter with different sides of diasporic existence. To preservationists, it is a vital link to a vanished world. To Eric and Martin, it conveys the still-nebulous status of Asians in America. Sporting hip apparel, gliding through the belly of America, they realize that they are constantly being resituated in terms of their racial identities and in relation to older worlds. This is sobering: "We hiked and skateboarded Manzanar, but the place should never be confused with a summer camp." Here history haunts the delirium of the future.

It is at the point where skateboard wheels touch an off-line road that Eric and Martin find involuntary memory. The weight of history descends, and an entire body of memory—theirs and mine—is driven into this trip like RAM into a hard drive.

Toward the end of their sojourn, Eric finds a large collection of pop artifacts resting atop a commemorative plaque relating Manzanar's history: stuffed animals, makeup, candy, a framed photo, a pack of Marlboro Lights, a tie-dyed handkerchief. They are votive offerings, a makeshift memorial. They remind me of an evening I once spent at the home of the Japanese Canadian novelist Joy Kogawa. Sitting on her couch, I watched as she pulled out a collection of newsprint books for children, mass-produced copies of *Agent K-47* and *Mickey Mouse*. No larger than a child's hand, they were part of her small collection in British Columbia's Slocan internment camp during the war years. Carefully supporting their cracked bindings, I flipped through them. The inside covers advertised the wonders of products long since forgotten: secret decoder rings, a comic book called *Air Adventures*.

Joy also brought out several lantern slides and assembled a small crank-driven Victrola, which her father had bought for family listening in the camp. Nowadays they're relics of a dead technology. But back then, chosen for their compactness and portability, they were links to the outside world. They represented a "virtual reality" that existed at the other end of the highway, beyond the gates of internment. This pop culture, lightly held and shared between youths and adults, did not prove to be the great social equalizer, but it did provide respite for an otherwise isolated and information-starved community.

At the time, Joy told me, the future we are now living didn't have a shape. The wired world was still a dream, the very idea that one could exit one's body a sign of madness or death. Joy's packed-away possessions, like the Yosemite tea towel, stand as small reminders of the quiet, mostly unnoticed, banishment of Japanese communities from North American society.

At Manzanar, at Slocan, the visibility of those incarcerated was essentially what led them there, victims of the era's giant robots or racist mind-sets. A half-century later at Manzanar, Eric and Martin find that the dream of futuristic technobeings, whose worlds fuse into one stream, expresses—for all its promise—a sense of emptiness and amnesia.

The ability of anybody to predict the future is largely chimeri-cal. Having travelled this far, I sense too that every highway chases its own vanishing point. In a troubled century's twilight, the race to the future is pervaded by a sense of congestion, rather like the insis-tent pounding of traffic waiting to be uploaded.

1997

"The Little Gypsy"
The Jazz Legend of Lenny Breau

| | | | | | |

David Hayes

| | | | | | |

A T DUSK ON A SUMMER'S DAY IN 1975, JAZZ GUITARIST
Lenny Breau was playing a breathtakingly delicate ballad on a
nylon-string guitar while standing ankle deep in cow dung in a farmer's
field. His eyes were closed, and a beatific smile crossed his face as a
cascade of notes travelled along, and occasionally over, the edge of
the key. His right hand was a blur, beginning with spidery, five-
fingered picking and then shifting to a fanlike flamenco strum. There
was a luminous quality to the sound, and sometimes Breau struck a
harmonic that strung a single note in the air as though allowing the
light to burnish it.

The occasion was an outdoor party held on the farm of a member
of the hippie community around Killaloe Station, a small town near
Algonquin Park. There were forty or so onlookers, most of them
dressed in the bib overalls, brightly coloured peasant dresses, and
tie-dyed shirts popular at the time. Breau looked out of place among
them. His black shoes, black slacks, black shirt, and mirrored sunglasses
were the uniform of an urban creature, and he had the pale complexion and distracted manner of an aesthete who lived most of his life
indoors. Breau's friend, a saxophonist named Glenn MacDonald, had
invited the guitarist to visit while he tried again to kick the drug and
alcohol dependency that bedevilled his life.

When MacDonald joined Breau in the pasture, the melancholy
moan of his horn weaving around the guitar's silky melody seemed

to embody the two main elements of Breau's troubled character. A gentle, introverted artist, Breau was devoted to his music like a monk to his faith, but he had trouble dealing with the simplest day-to-day responsibilities. He had been called an idiot savant, which overstated the case, but he was unquestionably a man whose musical genius and dedication to his art unbalanced his life. For the moment, though, as a cow ambled across the field and stood contentedly beside the musicians, Breau looked peaceful, as though his demons were at least temporarily at rest.

Two years later, Breau resurfaced playing brilliantly in the company of jazz star George Benson at a US music festival, and the predictions of overdue fame and fortune that arose whenever Breau's name was mentioned were reignited. Instead, his career continued its roller-coaster course as promising concert tours and recording opportunities were interrupted by periods of dissolution. When the forty-three-year-old Breau was murdered at his LA apartment complex in 1984—a case that remains unsolved—it marked the end of an extraordinary talent.

| | | | | | |

THE PUBLIC BARELY KNEW OF LENNY BREAU DURING HIS brief, misshapen career. He recorded relatively little and never committed to tape a masterwork that would have elevated him into the pantheon that includes fellow guitar pioneers Django Reinhardt, Charlie Christian, Barney Kessell, and Wes Montgomery. Nonetheless, he is regarded by musicians in North America, Britain, and Europe as among the most influential guitarists of this century. Chet Atkins, the legendary Nashville guitarist and producer, called him "the best guitar player who has ever walked the earth." A few months before Breau's death, Joe Pass, one of the giants of jazz guitar, said: "Lenny Breau is one of the most innovative jazz specialists currently playing." And US musicologist and critic Leonard Feather wrote: "If you haven't heard Breau, then you don't know how far the instrument can be taken."

Breau had an expansive musical vocabulary. He combined elements of old-fashioned country music, classical and flamenco guitar, jazz styles ranging from bebop to fusion, and eastern influences. He was a virtuoso, his playing shaped by his masterly technique.

Yet when he played a high-speed number filled with grandstand-pleasing, multinote passages, he rarely sacrificed taste for pyrotechnics. Although sometimes his approach was overly sentimental and his choice of material fell perilously close to kitsch, he had a sweet, melancholy way with a ballad, and his touch was always delicate; there was never any heavy breathing. He composed music, but he was most famous for taking a standard such as "My Funny Valentine" and altering the chords, tempo, and time until he had melodically and harmonically reshaped it into something that resembled a cubist painting.

As a guitarist, Breau played an instrument that was for many years an undervalued stepchild in the family of jazz. Brass instruments (trumpet, trombone), woodwinds (clarinet, saxophone), and piano dominated. During the early years of the century, bands were more likely to include a banjo, because it was loud enough to be heard through the din, rather than the more melodically versatile guitar. By the early 1930s, guitar manufacturers managed to make the instrument louder by increasing its size, altering its design, and experimenting with metal resonators, and it gradually replaced the banjo in even the largest bands. Musicians such as Eddie Lang and Belgian gypsy Django Reinhardt demonstrated the guitar's potential as a soloing instrument, but they were confined to recording studios or small ensemble settings where they could be heard. Eddie Durham, a big-band guitarist, is credited with playing the earliest amplified solos in the mid-1930s by pressing a microphone against his instrument's soundhole, but for the most part guitarists were relegated to a support role in a rhythm section until electrical amplification was invented in the late 1930s.

Modern jazz guitar emerged in the form of Charlie Christian, who came to prominence in the early 1940s as a member of Benny Goodman's immensely popular bands. An imaginative improviser with a dazzling technique, Christian played long, flowing lines (made possible by his use of an amplified electric guitar) that proved the guitar was as expressive a solo instrument as a saxophone or trumpet. Because Goodman was a widely recorded star of the swing era, Christian's playing was heard by musicians across the country, giving the guitar new legitimacy. Also, Christian was a key member of a gang that included alto saxophonist Charlie Parker, trumpeter Dizzy

Gillespie, and pianist Thelonious Monk who were experimenting with harmony and melody, which meant that the guitar was present when the foundations of modern jazz were laid. Over the next two decades, guitarists such as Barney Kessell, Tal Farlow, Wes Montgomery, and Herb Ellis refined and extended the instrument's potential.

Although aware of these masters, Breau slowly began to develop a style that was his own. There are two basic approaches to jazz guitar: the strummed chord style that, joined by bass and drums, traditionally provided rhythmic backing to solo instruments, and the single-note style, associated with soloing. A variation is "fingerstyle" playing, a technique adapted from classical guitar and commonly used in folk and country music. Breau developed a hybrid of all three. Where most fingerstyle guitarists used the thumb and first three fingers of the right hand, Breau also used his pinky, which allowed him to play with increasing complexity. Meanwhile, with his left hand, he used the thumb and first two fingers to chord while simultaneously playing single-note lines with his third finger and pinky. Sometimes he added a walking bass line, which made him sound like two or three guitarists and never failed to astonish audiences at live performances.

Breau came by these abilities through both nature and nurture. His right pinky was slightly bowed—he said that it was a peculiarity on his mother's side of the family—which gave his hand a subtly clawlike appearance, precisely the shape that a guitarist's right hand takes as it's poised over the strings. The remarkable dexterity of both hands was achieved through constant practise. As a teenager, he spent hours squeezing a tennis ball and strengthening his fingers on a board to which elastic bands had been stretched.

By the late 1970s, Breau was using a custom-built seven-string guitar that further extended his range. His use of harmonics—high-pitched, chimelike tones produced by lightly touching a string on the fingerboard while simultaneously picking it—was revolutionary. "I got the idea for the chime tones from Chet Atkins," Breau once said. "My ambition was to play like Chet. After that I sort of started studying music, using the same approach but only with a jazz style in mind."

Breau was probably best known for his complex harmonic arpeggios, a cascade of tones that sounded like a harp or, as he once described it, "like playing piano with the sustain pedal down." It was these various techniques that allowed him to execute intricate chord voicings previously confined to the piano, voicings that were his ultimate goal.

"I developed my style trying to sound like a piano," he told a writer in 1981. "A lot of the stuff I play on the guitar is supposed to be technically impossible, but I spent over 20 years figuring it out. There are always two things going on at once. I'm thinking melody, but I'm also thinking of a background."

LENNY BREAU'S BACKGROUND WAS STEEPED IN COUNTRY music. He was born on August 5, 1941, in Auburn, Maine. His parents were the itinerant country entertainers Hal "Lone Pine" Breau and his wife, yodeller Betty Cody. Hal, in his white suits embroidered with pine trees and rhinestones, and Betty, in her fancy, ruffled western skirts, were minor stars in the country music world. By the early 1950s, they'd had a few hits, including "It's Goodbye and So Long to You," "I Heard the Bluebird Sing," and "Tom Tom Yodel," recorded on the RCA Victor label. Although they'd been part of the Grand Ole Opry's touring show, they mainly worked alone throughout the northeastern United States and the Canadian maritimes. Radio stations in those days would often hire a travelling act to broadcast a couple of hours a day, host a Saturday-night dance, and perform in small towns within the station's listening area. Rather than an endless string of one-night stands, this meant settling down for a year or so, and Betty always made sure the children—Lenny and, later, his brothers Richard, Denny, and Bobby—were billeted with relatives or friends nearby so they could attend school and see the family regularly.

Breau began playing simple tunes on a small accordion when he was three. Soon he began appearing on stage with his parents, playing a tiny washboard and occasionally breaking into a jig. Once, when his parents were rehearsing Eddy Arnold's "Cattle Call," Breau waited for the chorus to come around and sang the third harmony perfectly. After impressing his father by playing some chords on a borrowed guitar, he received a flat-top Gibson, a real musician's instrument.

Over the next few years, Breau learned everything from boogie-woogie riffs to classic country tunes. His hero was Atkins, a multitalented guitarist, songwriter, talent scout, and record producer who was becoming an influential force in country music from his Nashville base. When Breau was ten and living in Wheeling, West Virginia, where the Lone Pine Show was part of radio station WWVA's *Jamboree,* he was mesmerized by a recording of Atkins's intricate, fingerpicking version of "I've Been Working on the Railroad." After months of practice, he taught himself the song.

By the time Breau was fifteen and living again in Maine, he was obsessed with music to the exclusion of almost everything else. "He was in the ninth grade at school when the principal called me," says his mother. "He said: 'Lenny is a good, good person in school. He's quiet and polite, one of our best boys. But he's a dreamer. He's into music, and I think our best bet is to let him go and be a musician.'"

In 1956, Breau joined the family act as a guitarist and was dubbed "Lone Pine Junior." He was a shy boy with a stutter that disappeared only when he was completely at ease. With his black hair, olive complexion, and soft features—he looked a little like actor Sal Mineo—he was a hit, especially with young people. After moving from temporary home to home as a child, he now joined his parents' life on the road, a world of cars and roadside restaurants, motel rooms and dressing rooms. That year, his parents were offered a long-term engagement by CKY radio in Winnipeg, Manitoba. Besides Hal, Betty, and Lenny, the band consisted of a pedal steel guitarist and a comedian named Crazy Elmer who doubled on bass. Elvis Presley was the teenagers' idol of the day, so when they reached Winnipeg Hal hired singer-guitarist Ray St. Germain, a local sixteen-year-old who modelled himself after Elvis.

The family lived in a house in Winnipeg and travelled around the region in Hal's white, seven-passenger Cadillac with the luggage stored on a roof rack. When they visited neighbouring towns, Hal would connect a speaker to the car's battery and drive up and down the main street announcing the weekend performance. When the Grand Ole Opry came through Manitoba with the likes of Johnny Cash and George Jones, the Lone Pine show joined the bill. For a pair of teenagers such as Breau and St. Germain, it seemed to be an idyllic life of performing and hanging out in pool halls while other kids were in school.

"He was the star of the show," says St. Germain, today an entertainer and businessman in Winnipeg.

The kid that looked great and played great. At the time, Chet
Atkins was the guitar player, and Lenny played exactly like him.
He knew every Chet Atkins record there was. He was a sensation; "the guitar wizard" is what they called him. The women
loved him because he looked like a movie star. He had an
orange Gretsch "Chet Atkins" model guitar with a white leather
case, and he dressed very sharp, in black, with white shoes.

He could pull in some pretty big houses for his parents, so they
let him alone. His life was being on the road; he never had to
do anything except play. The pressures of old-time show business—you know, never talk or laugh behind the singer—were
being drilled into us every night by his father, but they never
asked him to take out the garbage or anything. He was always
forgiven for any mistake he made. There was no one to say,
"You're being an asshole, Lenny." He didn't have any real life
skills because he was never taught any.

By 1958, Hal was living the show business stereotype of hard
drinking and womanizing, and he and Betty separated. She returned
to Maine with the three youngest children, leaving Hal in Winnipeg.
Around that time, Breau, who had elected to stay with the band,
became interested in jazz. For his seventeenth birthday, St. Germain
bought him an album by Barney Kessell, and a week later Breau
could play every song. He began studying music with a local jazz
pianist and sitting in at local clubs. One night, when his father was
singing Don Gibson's "Oh, Lonesome Me," Breau improvised a few
fancy licks during the guitar break. At intermission, Hal slapped his
son. "I warned you about this," he yelled. "Don't ever play jazz on
my show again!"

Tired of the escalating conflicts with his father, Breau quit the
band, moved out, and began playing in clubs. When he couldn't get
work playing jazz, he played pop music; when he couldn't get work
as a guitarist, he played electric bass or gave lessons. At one time, he
was the guitarist in the house band on the Winnipeg portion of a
national CBC TV show called *Music Hop,* hosted by Ray St. Germain.
But jazz was still his passion. In one of his earliest solo recordings,
done at the CBC's Winnipeg studios, he performed an arrangement

of Duke Ellington's "Caravan." Although he showed impressive musicianship, his style had not coalesced; there were awkward moments that sounded like a shotgun wedding between country picking and jazz ambitions.

Breau, like so many musicians in the late 1950s, became entranced by the music of pianist Bill Evans. Evans appeared on Miles Davis's landmark *Kind of Blue* album in 1958, which launched the cool movement, and his early trio recordings were making an enormous impact on the jazz world. Evans had devised a system—it was more like an Eastern philosophy—of tinkering with chords, the basic building blocks of music, and weaving melodies as intricate as clockworks. Until then, Breau had been studying country and jazz guitarists and flamenco giants such as Sabicas and Ramon Montoya. In Evans, Breau found inspiration for his own musical evolution.

One of Breau's closest friends was David Young, the bassist on *Music Hop* at the time who would become a leading jazz accompanist and work with, among others, Oscar Peterson. He and Breau used to spend hours practising jazz, learning the songs on Evans's albums. Says Young about Breau: "He had a wider experience [than many jazz players] because he'd played country, rock, classical, everything. Sometimes I'd recognize Bill Evans voicings he'd managed to learn. He synthesized it all. Nothing was sacred, or maybe everything was sacred. The beauty of what he did is that he created his own style of playing."

Breau had married Ray St. Germain's sister, Valerie, when he was eighteen, and the couple had two children, a boy and a girl. But he would never be a stable provider, and his nomadic upbringing and artist's personality apparently made him temperamentally unsuited to settling down. He moved to Toronto in 1962 and began working within the city's active jazz scene. Soon he joined actor and singer Don Francks and a string bassist in a trio Francks called three. Their repertoire ranged from jazz standards and Broadway hits to country tunes. Francks used his voice like a horn and treated words as though they were notes, cleverly mixing and transposing lyrics and employing a variety of accents. In doing so, he injected a Greenwich Village hipster's attitude to what was in essence a mainstream nightclub act, and the result was a hit on Toronto's jazz scene and on CBC Radio and TV variety shows.

Upon meeting Breau, Francks says,

I didn't believe what I heard, this stuttering, beautiful young guy who knew about jazz but also knew about country music and was open to everything. He was a nonverbal person; he spoke through his music and listened to everything. It would be silly for me not to say that the birds in the trees influenced him. He'd say: "L-l-l-ike, like m-m-m-an, dig this," and play something extraordinary.

He had a quirky sense of humour. Really corny. He probably picked it up from his father and those old country guys he'd hung out with on the road. When we were leaving somewhere, he'd actually say: "L-l-like man, don't take an-n-n-y wo-o-o-den nickels."

Publicity photos of three show a boyishly handsome young man, wearing an expression of moody intensity, posing with his guitar. "He was clean, you can see that," Francks says.

He didn't drink alcohol very much. He and I would smoke the occasional reefer, some tea as it was called, just to get right into the music. But he didn't need drugs then; the guitar was his drug. To be involved in what we were doing, you needed to be on top of it. We didn't want any trouble with police or at border crossings. We wanted to make it.

I once said that he was capable of tripping over his own shadow, but it wasn't meant in a nonloving way. That's the way Lenny was: you took care of him. You lifted everything, including his six guitar cases, because the fingernails on his right hand were very long, and he didn't want anything to happen to his hands. If we needed tickets, I got them. I made sure nothing upset him.

Scouts from New York's William Morris Agency were interested in Francks, so in early 1963 the trio was booked for a three-week stint at the Blue Angel, a trendy Manhattan nightspot. On April 24, they appeared on Jackie Gleason's national TV show, and a few weeks later they made a live recording at the Village Vanguard, one of the city's premier jazz venues. The album, entitled *Jackie Gleason says: "No one in this world is like Don Francks,"* was released later that year, and Billboard, the record industry trade magazine, wrote: "This album will appeal to sharp, hip people." But Francks moved on to a Broadway production of *Finian's Rainbow* and the bicoastal acting career that followed, and three was dissolved.

Throughout the rest of the 1960s, Breau travelled back and forth between Toronto and Winnipeg. In 1967, he came to the attention of Chet Atkins, who was by then running RCA's Nashville operation. "He had assimilated all these ideas from flamenco players and from country players and jazz players," Atkins said at the time. "He had this bag of tricks I'd never heard before. He could play every tune I'd ever recorded, but he was modern with them."

Atkins, who called his new friend "the little gypsy," was so impressed that he offered to produce Breau's first record. On *Guitar Sounds from Lenny Breau,* Breau sounded comfortable accompanied by drummer Reg Killn and bassist Bob Halderson, his regular backing musicians from Winnipeg.

One track—an arrangement of the folk song "Freight Train"— provided a catalogue of his tricks, illustrating why he made so powerful an impact on guitarists everywhere. He played the first chorus traditionally, using a jaunty country and western fingerpicking style, then broke the rhythm into complex syncopations for the second. For the next three choruses, he shifted between densely intricate flamenco picking and a series of harmonically challenging chord voicings that reduced the familiar tune to fragments. Killn and Halderson joined as Breau returned to jazz orthodoxy with fluid, single-note soloing (while simultaneously chording). He ended the song with a flourish: a few bars in classical style, a bluesy ragtime passage, and a shimmering of harmonics. It was a bravura performance that demonstrated a breath-taking mastery of the instrument.

The rest of the material was a weirdly eclectic assortment of songs ranging from Roger Miller's "King of the Road" and Bob Dylan's "Don't Think Twice It's All Right" to standards such as "My Funny Valentine" and "Georgia on My Mind." "There was a time when I would have been afraid to record in Nashville because I wanted to be known as a jazz player," Breau told a CBC interviewer. "But now I don't really care what I'm called as a player, because I feel it's just music."

Which raises the problem of categories and labels: where did Breau belong? Radio programmers, notoriously uninterested in such epistemological concerns, for the most part ignored him. *Guitar Sounds* was too country for pop or jazz stations and too jazzy for country stations. His arrangement of "Freight Train," for example, may have been revolutionary to musicians' ears, but to many ordinary listeners it was simply confusing, filled with parentheses, asides, and digressions. A few months later, RCA recorded a two-night perform-ance at Shelly's Manne-Hole, a Los Angeles jazz club, again with Killn and Halderson. This time, RCA executives were eager to get Breau radio airplay but needed a three-minute track that would showcase Breau's talents. Breau said he understood what they wanted, but whenever he began playing he lost himself in his improvisations and most of the numbers ran between six and ten minutes.

The Velvet Touch of Lenny Breau Live! was as eclectic as *Guitar Sounds*. It included a clever reworking of saxophonist Cannonball Adderley's hit "Mercy, Mercy, Mercy," an arrangement of "A Taste of Honey" that sounded like at least two guitars at once, and a whimsi-cal version of Merle Travis's country classic "That's All," which Breau sang in a laconic, nasal drawl. Elsewhere he touched on Latin, Spanish, and blues influences.

Even though *Guitar Sounds* and *Velvet Touch* were unfocused creations, Breau was reinventing jazz guitar. Both albums were enor-mously influential among guitarists, establishing Breau's reputation throughout North America. In terms of guitar technique, his style was as artistically innovative as it was mathematically precise. The myth-making was also beginning. One of the earliest legends surrounding Breau—recounted in the liner notes for *Guitar Sounds*—was that he mastered Les Paul's 1952 recording of "Tiger Rag" without realizing that Paul had achieved his multilayered sound through his early exper-iments with overdubbing separate guitar tracks onto several tape recorders. The self-effacing Breau later discounted the story, saying that he knew Paul had overdubbed the parts, as though that admis-sion diminished the fact that he'd managed to duplicate the sound of several guitars singlehandedly.

Larry Carleton, an LA session guitarist who played with musi-cians such as Andy Williams, Joni Mitchell, and Chick Corea as well as recording his own albums, said: "For players like myself, who've been playing guitar since we were six years old, it happens maybe once in a decade that you hear something so unique that you get excited. Lenny was one of those players you listen to and go, 'What the heck is this guy doing, and how is he doing it?'"

But neither album was commercially successful. They would mark the last time Breau recorded on a major record label.

| | | | | | |

THERE HAD BEEN TROUBLING TALK ABOUT LENNY BREAU FOR some time. He used to tell people that he'd recorded *Velvet Touch* after taking a partial dose of LSD. Once, after he had visited Atkins and his wife at their Nashville home, they found tinfoil and matches in their bathroom, and Atkins realized his protégé was doing drugs of some kind.

The Toronto jazz scene, of which Breau was a part, was made up of two segments. Many respected artists who wrote and recorded original music also earned much of their incomes doing sessions for jingles or TV programs. Being an instrument-for-hire was lucrative, but it demanded disciplined musicians who could read music fluently, follow directions, and show up unfailingly for morning calls. At the other end of the spectrum were the "street musicians," a subculture populated by talented players with unruly souls, hangers-on, and genuine artists like Breau whose demons were overtaking them. For them, the demands and obligations of music as a business were anathema to art, to say nothing of being impossible to fulfil. Besides, a nocturnal lifestyle and ample substance abuse were an integral part of a jazz musician's life, as the tragically romantic sagas of Bix Beiderbecke, Charlie Parker, Billie Holiday, Chet Baker, and countless others proved.

Breau played on sessions from time to time, even though his reading was weak. Usually, one or another of his friends among the studio players would hire him and coach him through the number. But the self-destructive side of his character was growing stronger. He couldn't be counted on to show up for a session. He was even cancelling his own engagements with increasing frequency. A newspaper ad for a 1971 gig reported that another act was replacing an "ailing Lenny Breau." He spent that summer recuperating in Maine with his family.

In spring 1972, he was hired as the guitarist for Anne Murray's backup band. Once, in a hotel in Chicago, Breau and several other musicians rode the elevator to their floor. As the musicians walked toward their rooms, they noticed Breau was no longer with them. Hearing a strange rhythmic thumping, they retraced their steps. Breau, stoned on LSD, lay facedown in the corridor while the elevator doors opened and closed on his head. He was, as it turned out, also using methadone, a heroin substitute used as part of addiction treatment programs, although he insisted it was prescribed to help him with the effects of LSD, not heroin. In any event, he shared it freely with his bandmates. With his behaviour becoming increasingly erratic, Breau left the band in Winnipeg, midway through the tour. His old friend, Ray St. Germain, hired him to play with a band in a club he was managing. Breau was so unstable that St. Germain agreed to pay for whatever he needed but give him no cash. One night he failed to appear. At 1:30 a.m., as the club was closing, he calmly walked in, set up his amplifier, and plugged in his guitar, apparently unaware of the time. St. Germain later found out that he had been charged that night with possession of heroin. (At his trial a year later, he was given a conditional discharge and ordered to attend a methadone clinic.)

Despite all this, Breau's career hadn't entirely deteriorated. By the mid-1970s, he was performing for modest fees at clubs and small theatres and giving guitar clinics. His restless experimenting meant that he still hadn't settled into a distinctive musical niche, a shortcoming exacerbated by his personal problems. Around this time, the *Toronto Star* wrote: "Guitarist Lenny Breau is the type of jazz musician whose appearances are always overshadowed, confused and preceded by his reputation."

Then, in 1975, on Hallowe'en, Breau answered a knock at the door with a bag of candy to find narcotics officers with a warrant. One of his roommates had been selling pot, and everyone in the house was charged. Frightened at facing a second drug charge, Breau fled to Maine, where his father, who had retired years earlier, was in poor health. When he failed to appear at the preliminary hearing, his roommates proclaimed their innocence, and Breau was charged with trafficking.

In Maine, he was enveloped by an extended family that included his mother, brothers, and a sympathetic uncle who was a recovering alcoholic. "He'd say, 'I've gotta have a rest, mom. Can I come home?'" Betty Cody said. "We'd never say no to him, because we all wanted to protect him. We tried to talk to him, and there'd never be a harsh word out of him. Always quiet, always humble, agreeing with us. At one time, he stayed for six months. The doctor would tell him, 'Lenny, you're going away too soon. You should be here a whole year.' He'd say, 'Oh, no, I'm strong enough now, I know I can make it.' And he would stumble again."

For the rest of the decade, his life was characterized by peaks and valleys. Although Breau attended drug treatment programs, periods of recovery were punctuated by drinking binges with his father or drug taking with the musicians and hangers-on who sought him out. His 1977 appearance at a Georgia music festival with George Benson was thought to mark the beginning of an upswing. Then, one night in February 1978, a nearly fatal mixing of alcohol and methadone left him unconscious in a New York City snowdrift. Only an alert police officer prevented him from freezing to death. He entered still another drug rehabilitation program.

Breau made frequent trips to Nashville, where Chet Atkins, who was like a surrogate father to him, gave him session work and encouraged him to regain control of his career. Breau was coleader on *Minors Aloud,* a remarkable recording with noted pedal steel guitarist Buddy Emmons that seamlessly blended country and jazz, and he made a duet album of country standards with Atkins. Once, during a visit to Atkins's farm when the two had been together for most of the afternoon, Atkins noticed that Breau had somehow managed to get high. Driving back to Nashville, Atkins said: "Lenny, what happened to you?"

"Well, man," Breau replied, "I went in the bathroom and looked in the medicine chest, and there was a bottle of Valium there. So I took five of them."

"Man, why did you do that?" asked an exasperated Atkins.

"W-w-well, like, man, I'm a junkie," Breau said in his childishly earnest way. "It's like seeing candy."

IN THE MUSIC BUSINESS, MAINTAINING A PROFILE IS CRITI-cally important, and success is measured by the quality and the quantity of an artist's recordings. Only two albums had appeared under Lenny Breau's name since *Guitar Sounds* and *Velvet Touch—Five O'Clock Bells* and *The Legendary Lenny Breau . . . Now!*—both released on tiny independent labels in 1978. In Nashville, he'd played on three innovative country jazz recordings and accompanied Chet Atkins on two of his albums (all of which were out of print by the early 1980s). He had become the reclusive prophet of the guitar world. Everyone from aspiring teenagers to seasoned pros traded homemade tapes recorded in living rooms and at music store workshops. Many sought him out, bringing with them their instruments and tape recorders. One of them was Scott Page, an LA-based saxophonist and guitarist who had performed on hundreds of sessions. In the fall of 1978, Page was travelling with folk-rockers Seals and Crofts when he learned that Breau was living in seclusion in Maine, not far from one of the tour stops. He took a lesson, then encouraged Breau to move to Los Angeles, even offering him temporary lodging in his house. Breau accepted the offer.

In February 1979, Page, a hustler with a keen business mind and an enormous number of contacts, booked Breau into a local club despite the owner's misgivings about hiring a guitarist he'd never heard of. The club was filled to capacity and a lineup stretched down the block for the entire two-week engagement as just about every guitarist and jazz fan in Los Angeles came to hear the legend. "If they would've dropped a bomb there, the whole guitar world would have been finished," joked Page.

The "guitar world" is uniquely insular and narcissistic. The instrument, which Beethoven called "a miniature orchestra in itself," can be played poorly with minimal effort but is exceptionally difficult to master. Aspiring musicians can grasp the mechanics of trumpet, saxophone, and other members of the brass and woodwind families relatively quickly and move on to artistic concerns, whereas guitarists struggle with fundamentals for years. Even piano, a highly complex instrument, features a keyboard laid out in a linear fashion that's easy to see and play. By contrast, a guitar's fingerboard is difficult to see and awkward to play, in part because the standard tuning dates back six centuries and is unaccommodating to modern techniques and ideas; it's like playing six pianos sideways. For centuries, classical guitarists mainly wrote and performed solo pieces because they couldn't be heard in orchestral or chamber group settings, and something of that isolation characterizes the guitar world to this day. Despite its predominance in rock, blues, and country—all derivatives of folk music—it's still not considered a frontline instrument in jazz.

"A professional guitarist relies to an unusual extent on the guitar world," says Jim Ferguson, a guitarist who teaches, writes instruction books, and was for years an associate editor with *Guitar Player* magazine. "Take a great jazz guitarist like Joe Pass. He's out playing with famous jazz people, but a large part of his audience is still guitarists. He plays at clubs that feature only guitarists and gives clinics and workshops. That doesn't happen with other instruments."

Breau was sustained by this world. He continued to play clubs and give workshops, but he remained a guitarist's guitarist. By this time, he was using a custom-designed seven-string guitar fitted with a wide classical guitar's neck that gave him even more opportunity to create his distinctive piano voicings. But despite the sophistication of his musical explorations, his work was so intensely personal and, at the same time, profoundly technical that it turned in on itself. He was so obsessed with the purity of improvisation that his few recordings were spontaneous, one-take efforts complete with fumbled notes and miscues. It fascinated guitarists but didn't conform to the commercial recording standards and polished performances to which most listeners were accustomed.

Still, one of the records, *Five O'Clock Bells,* became a collector's item among guitarists. Although some of the material sounded like a grab bag of tricks rather than fully realized compositions, it included a stunning version of pianist McCoy Tyner's "Visions," a number that many would consider unplayable by a solo guitarist. But Breau's low profile and limited recordings made him a spectral presence on the music scene. People talked about his appearances and recordings the way birders discuss sighting a rare species.

Furthermore, Breau, unlike many artists who are reluctant to reveal their trademark licks, was always willing to demonstrate and explain in detail his techniques. One of his admirers, Larry Carleton, remembers the impact Breau's generosity had on the music business even while his own career remained in limbo. "The second that I realized there were twelve guitar players doing sessions in Los Angeles who were using harmonics the way Lenny did, I discontinued doing it. His vocabulary was becoming clichéd, not because of him but because of those of us who stole from him."

Finally, in 1981, Breau was determined to clean up the many loose ends in his life. He had been unable to return to Canada because of the six-year-old drug charge, so Don Francks hired Toronto lawyer Austin Cooper, who, in 1978, had defended Rolling Stone Keith Richards on a heroin charge. Breau was fined $1,000 and released. Next Francks hired an accountant to help Breau with his back taxes.

His inability to cope with life was painfully clear to Francks during one session with the accountant. Rather than asking specific questions, a bewildered Breau turned to Francks and plaintively asked: "What does it mean, Don?"

With Francks's help, Breau began his comeback. Bookings across Canada were arranged, and he was paired with David Young, his old friend from Winnipeg. With Breau apparently in good shape, the duo began by playing dates in Montreal, Ottawa, and Toronto. But the confusion and conflict that had dogged him for years hadn't disappeared. When he arrived in Winnipeg for a sold-out concert, he learned that a judgement had been reached charging him with $20,000 in back child support and alimony payments. At his hotel, a sheriff served an injunction preventing him from performing until the bills were paid. Breau's Winnipeg promoter arranged a meeting between Breau, his former wife, Valerie, and her lawyer, and a settlement was reached hours before the concert.

But the damage had been done. A badly rattled Breau arrived that evening at the Pantages Playhouse Theatre having consumed a combination of alcohol and pills. After a rambling introduction, he stumbled several times on the opening number, groaning at one point as he tried to make his fingers do what he wanted them to do. Later, in a slurred voice reminiscent of Billie Holiday's last recordings, he sang a country tune: "How high's the water, mama, / Five feet high and risin' / How high's the water, papa." Forgetting the words, he stopped. "No, that's not it. I got off on the wrong foot. . . ."

The concert was a disaster, and upcoming shows in the West were cancelled one by one. The pain and confusion in his soul, which seemed to be the dark side of his genius, were dogging him again. An interview given to a CBC reporter demonstrated his fragile, emotionally unstable state at the time: "Long story, man, it's a long story," he said, with resignation in his voice.

It's just one of those things. IT'S ONE OF THOSE THINGS, man. It's like, I was hanging out with guys who were doing it. At first, I did it for inspiration, you know. I got the inspiration at first, but in the end it turned against me. It turned against me. It wasn't inspiring anymore. It was a habit. It was a drag. It was a necessity.

So a little piece of this and a little piece of that can be inspiring sometimes, but if you use it every day and you make a pig of yourself, then it ain't inspiring anymore, then it's nothin' but a habit. It robs your soul after awhile, man, it robs your soul. It's like a seductress. It's like a prostitute who takes more and more and more and more and more and after awhile you're spending so much money doing it that you really can't enjoy yourself and it takes all your money and you get to the gig and you don't even enjoy it because you're not getting off. . . .

Breau returned to the United States, again dividing his time mainly between California, Maine, and Nashville. In 1981, *Guitar Player* hired him to write a column called "Lenny's Fingerstyle Guitar" but had to make special arrangements to accommodate the unpredictable Breau. "Most columnists for *Guitar Player* wrote their own columns," says Jim Ferguson, the magazine's associate editor at the time. "This was one of the first that was ghostwritten. We'd get him a hotel room in San Jose, and I'd spend two days gathering enough material to keep the column going for six or seven months, just in case he didn't show up again."

It was revealing that Breau compared drug addiction to seductresses and prostitutes, because he'd recently remarried. His wife was a tough, big-boned Lebanese American named Jewel Glasscock, an aspiring singer and self-proclaimed born-again Christian who had met Breau in RCA's Nashville studios. (She had previously been arrested on prostitution charges in Las Vegas.) By all accounts, her behaviour bordered on the psychotic.

"I think she must have had a chemical imbalance," says Betty Cody.

She was always in high gear. She was so jealous and possessive she would scream at him because he was paying too much attention to me. She called me at all times of the night, screaming and crying. When he was staying with his uncle, she brought him a bag of peyote. When he was in a rehabilitation centre, he wasn't supposed to see her. She arranged a visit and brought him a cake with LSD in it. I once said to her, "Don't you want him to get better?" She said, "I'd rather have my old Lenny back, on drugs and drinking." That was how she controlled him.

Between late 1981 and 1983, whenever Breau was in Nashville, he performed with a successful studio singer named Jim Ferguson (unrelated to *Guitar Player*'s Ferguson), whose first love was playing jazz bass. Their first job together was at a restaurant called Faison's. Breau and Glasscock were separated at the time, but at the end of the night she cornered him near the stage and shoved him across a table, hurting his hand.

"When they finally got back together, she would come to the jobs," Ferguson says.

She'd get her hands on the money, and it would be all hell to get the sidemen paid. Lenny was such an addictive personality, though, that if someone would supply him he would do it. When I worked jobs with him, guys would just hum around him, wait till he got paid, and see what they could do. I worked jobs with Lenny where he spent the entire door take on drugs. He'd take rent money and spend it on drugs.

When Lenny was straight, he could be one of the sweetest, gentlest guys around. But when he was straight, he was real nervous unless he was in the company of people he was comfortable with. I remember doing some TV shows with him where he would be shakin'.

I suppose it was a love-hate relationship. I hated that Lenny was addicted, trapped in that kind of lifestyle. If he'd been even half sober, he'd have been internationally famous. But I guess it's like if you were a cellist and you found out Pablo Casals was a junkie. That wouldn't mean you didn't love him and respect the beautiful things about him and the way he played.

In 1983 and 1984, Breau was living in Los Angeles with Glasscock and their baby girl, Dawn. To some of Breau's friends, things seemed to be improving. In June 1983, performances in Toronto at Bourbon Street accompanied by his old friend David Young were recorded and sold to a small US independent label, which issued them under the titles *Quietude* and *Legacy*. But his past haunted him. "We could have gone to Europe after the Bourbon Street date," recalls Young, "but you couldn't count on him. He couldn't convince people he was a responsible guy, and no agent's going to risk that. In the last five years of his life, he could've capitalized and become a big name, but he was too emotionally disorganized."

His personal life was as unsettled as his career. On many occasions, Breau tried to leave Glasscock, who alternately threatened his life and their daughter's. On one occasion, he was staying with jazz guitarist Phil Upchurch, who had hired him to play on his latest recording. Breau told Upchurch that Glasscock sometimes hid his instruments to make him obey her. Once a thug sent by Glasscock came to Upchurch's house and bullied Breau, then left with his guitar.

Breau and Glasscock were living on the seventh floor of the Langham Apartments, a building originally built in 1927 as an opulent mansion for Al Jolson and later a tony address that was home to Clark Gable and Ronald Reagan. It was later converted into luxury rental units, but by the 1980s it had become just another rundown apartment house in a rough area of East Los Angeles, on the fringe of Koreatown.

At 6:30 on the morning of Sunday, August 12, 1984, Breau called his mother. "I need advice, mom," he said, sounding agitated and depressed. "I don't know what to do. It's getting violent here. Last night we had an awful argument, and I walked out and got drunk, the worst thing I could do. I've been keeping clean, too. I came back, and she's not here." His mother told him to come home, and he said he would call back.

Four hours later, Breau was found at the bottom of the building's rooftop pool by a tenant, apparently the victim of an accidental drowning. The next day, the county coroner announced that he had been strangled before being placed in the pool. Larry Bird, a detective with the LAPD homicide division, and his partner spent more than three months investigating the case. "We knew he had been strangled somewhere in or around his own apartment," says Bird. "Then the body was carried up the two flights and dumped in the pool. We feel we know who did it, because we eliminated all other motives or suspects, but without an eyewitness or a confession, we didn't have enough evidence to file charges."

| | | | | | |

ASIDE FROM THE DEBILITATING EFFECTS OF DRUGS AND alcohol, Lenny Breau's greatest handicap was genius without vision. Although Breau played with passion, his style remained unfocused throughout his life, a set of brilliant techniques that was a guitar student's fantasy but too fragmented and abstract for popular appeal. His love of spontaneity meant that he usually played solo (or accompanied by a sympathetic bassist), an arrangement that, along with the spiritual exile of the addict, encouraged his tendency to self-absorption. "The soloist is a narcissist," wrote jazz critic Whitney Balliet, "who sets his own boundaries, goals and speeds, who makes his own weather." Breau had a pure artist's soul—he wanted to create when the muse touched him, not on demand like a musician specializing in advertising jingles. But his life was in such a shambles that it blocked inspiration and prevented him from progressing further with his revolutionary guitar ideas.

Even all that might have been corrected with the help of a dedicated manager or a perceptive record producer. But Breau was a labour-intensive client; what manager wanted to handle an artist who might appear for a show incapable of performing, if he showed up at all? What record company wanted a drug-addicted genius who was impossible to control and whose music—assuming he remained lucid long enough to record it—was difficult to market?

Breau often said he drew his greatest inspiration from painting. He carried a Renoir reproduction in his case, and he once said: "I'm trying to paint with the guitar. Not just play the tune, but paint colours and tell a story. . . .

"The type of music that I play thrives on quietude. With quietude I can use the approach of the Japanese painters who paint a little man on a boat fishing, and in the back there's nothing but emptiness. It looks unfinished. Once in awhile I'll just play a note and there will be a great, long space. The space becomes really dramatic. Dead silence is intense."

1992

| | | | | | |

The Translators' Tale

| | | | | | |

Stan Persky

| | | | | | |

I T WAS REPORTED IN THE PRESS THAT THE TWO MEN, TRANS-
lators in Tirana, Albania, had shared "a tiny, Spartan office" in the
state publishing house for most of the past twenty-two years. That
touching detail particularly fascinated me. "Behind battered type-
writers," the article said, perhaps a bit melodramatically, "they have
battled to keep fragments of literature alive in the darkness of Stalinist
orthodoxy."

The story was published in April 1991. Reading the brief account
of the two men, now middle aged, I wondered the simplest things.
How had they spent their time? What had they talked about? Kept
necessarily silent about? What loyalties had caused them to perse-
vere? How had they maintained their sanity? (for it seemed like an
ultimate test of sanity). It was something like those stories one occasionally ran into ages ago in which a pair of Japanese soldiers emerged
from a jungle in Burma or Java twenty years after World War II, never
having heard that it had ended.

In the case of Mr. Simoni and Mr. Qesku—those were their
names—the endurance had been similar, but the cause was more
familiar to us. The convulsions that swept away regimes across Europe,
from Warsaw to Bucharest, in the late 1980s had at last, in the early
1990s, reached the hills of what was once ancient Illyria. And blinking in the uncertain sunlight—for it was hardly clear that our vaunted
free markets would provide a panacea for their woes—there appeared

the translators of Tirana, having, you could say, kept the faith. It was a faith that transcended the generations of remoteness that shrouded their land. Albania was neither a Burmese jungle nor an island in the Indies but a southern European nation wedged between Greece and what was then Yugoslavia, a mere eighty kilometres across the Adriatic from Bari or Brindisi in Italy; yet it might have been as distant as the moon, so successfully and for so long had its Glorious Leader sealed it off as the last and purest bastion of communism. That spring and summer, I was in Berlin, writing about the fall of communism (it was more than a year since the collapse of the Berlin Wall), reading a little philosophy (that's the subject I teach at a college in Vancouver), and pursuing the amorous adventures that leisurely evenings in bars and cafés sometimes yielded.

I was often to be found at a table in the Café Einstein in the late afternoon at the beginning of summer, like many of the other patrons, engrossed in a book or newspaper. Although Joseph Conrad's *Heart of Darkness* was something of a reading-list staple when I went to school, somehow I had never gotten around to reading it until now. Or perhaps I had and had merely read it carelessly as a student—because, upon taking it up now, it seemed fresh yet strangely familiar to me.

As I began (or began again) the tale of a journey to what had once seemed like the ends of the Earth, it called up the ideas I had about Albania, a preoccupation that had been inspired by the brief newspaper article about the translators I'd read that spring. (In fact, I'd clipped the story and tucked it into the back of my notebook.)

I never really admitted to my friends in Berlin that I intended to go to Albania. At most, I'd say something casual and indirect, such as "I wonder if it's possible to fly to Tirana from here." Perhaps I didn't even want to admit my intention to myself, fearing that a glimpse of its foolishness might put me off. Nonetheless, however desultorily, I made the necessary phone calls, inquired at a travel agency, checked the airline office. One day, I got my friend Manuel (he was also my current amorous adventure) to accompany me to the Albanian consulate in east Berlin, only to find the dilapidated building locked and to be informed by a caretaker that I needed to contact the office in Bonn.

My method—to use a word that appears prominently in Conrad's tale—was circuitous at best. Indeed, it was a sort of game that I called

STAN PERSKY

"following the story," in which one set certain events in motion, or
created the possibility of setting them in motion, by some ordinary
but deliberate act—reading a book, walking a certain route, going to
a particular place (say, the bar where I met Manuel). And if something
happened as a consequence, the challenge then—the whole point of
the game, really—was to attend to the ensuing possibilities in such a
way that the pattern of meanings we call a story resulted.

Reading the opening pages of Conrad's story, I found it easy to
identify with its narrator, Marlow, the veteran sailor who makes his
way about Brussels to secure a posting on a Congo riverboat of the
Belgian trading company that, for all practical purposes, ruled that
distant African land. I had also been to sea. As I read—while at the
same time arranging my own curious journey—Albania seemed as
distant as Marlow's destination, and Comrade Enver Hoxha, who had
ruled it, was a figure as forbidding as Kurtz, the god-man who domi-
nates the Polish writer's tale.

Of course, I was aware of the cliché of reading Conrad in that
way. The "heart of darkness" was everybody's metaphor; whoever travelled to what might be regarded as an obscure part of the Earth
invoked it. But there was nothing I could do about it. If you're a
reader, sooner or later you read Conrad, and by happenstance I was
reading *Heart of Darkness* at that moment.

In the end (the end of the beginning, that is), I found myself filling
out a visa application form while seated at a table in the Café Einstein.
I was in the high-ceilinged room of the villa that overlooked the café
garden, which was more than half-empty that particular afternoon,
leaving to the tame sparrows that hopped up onto the tables almost
no one from whom they might filch a stray crumb of Apfelkuchen.
Wettest, coldest June in memory, the German tabloids blared, along
with requisite references to "global warming" and other climatic disturbances. And still chilly, even into July. The black-jacketed waiters
moved among the bundled-up patrons at a glacial pace, carrying hot
drinks on sterling trays.

When I asked my friends, in that studiedly casual voice I'd
adopted for the purpose, "I wonder if it's possible to fly to Tirana
from here," they invariably replied, with barely restrained politeness,
"But why would you want to go there?" Or, because I was a Canadian,
they assumed I was saying "Toronto," which necessitated my having

to distinguish the two: "Not Toronto, Tirana." In any case, they would often fail to hear me correctly and make me repeat the name of the Albanian capital, and then they, who had been almost everywhere, would quizzically repeat it themselves—"Tirana?"—in the slightly astonished tones reserved for impossibly distant places or vanished cities of the past.

Sometimes they would attempt to dissuade me by pointing out the difficulties of acquiring a visa.

"I phoned," I reported.

"To Bonn, of course," one of them assumed.

"To Tirana," I said.

"You can phone Tirana?" they warily asked.

"Easier than east Berlin," I replied, drawing a wan smile among my friends for all the times we'd tried to make an appointment across the once-divided city.

The attaché in Bonn suggested that I needed an invitation from someone in Tirana in order to complete my visa application. When I asked him if he happened to have the number of the state publishing house in Tirana, he supplied it, and soon after I attempted to phone Simoni, one of the men mentioned in the newspaper story. Astonishingly enough, after bursts of static on the line and a babble of languages (Albanian, English, German, Italian), then a long pause (he had been walking down a flight of stairs), I was speaking with Simoni himself. He promised to send a note of invitation. Thus, I "followed the story," even as I was following other stories (the blond-haired Manuel, for example, with whom I was in the midst, or perhaps at the end, of something, had abruptly—but only temporarily, I hoped—decamped). Well, if the invitation from Tirana arrives, if mail service from Tirana even exists, I told myself, then I guess I'll get some snapshots from the photo booth at the train station to stick onto the application form. And indeed, one by one, each of the items appeared, until at last I signed my name in the Café Einstein and sent the papers off from the nearby post office.

A few nights later, a Saturday evening, while I was in the bath at the place I was staying, the phone rang. Annoyed, and dripping down the hallway, I picked up the phone to be told by the Albanian attaché in Bonn—unusual that he should be working on a Saturday night, I marvelled—that my visa had been approved.

In the post, along with the papers, he sent me a picture post-card, signed with his best wishes. I didn't know what to make of such an unbureaucratic gesture. It was a picture of an ancient boy's head, marble, from Apollonia, one of the places down the Adriatic coast that the Greeks had set up in the fifth century or so BC. "Best wishes," the picture postcard said.

I was on the Berlin-Zurich-Tirana flight, with a date to meet the two translators at 7 p.m. at the base of the Skanderbeg statue in the town square. I hastily acquired the necessary background from *Eastern Europe on a Shoestring*. Skanderbeg (the potted history tersely informed me): fifteenth-century warlord; castle in the hills at a place called Kruje, a bit north of Tirana; fought the Turks twenty times, never beaten. National hero. Of course, once Skanderbeg was out of the way, it was the Ottoman Turks for the next 500 years. Succeeded by King Zog, then the fascists, and finally by the Glorious Leader, Comrade Hoxha.

I don't know what I was after. Oh, to find Simoni and Qesku, certainly. And to find out how a country in the middle of Europe could more or less disappear from the face of the Earth for half a century. But I think I also wanted to know what was there. As if to make up for an oversight on the part of North Americans. Sure, Albania had been sealed off for God knows how long, but was that sufficient excuse for our failure to consider it? Of course, if we had, would anyone have bothered to pay attention? Marlow's celebrated utter-ance (I'd tossed my copy of *Heart of Darkness* into my bag) echoed in my mind: "And this, also, has been one of the dark places of the earth."

So, I had a rendezvous. But first there were the "pilgrims," to use Conrad's term for them. I mean, if I could think of it, then surely the business pilgrims would already be figuring out how to turn a dollar. He was a Swiss engineer, named Weber. Boarded at Zurich. The Texans were seated in front of us. As soon as we were up, the engi-neer had a powerful thirst. Scotch doubles, and beer to wash them down. By the descent, he had persuaded the flight attendant to sell him some cans of beer in a paper bag. But he knew the country, I had to give him that.

When Weber wasn't courting the woman in the window seat, I asked him the usual traveller's questions. I'd heard of the Hotel Tirana.

No, the Dajti, he firmly recommended. Reservation? No problem, he'd fix it up if it came to that. And was there a bus into town from the airport? *Kein* problem, I could ride in with him. Hail fellow, well met. Well lubricated, too, by the time we were on the ground.

The airport was a tiny patch of cement in the countryside. Thirty degrees on the ground at 4 p.m. Walking down the double row of palm trees into the terminal, I was poached in my own juices. Lads in green with machine guns. The usual madhouse—babies, relatives, heaps of baggage. "Fixers" everywhere. I'd heard the term back home during the Gulf War six months earlier, at the beginning of 1991.

Weber had several thousand dollars in trading goods, by my estimate. Cigarette lighters, Swiss army knives, textiles, camcorders, the whole store; vast amounts of personal belongings, bottles of Johnny Walker, cigars, suitcases for an expedition. We showed our papers, then lugged the whole caboodle past the boys with guns into the courtyard of the terminal. I had barely a moment to get my bearings. Sheer confusion it was. Crush of relatives, officials, much weeping and kissing on the cheek, the yard crammed with cabs, children begging for coins, the swelter. A whole family to greet the engineer, with hugs, kisses on both cheeks, bouquets of flowers already wilted in the heat. I was introduced, our party divided into two cabs, the engineer's trading goods stuffed into the trunk (he was already passing out cigarette lighters), and then we were off.

It was the moment of pure exultation in a strange place, whether there was anything to be had or not. Soon enough there would be the practicalities, interviews, putting together bits and pieces of history. But for now, we're barrelling down a country road, honking at peasants on horsecarts or bicycles, sheep on the road, shirtless men in a field, squinting through the sun at you—just an instant to glimpse their bodies.

The countryside was dotted with concrete mushroom caps, overgrown now—apparently defence outposts, gun emplacements, and the like. The Glorious Leader was ready to fight the Turks, imperialists, Titoists, Russian revisionists, Chinese renegades after Mao—everyone he'd broken with in the name of Marxism-Leninism, in the name of Comrade Stalin, of the truth. I had the unnerving sense—for the briefest moment—of peering into Hoxha's besieged mind.

At the fork halfway between Durres on the Adriatic and the capital inland, we took the turn for Tirana. And all the time, the engineer, sitting in the back between a pale girl, in a white blouse, and her father, lectured the lot of us. I missed most of it, I confess. Words lost in the wind while the driver ran peasants on bicycles off the road with his terrible honking. Of course, the pilgrim had a plan to set the country right, something about playing Beethoven on the radio and the sentence "They're really children, you know"—how often had I heard that one before?

Finally, we came upon the city. All the main roads of Tirana converged on Skanderbeg square. It was a huge open space. I marked the equestrian statue as we passed; that's where my rendezvous would take place. Around the edges of the big traffic circle in the square were various official buildings, "people's palaces," windows bashed in and boarded up after the recent rioting. I was informed right away that the towering statue of the Glorious Leader, set in the middle of the traffic circle, had been pulled down by the people three months ago.

We dropped off the girl and her father and some of the engineer's booty. Weber genially ordered them about, drank his beer, handed out gifts; he was a lean, nervous pilgrim, but no fool. Then back to the square, this time south, past yellow and red stucco buildings—government ministries, he said—and down the martyrs boulevard a block or so to the Dajti. A four-storey job done by the Italians before World War II, big Mediterranean pines all around shading it, and facing a spacious public park. Crowds of fixers, drivers, cadging children, and arriving pilgrims in the driveway. Naturally, no available rooms. But the engineer was jovial, extra bed in his suite, no problem for the night, fix you up in the morning, he'd enjoy a bit of company—more like an audience for his unpacking. I barely had time to splash a few drops of water on the dusty wraith I'd become before the engineer was off for business in Durres, I think it was. An hour later, at the onset of dusk, I made my way to the square. I sat beneath the fearsome Skanderbeg perched on his mount. Presently, two men arrived, as ordained. The younger one, Pavli Qesku, struck me as rather elegant—mid-forties, lean, prematurely grey hair, tinted glasses. The older man, with one good ear, had to position himself on the left to catch the conversation. That was Zef Simoni.

I'd brought books for them—I suppose I was a pilgrim in my way too—but they suggested we take a stroll down the martyrs boulevard. They pointed out where the statues of Lenin and Stalin had flanked the thoroughfare; now only pediments remained. Everything had come down in the last six months, more than a year after the wave that swept the rest of central Europe, more than five years after Hoxha's death. The party attempted to make the transition, assuming that everything would continue forever—simply parade the image of the old Glorious Leader and gradually add that of the new one, a man named Ramiz Alia. But now everything was breaking up. Statues toppled, street names altered.

I'd noticed on a map that the continuation of the boulevard north of Skanderbeg Square had been named for Stalin. I wondered if it still was.

"Oh, we never called it that, anyway," Zef said, dismissing the issue in an understated, slightly ironic way I would quickly get used to.

"But this is still the Boulevard of National Martyrs?" I inquired, just to check.

"Well, after all, this is true," Pavli said. "We are still a nation, and indeed there have been martyrs."

"So there is no need to change it," Zef added. They had been in each other's company for so many years that they had acquired the habit of completing each other's sentences, as old couples do.

I was impatient to get to the heart of it, to the only question I really had for them, namely, how had they survived? As we passed the Hotel Dajti on the left, and as twilight came down on the big park facing it, they represented themselves as timid, unheroic, cautious men, never members of the party even though they had worked in the state publishing house translating the Glorious Leader's works and speeches all those years, Zef into German, Pavli into English. Another translator, Jussef Vrioni, had put Hoxha into French. I'd seen Vrioni's name—about a month before in an article in an American magazine, where he'd been cited as the French translator of the great Albanian novelist Ismail Kadare, who was now living in Paris. I'd even glanced at *The General of the Dead Army,* one of Kadare's novels.

But the immediate answer to my question was relatively simple. They had translated literature—Dickens, Conrad, Lawrence, Orwell even. I knew that already from the newspaper piece. But they also compiled dictionaries. It was an obvious thing for translators to do, now that they mentioned it, but it hadn't occurred to me. "So," I said, "in a sense, words saved you."

We crossed a trickle of water just beyond the hotel, the Lana River. It flowed in a ditch below us, beneath the boulevard over-pass—grass slopes, a bit of paving-stone embankment; to the right, from the west, the last of the light hit it.

"Working with words saved us from the situation in which we lived, sort of," Pavli replied. Then he added, almost more to himself, "Yes, to a certain extent, it is true."

"A justification," Zef explained. "In our work as translators, we used words to express other people's thoughts—and we were not in agreement with those thoughts. So we wanted to use the same words to express, not our thoughts, but something neutral at least." It was put with perfect modesty. My curiosity was at once satisfied. Strange how quickly it went. Now we were simply evening strollers, casually conversing.

The boulevard, a broad four-lane thoroughfare, abruptly ended at the university, which was set at the base of a hill. The students had demonstrated here the previous December and then again in February. That, apparently, was what had started the revolt. We took the footpath that wound around and up the wooded rise. St. Procopius hill, Zef informed me.

Somehow we got onto the subject of China. I don't remember what led to it. Perhaps something about Zef's bad ear. He had been to China during Hoxha's alliance with Mao, and the Chinese had restored some of his hearing. Even now, he had only one good ear, supplemented by a bit of lip-reading. Anyway, it got me thinking about my time in China, in 1977, just after Mao's death, around the time of the breakup of Albania's "firm and eternal friendship," as the formula went, with Beijing. I found myself recounting an odd little conversation I'd had with my minder. We had been talking about sexual practices, and I'd asked, a bit mischievously, if there was homo-sexuality in China. My guide had affected to be shocked. No, none at all, he had firmly assured me. None whatsoever. So I had asked him if the Chinese masturbated. Oh no, he had said, and then, curiosity getting the better of him, he had asked me, And you, in the West, do you masturbate? Why, yes, I had replied, all the time.

Zef and Pavli burst into laughter, got it right away. "So, there was even a correct line on sex," Pavli chuckled.

I was about to rattle on when Zef interrupted to point out some buildings to our right. "The barracks of the National Guard," he said, making it clear by his tone that the institution wasn't exactly loved. The path switched back up St. Procopius, but an unpaved road forked off toward the barracks. It was dark now, and all we could see were some lighted windows and boys in uniforms inside.

At the top of the hill, we came out of the pines onto an outdoor café, which was our destination. It was well attended, mostly by couples and some guardsmen in pairs. A table was found for us, and the waiter brought us drinks.

"Raki," Pavli said, naming the alcohol. "Perhaps you won't like it."

It was acrid stuff, perfectly drinkable, of course. And there was bread, soup, and some roasted chicken. My hosts half-apologized for the poor quality of everything, but it was fine. A perfectly delightful café on a summer evening, and a bit cooler up there on the hill. After the food, more raki, and then we smoked cigarettes.

One of the young guardsmen broke away from his friend and came over to our table to ask for a light. I held the flame to his hand-rolled smoke.

"You've just lit the cigarette of a National Guard," Zef said.

"Of a boy," I insisted.

"Who might masturbate in the barracks," Zef quickly added, accepting my distinction. We all laughed at that.

Oddly enough, we didn't talk about politics at all that evening. Zef mentioned that he had learned to read Greek and had read Plato's *Phaedo* in the original. It was a work I was familiar with; I often taught it at school. Indeed, I had opinions about the death of Socrates.

I confess that I did most of the talking. As I said, I had views. The part about Socrates' last day in jail, his weeping friends, the hemlock he drank—all that was true in my opinion. But the part about the immortality of the soul, I insisted to Zef and Pavli, that was added by Plato himself. I don't think Socrates believed any of that. He simply thought you died and consciousness ceased or—well, it doesn't matter about my views. But it was all so wonderfully odd. I'd come all this way, to the moon, to the last outpost, to inquire about the fall of communism and, instead, ended up talking about Plato, just as civilized people anywhere might have done. Of course, I had to acknowledge that the places where civilized people could talk of such things were much diminished in our time, even in my part of the world.

It had grown late, the café had emptied, the guardsmen were back in their barracks. Zef and Pavli walked me down the hill, back into the heat of the town, now in darkness. Behind the hotel was a sleek building that bore the only electric sign I'd seen. It alternately flashed the temperature and the time, lighting up the night. The Institute of Strategic Studies, Pavli informed me. They went into the Dajti with me for a minute so that I could give them the box of books I'd brought, and arrangements were made to collect me in the morning.

The engineer soon returned from Durres. He produced a bottle of Johnny Walker, and we sat on the balcony outside the room, over-looking the martyrs boulevard—little traffic at that hour, only the gear-grinding of the occasional truck, a late-night bus.

In the morning, the engineer and I took breakfast together. The other pilgrims were there, impatient with the service, anxious to get on with business, to make the world go. Weber was soon off, the brooding Swiss of last night—he, too, read some philosophy—giving way to the nervous energy of the deal-making pilgrim.

Across the corridor from the breakfast room was the bar, where the engineer left me with one of the fixers he knew, in case I needed anything. I escaped onto the cement front veranda of the Dajti. The flashing digital sign reported nearly thirty degrees before nine o'clock, but a nice breeze came in from the park across the boulevard. Below me, in the driveway, the taxi operators were taking the pilgrims off on their business. There were all sorts of kids hanging around. Small ones, teenage boys.

One boy in particular attracted me. He was in his mid- to late teens, blue eyed, with pale sandy hair and a quick smile. He was with a couple of his friends, and at first all I noticed was the boys' friendliness between themselves, the way they leaned against each other, casually draping an arm over the other's shoulders. Then the blue-eyed boy and I exchanged glances, and there was a brief, word-less encounter, the sort of meeting I might have forgotten if nothing else had happened. Our eyes met again, and he offered a smile. It was nothing, really. But as he passed behind me on the veranda, he touched me. He ran a feathery hand across my shoulders, just as he did with the other boys. Then, as quickly as he'd appeared, he was gone.

Just then, Zef and Pavli turned up to show me around. I tried to make apologies for my chattering on about the *Phaedo*.

"No doubt, you like the part about the soul," I said to Zef. He had told me he was a Catholic. But apparently there was no harm done.

"It was very good conversation," Zef assured me.

"Yes, nice to talk," Pavli seconded.

We crossed the square—already we could feel the morning heat—and were soon in a maze of side streets and then back lanes. There were some market stalls set up on the walks. Little potatoes, green onions, dark fresh figs, all in small quantities. The women spent hours gathering the day's provisions.

"Looking for things that don't exist," Pavli said.

"Or hunting for things," Zef amended, "this is called shopping."

We came to a five-storey building made of bricks oddly spaced, a hand-done job it seemed. "Zef's flat is on the top. He built it himself," Pavli told me. Looking up, I could see from the fresher colour of the brick that the top floor had been added recently. I could imagine the difficulties of a man in his fifties hauling the bricks up those stairs, mixing the cement, mortaring them in himself.

By the time we climbed to the top, my shirt was soaked through. Zef's wife met us, and while we settled in she brought us bottled water, raki, some Turkish Delight, and then coffee. I reminded myself that I was in one of those southern European cultures where they give you everything they have, however little it may be.

There were shelves of books along the back wall. With a slight ceremonial gesture, Zef presented me with a copy of the German-Albanian dictionary that he had compiled and that had been published the year before. He quoted Milton on justifying God's ways to humans. "I had to justify myself to myself," he said, by way of explanation. "To do something useful."

About noon, we went down and made the short walk to the publishing house where they worked. First there had to be a formal meeting with the director in his suite of offices. Pavli translated. I had been through this sort of thing before. Formalities to be observed, cups of bitter coffee served. I intimated that I had some access to paper supplies, something the director—who, of course, was a party member—could note in his report, if necessary. Even though it was all breaking up, the party in the midst of a chameleon-like effort to appear in more acceptable colours, much of the infrastructure was still in place. And all the old habits. Although the director was the only party member I would meet, I was little inclined to question him about his view of the recent political changes. I knew I'd only get the current official line, and in any case the shade of "the last communist," Hoxha himself, still lurked everywhere. On the stairway, going up to their office, Zef said, "Very good," appraising my performance, and the three of us laughed about it.

Then we were in the "tiny, Spartan office" that I'd read about in the newspaper piece. Well, a professional quibble here, a detail. It was Spartan in the sense of equipment, absence of books, of course. But not tiny. Larger than the cubbyholes most journalists and instructors had in the newsrooms and college offices I was familiar with back home. It was spacious enough for facing desks, walls a bright, pastel green, and there was a big window with a breeze coming in and a view from the second floor looking west to the hills, in the direction of Durres on the coast.

We talked about making dictionaries. There was a large, old one on a revolving stand on Pavli's desk. I'd never thought about them before, not in this way.

"Where do you start?" I wanted to know.

"You begin from anything you like," Pavli said. "Just collecting words, finding phrases, putting them on cards, keeping files. But that is only preparatory work. The real work begins when you touch a typewriter and put a white sheet in and write A. What shall we write about A?" he asked.

I'd wanted to know how they had survived all those years, and here was a clue under my nose. You know how you're so familiar with an object that you barely notice it? You're looking for a big answer—something about the spirit or history—but the answer is right in front of you in a simple, material thing. In the German-Albanian dictionary Zef had given me, in the old dictionaries in their Spartan, but not tiny, office. It's a matter of seeing it, of resisting your own familiarity.

Zef had said, "So we wanted to use the same words to express, not our thoughts, but something neutral at least." Harmless things.

Words. And in the pages of his dictionary were thousands of words—tree, sky, beach, sea—each one an expression of thought uncontaminated by the regime.

"Something neutral," Pavli repeated, adding, "despite the fact that, sometimes, other people, outside us, put in words that expressed the reality that existed at that time. Like they did with Zef's dictionary. They put in expressions like 'the dictatorship of the proletariat,' and 'scientific socialism,' and so on."

"Not very 'scientific,'" Zef commented wryly.

"But also the definitions," Pavli said. "Here, look." He came to the word liberal. "'One who makes concessions towards shortcomings and mistakes,'" Pavli read, "'who is not exacting towards others; who allows irregularities which harm the work of society.' This dictionary is full of such stupidities."

Over the years, they slowly compiled words at night, whereas at work they duly translated documents, position papers, the works of Comrade Hoxha. On the far wall facing the open window that looked out toward Durres was a bookcase containing the books of the Glorious Leader. Zef went to it, pulling out a couple of paperback volumes to give me. He made a show of banging them against the side of the case to shake the dust from these translated, but never-read, memoirs. On the cover of one called *With Stalin* was a photograph of the two men, shot from below, standing on a rampart. Later, in the hotel, I skimmed its hagiographic, childishly humble accounts of Hoxha's reception in Moscow by "Comrade Stalin."

Pavli walked me back through the midafternoon heat to the Dajti. We arranged to meet again in the evening. The desk clerk had a room for me. Weber, the engineer, was still out when I moved my things to the new room. It was small but sufficient—a bed, a writing table, lace curtains, a shower, a little balcony, and a roll-down metal shade to keep out the heat. The room faced east, looking directly onto the blinking electric sign with the time and temperature. By the time I came up from the bar, bringing back a litre of mineral water, I was soaked from my exertions. I showered, made my notes, replenished myself with liquids, read a page or two of Conrad, and then napped.

Pavli came to get me in the early evening and took me to his apartment, where Zef was already waiting for us. Pavli's wife brought us raki and then went into the kitchen while we watched television.

There was an interview with a visiting Albanian political leader from Kosovo—the southernmost, so-called autonomous, province of Yugoslavia but actually under the thumb of the Serbians. Two million Albanians lived there, and now, with the disturbances in Yugoslavia, the old dream of Greater Albania was in the air again. I happened to learn a little about it only subsequently when I read a translation of a novella by Kadare, set in Pristina (the Kosovan capital), about a failed uprising a decade or more ago. Zef and Pavli watched the interview intently; such discussion was still something of a novelty on Albanian television.

Then Pavli's wife brought in food, and they switched channels to an Italian game show. It was announced as a "light supper," but it was a full plate, carefully laid out. Mussels, olives, tomatoes, onions, hard-boiled eggs, and then a fruit compote for dessert. All the time we were watching the politician from Kosovo, Pavli's wife was working in the kitchen. The women evidently did all the domestic work; the arrangements were quite traditional, as we say (giving much more dignity to the word traditional than it deserves). I thought of a feminist friend of mine back home, and I knew exactly what she would make of it.

After Mrs. Qesku cleared the table, I turned on the tape recorder for our formal interview. Now I was at work, as I had been a hundred times before, in many places. And later, in some faraway place, I might hear those voices again, or they would be transcribed into a sheaf of notes, which would find a place in a manila folder or in the depths of the maroon-coloured gym bag I lugged around with me, a familiar object I sometimes described in jest as "my office."

Zef Simoni was born in 1933 in the northern town of Shkoder to a well-to-do Catholic family. As in neighbouring Yugoslavia and Greece, the end of World War II in Albania inaugurated civil war. Whereas Greece was allotted to the Allies, in both Yugoslavia and Albania the partisan triumph was not impeded.

"Immediately when the partisans came into Shkoder," Zef recalled, "they started shooting people in batches. Behind the town graveyard. And after having a batch of people shot, they put up a proclamation with the names and the crimes they were supposed to have committed." Zef was eleven.

"So they came in 1944?" I calculated.

"Yes. And they were my first exercises in literacy."

I was momentarily puzzled.

"To read the names," Pavli supplied.

"It was just reading matter for me," Zef said.

I had a glimpse, no more, of a boy peering up at a freshly pasted sheet on a brick wall, absorbing the litany of the newly dead with a chilling innocence that separated the act of reading from the acts to which the proclamation referred. Outside, in the night, we could hear the shouts of children at play.

Pavli's wife offered us brandy. "It is a very fine brandy made at home," Pavli recommended. "Wild cherry." We each accepted a small glass.

"They were people of a conservative mind," Zef said, recalling his family. "Right-wing, I would say now. My father was first an import-export merchant; then he had a printing shop, then a magazine, and he made some translations. He was the first Esperantist in Albania."

"He has translated the *Pinocchio,*" Pavli added.

"Into Esperanto?" I wondered, slightly amused at the mention of the strange dream of creating a mutually understandable artificial language. But no, he had put the famed children's tale into Albanian.

"He has translated the biography of Skanderbeg into Esperanto," Zef said.

"So, you're a second-generation translator," I observed.

"Second-generation," Zef nodded, laughing.

Once again, it was a matter of words. Words for civilization, words in self-defence. But wasn't the party's concern also the use of language?

"Propaganda is made of words, of course," Pavli agreed.

"But everything is distorted," Zef pointed out. "You are told you have freedom, which others, you are told, have not. And you have not freedom. You are told you have free speech—it is written in the constitution—and you land in jail for saying the wrong things. You are told you are free to move about, and you must have documents to move from one city to another. Everything is told it exists, and it doesn't exist, or exists its counterpart." Zef spoke rapidly, forgoing the niceties of English grammar in his excitement.

"My own family," Pavli said, "was a little more exposed to such propaganda. My father was a partisan, then a communist, and fought in the brigades of the national liberation army. After the war, he began to realize that there was something amiss. But he couldn't grasp what it was. He was a tailor. In a small town in central Albania. Slowly but surely he began to realize that the cause of the situation was the party itself, and he began to dislike it, until, in 1949, after five years in the party, he refused to be a member." Pavli was five then. "But in my family there are still some people who believe that the party is good, just that something went wrong somewhere. There are some people who are still Utopians, who have the hope that socialism is something good for humankind."

I was curious to know how they had become friends.

"We worked together," Pavli said.

"They just put us in the same room," Zef added, "and they just said work together."

The two of them laughed at the simple absurdity of it.

"And this has gone on for over twenty years," I said, laughing also.

"Yes, twenty-two years," Pavli confirmed, "except for a period of three years when I was in Peshpatia, a small town in the mountains."

They had escaped the terror of jailings and executions, but not entirely. They had spent the years together carefully. "Very careful," Pavli reiterated. "What we said in the streets, what we said in the café."

"We expressed our more delicate thoughts in English, just in case," said Zef. "We were very careful about where we talked, how we talked."

"Or we had code names for things."

The way their voices alternated reminded me of the strophe and antistrophe of a Greek chorus. "Code names?" I repeated.

"For the government, the party, the leaders, our party secretary."

Like a children's game, I suggested.

"It was very childish," Zef said, "and very horrible."

"But it was not Newspeak," Pavli added, glancingly referring to Orwell's account of totalitarian rhetoric.

Yet their caution did not protect them completely. Pavli was shipped off for three years in 1975 to a sort of internal exile.

"The reason they gave Pavli for sending him to Peshpatia—" Zef began, "well, the true reason was that he didn't accept to become a member of the party—the specious reason they gave him was that you keep too much Zef's company. They kept me in Tirana."

"But Zef was frightened then."

"In their sick mind, I was infected, hopelessly. There was some hope for saving Pavli."

So Pavli was shipped off to work as a schoolteacher in a mountain village. "Did you think that you would ever return?" I asked.

"It was a closed chapter," Pavli replied. "I just took my bag, my typewriter, and my books."

"Were you married?" I asked.

"Yes, but happily we had no children then. My wife could go on working here. Fortunately, the government needed her work because she was chief engineer of the porcelain factory. She kept working in Tirana, and I went to Peshpatia."

"Chinese style," Zef said.

Pavli's wife was sitting in an armchair, away from the table the three of us were gathered around. For all her fulfilment of the traditional duties, she was an educated woman, skilled, and able to follow our conversation in English, occasionally supplying a correction to their account. I saw her then as if for the first time. I had only a moment to imagine their three years of separation, caused by an ideological whim, which they treated, in retrospect, as a minor inconvenience.

Pavli went on, speaking of Peshpatia. "The headmaster of the school was a very nice chap, very understanding. He gave me a whole room to myself, a bare room of course, but it was a room. There was a round stove which the schoolboys were careful to supply with firewood. It is fifteen or twenty degrees below zero in winter there. I was all by myself. The dictionaries were there, and whenever these people, security people, came from time to time, unannounced, to search my room, they saw that they were harmless books. I never gave them cause to suspect."

"And in the place of Pavli," Zef said, picking up the other end of the story, "into the office stepped a chap who had been Pavli's schoolmate. He had some connections with the minister of internal affairs, and I am sure he informed on me, but he informed only on the good side." Zef laughed at the small irony of informing "on the good side," then added, "I was very careful, of course."

"My former schoolmate didn't do anything while he was there," Pavli noted. "He was supposed to be a translator, but he couldn't do the job. When Zef was away, he just sat there doing nothing." The pride in their ability to do good work, regardless of its futility, gave an edge to the tone of contempt with which Pavli referred to the plant from the Ministry of Internal Affairs.

Sitting there, comforted by cherry brandy, I had to remind myself that I was listening to an account of political terror. Not executions, torture, jailings—though there were those forms of terror, of course—but quiet terror, everyday terror.

"When we translated that book which I gave you, *With Stalin,*" Zef began again, "we worked night and day."

"Three months of hard work in the midst of summer," Pavli said.

"Then they gave us four or five days to recover," Zef continued. "On one of these days, the chief of the enterprise came to me and said, 'You are invited to the Tirana branch of the Ministry of Internal Affairs. I don't know what they want from you, but you must go.' I went there. Certainly, I was very afraid. But I tried to keep control of myself. I told myself maybe they had some translations for me to do. I was ushered into a room, and there were two armchairs, and they smelled of sweat, a heavy stink of sweat. Because the people who went there sweated profusely under interrogation."

They asked Zef about various people he knew. Zef offered bland replies. The fencing went on for some time. Then the interrogators asked about a certain person. "I said, 'Yes, I know him.' I couldn't say I didn't. 'And what are his opinions?' they asked. I said, 'The generally current opinions.' 'And what are his literary tastes?' I mentioned the most conventional tastes I knew of. Then they told me he had been slandering the party, and 'You must know.' 'I know nothing; I have not seen him for six months.' After that, they gave me a cigarette. They did not make direct threats to me. They told me, 'Look, we are going to arrest this man. If you warn him, first, it would be useless, and, second, you will be arrested too.' So I went home. On my way home, I wanted to have a double portion of cognac just to steady my spirits." He laughed in recollection of his fear. "Then I thought that I might be followed. If they saw me drinking, they might think I had something to fear. So, instead, I went straight home and lay in my bed for about half an hour. Only then did I come out and go to the café, where I had my double portion of cognac. In about six months' time, Pavli, who knew nothing about these things—"

"Zef didn't whisper a word," Pavli interjected.

"Had I told Pavli, he would think, first, that I was a hero, second, that I must have blurted out something. So I said nothing. And six months later, it was Pavli who mentioned to me that so-and-so had been arrested. And still I said nothing."

"You didn't tell Pavli about the interrogation?" I asked Zef.

"I learned of it only last year," Pavli said.

"When did this incident happen?" I asked.

"In 1980," Zef said.

"You only told him ten years later?" I said in astonishment.

"Ten years," Zef said, and we all broke out laughing, but perhaps for different reasons. They laughed simply at the mixture of absurdity and horror, and because now it was possible to laugh at it, and because it was a small thing compared with what others had endured. And I laughed nervously, almost embarrassed to be made a party to this terrible intimacy.

"After six months, Pavli told me, 'You know this chap so-and-so has been arrested,'" Zef repeated.

I turned off the recorder and stuffed the tapes into my gym bag.

It was a story no different from those we had heard countless times in recent years. But that was the point of it. There was nothing "Albanian" about the anecdote. The insidious method was ubiquitous: anyone, even the most intimate of one's friends, might inform. A remark you'd made, in the sanctity of your home, thoughtlessly parroted by your child at school might bring the authorities to your door. No letters unread by the censors, no movement without approved documents, and, of course, no passports. Your fate decided in rooms, committees, none of which you had access to, but in whose anterooms you waited. And though the digital clock recorded the minutes, the Glorious Leader had made time stand still.

Yet, from the outside, to a visitor, the place must appear but a small, dusty, inconsequential city of barely a quarter-million inhabitants baking in the sun—poor but going about their business. There was little visible sign of the oppression or the methods that made it possible. It was as if I had travelled the length of a river—like that in Conrad's story—to reach, as Marlow does, the kingdom of a madman.

The parallels were eerie. Like Kurtz, Hoxha had not always been mad. He had begun with the intention of improving the lot of humankind, the great dream of our time. And those of us on the left had even grudgingly admired him as the ruler of a tiny, mostly agricultural, country who had rather heroically broken first with the

Soviets, for deviating from Stalinism, and then with the Chinese, for abandoning Maoism. But in his obsessive effort to perfect human beings, to create, like a god, "the new man, the new woman," he had gradually turned the inhabitants into slaves.

"You translated Conrad," I said to Zef.

"And perhaps you think you are a bit like Marlow?" Zef joked, intuiting my pretension.

But there was no Kurtz at the heart of this darkness, no self-critical last cry of horror to ponder. All that remained was the rubble of Hoxha's rule. And the inhabitants, of course. We had thought of them almost as savages, just as men of the imperium had thought of distant peoples of a different colour a century ago. Yet I had discovered, as had Conrad, that they were the same as us.

I didn't think all that at the moment—only later, when the voices recorded in my little machine had become words on pages. But there was something more, something that did occur to me as we spoke, though I didn't mention it to Zef and Pavli. I had yet to free myself from the human dream that had given way to the dictator's inhuman methods. Does Marlow murmur, quoting a forgotten poet, "Spirit of the night, teach us to bear despair"?

It had gotten well on into the evening. There was more to ask, of course, but Zef and Pavli had arranged for me to do interviews with some other people beginning early the next morning, a Saturday, and the following day we would hire a driver and go to Durres, so there would be time to talk then. However, I couldn't resist asking about the present now that the nightmare was over or almost over.

"The change can be seen if you follow a couple of people walking in the streets," Pavli said. "They have stopped turning their heads back to see if we're following them. We no longer turn our heads back."

Zef walked me back to the Dajti through the silent streets of Tirana. From the balcony of my room, I faced the electric sign flashing in the night. It was almost midnight. Just under thirty degrees. The sign blinked on and off, flooding my room with pale light and then plunging it into darkness. In bed, I turned away from the wall where light flared every few seconds.

Six hours later, I woke up. Beyond the Institute for Strategic Studies, beyond where the town ended, were pale brown mountains, with Mount Dajti to the east. A haze lay between it and the edge of the city. I stood on the balcony drinking coffee. Directly below me, three floors down, was the raggedy, semiabandoned garden of the hotel. Palm trees, an empty fountain, untended bushes. A skinny yellow cat prowled through the brush.

The opposition Democratic Party was headquartered in a sort of villa, set back from a busy street, with a wide gate at the front to admit vehicles. Inside, even at 8 a.m., clusters of men were gathered in the driveway-courtyard, petitioners or local functionaries perhaps. An outside staircase led up to a warren of offices. Zef, Pavli, and I were ushered into a large room with a long rectangular table. At the head of it, talking on a telephone, was a stocky young man in his late twenties, with unkempt curly black hair. There was a window behind him, covered with shutters through which slivers of sunshine filtered, playing upon the gauze curtains that hung before it.

When he put the phone down, we were introduced. His name was Azem Haidari, a graduate student at the university who had come from a small mountain village, Treppoja, in the north, married, with two children.

"If you want," Haidari said, via Zef's translation, "I will tell you about the democratic movement in Albania, the Democratic Party, the political life, and the Parliament." As a result of the elections in the spring, he now sat as a member of that body. We had about an hour's interview, variously interrupted by the urgency of the telephone and people poking their heads through the double doors with brief messages for the young politician. It was a standard interview; he spoke as a man with responsibilities. But I saw that both Zef and Pavli rather admired him. They liked his vigour and, apparently, the colourful mountain villager's way of speaking—Haidari didn't mince words. When he was on the phone, I got a hint of a more animated indigenous style that no doubt had popular appeal. But with me he was diplomatic, without irony.

As much as anyone, here was the person who had loosened the grip of Hoxha's successors. "The dictatorship was so savage there was no possibility of even thinking of establishing another form of government, because the mere thought of it put your life in jeopardy," Haidari said. But the explosions in Eastern Europe had had their echoes even in Albania. "Mr. Alia, recalling the fate of Ceausescu," he went on, "saw that he had to do something for democratization."

"So Alia was watching television," I remarked, recalling the footage of the execution of the former Romanian dictator and his wife that we saw the Christmas after the opening of the Berlin Wall.

"But his speeches, his manoeuvres, were only intended for export," Haidari said dismissively. "They were intended to give the impression that something was being done, whereas nothing was being done." It was that impasse that led Haidari to take political action, organizing the students. The way he put it was very innocent—it was the language of the nineteenth century's "springtime of nations"—yet it had the self-deprecating awareness of a man standing before a mirror, giving an account that would later be read as history. "When I was a student, I always recalled President Kennedy's words, 'Ask not what your country can do for you, ask what you can do for your country.' So I decided to give my all to Albania, even my life. At first, the possibility of emerging alive from the first demonstrations after forty years of communist rule was very slim indeed. Nevertheless, against all these odds, we succeeded in carrying out our peaceful demonstrations. The moment came to do something for Albania, and I am very happy this offer of sacrifice was accepted." That was all it took, if not to topple the regime, at least to shake its foundations.

Later, toward the end of the hour, the mountain man declared, "I love life, but I have the opinion that life should be loved only for as long as it lasts, and we should not think to prolong it more than its course. You can't escape your fate." It was not the first time I'd heard young men fearlessly proclaim such things, and I've seldom doubted them. Yet it was always eerie to hear someone say it. I couldn't imagine dying for my country.

Just at that moment, the phone rang. Haidari picked up the receiver and soon was speaking most animatedly. I saw alarm in Zef's and Pavli's eyes.

"There's been a shootout," Pavli said, following the progress of the conversation. "One of his cousins, a young cousin of his, has been shot."

"Where?" I asked.

"In Treppoja."

"How did it happen?"

"The situation is stable," Pavli said, ignoring my question.

"But who was shooting?" I wondered.

Haidari's voice subsided.

"He made a speech in parliament about Kosovo," Pavli explained.

I put the story together in bits and pieces—the arrival of the visiting politician from Pristina we'd seen on television had heated the political atmosphere—then there was Haidari's speech on the suppression of the Kosovan Albanians by the Serbs—no mincing of words, apparently—and somehow the news of the speech—was it heard as a call to arms?—was connected to the flare-up in his home village, not far from the border.

On the outside staircase going down, Zef said, "In six months, he could be dead." Meaning young Haidari, courting fate as he was. Then we were back in the streets, in the unforgiving heat. Mid-thirty degrees before noon. As we walked, Pavli recalled that the former student leader had accurately predicted that the newly elected government would be forced to form a coalition with the opposition "by the time the cherries were ripe."

"And when do they ripen?" I asked.

"In May and June," Pavli said. "And it happened. Now he says the present government will fall by the time the watermelons are ripe at the end of the summer. By the time the watermelons ripen." Pavli seemed taken with Haidari's agricultural turn of phrase.

Our next interview was with a writer named Trebeshina. It was held at the apartment of a young friend of his, also a writer. Trebeshina was in his mid-sixties, but I could see he had been badly used. He spoke in a hoarse whisper through yellowed and broken teeth. His was a tale of jailings and neglect. He had been imprisoned twice by the fascists, against whom he had fought in World War II, and three times by the communists. The first time, in the 1950s, was a literary jailing. "I was always against the socialist realism," he said. "I was of the opinion if there is realism, there is no need for socialist or fascist [realism] or so on." He wrote an open letter to Hoxha and got three years for it.

I didn't quite catch the reason for the next incarceration, but the third one, in 1980, came about when he publicly declared his refusal to vote. For that, he got a long stretch. He'd only been released in 1988. And though he'd written much after the open letter, none of it had been published. He had been ignored, neglected, always at odds with the Writers' League. He didn't share the conventional estimate of the great Kadare. "A collaborator," Trebeshina rasped. When I asked him about hearing of Hoxha's death while he was in prison, he replied, "He's not dead." At the end of his fragmented recital, Trebeshina said, "I always wanted to ring the bell for the others, but I did not. During all my life, I was a Don Quixote."

Pavli walked me back to the hotel. We went along the Lana River. A peasant sat on the grassy embankment, tethered to a couple of grazing sheep. The electric sign now registered thirty-six degrees. Pavli left me in the driveway of the Dajti. He and Zef had arranged a meeting with Kadare's translator, Vrioni, for the evening.

I had worn my lightest short-sleeved shirt, but I was soaked through and slightly dazed, grateful to get to the shade of my little room, clutching the bottles of water I'd acquired in the bar on the way up. Before I showered and napped, I made my notes, the paper practically melting under my hand. It was as if all substance had dissolved into a primordial ooze—the water I drank greedily, the perspiration pouring out of me, smearing the ink, dampening the pages.

The interviews with Haidari and Trebeshina had been ordinary enough, tales of courage and suffering in a heretofore almost unknown place that are then inadequately condensed into the columns of the dailies. But this time I had been affected. I could feel the ends of my nerves. Perhaps I, too, like Trebeshina, was a Don Quixote. It seemed to me that your entire life as a writer leads to the one street you are walking down, to the miserable little pile of dark figs you are looking at, to the rasping, bitter voice you are listening to. Everything has led to this moment. Yet you do not know the story, except as it unfolds before you. You do not know the story, I repeated to myself.

I went down to the veranda of the hotel early. The boy was there, the one I had seen before. Perhaps I went down early because I'd gathered from Zef's tone that the meeting with Jussef Vrioni that Zef and Pavli had arranged for that evening was a rare prize, and I didn't want to be late. Or perhaps because I hoped to see that boy again. I had thought about him, several times in fact. He had made an impression.

We greeted each other like old friends. We shook hands, and he touched me on the shoulder. Blue eyes, nut-brown tanned skin, radiant smile. His name was Ilir. Ilir as in ancient Illyria. It was impossible not to think of the head of the boy in the postcard that the consul in Bonn had sent me, not to see something in it more than a mere well-wishing.

Ilir was with a friend, his own age, to whom he introduced me. They both had a little English, though I had some difficulty following the anecdote they were trying to tell me. His friend was a music student, as was Ilir, or perhaps a dancer; I couldn't quite get it.

They knew all about current music. "Michael Jackson," Ilir said, naming the pop star, "he is a great man. And M. C. Hammer, very beautiful."

I was rather amazed by their knowledge, though also appalled that, of all things, this was what had penetrated the ideological defences of their shrouded land. "But how do you know all this?" I asked Ilir.

They had seen it on television from Belgrade, which apparently transmitted the European version of the American music channel MTV. So, score one for the Global Village. I was too charmed by Ilir to be contemptuous of the pap the world wanted to feed him. Indeed, it seemed to me remarkable that in this remoteness he was nonetheless a thorough contemporary of lads his age anywhere in the world. If I had to choose between Hoxha and MTV, well, why not the latter?

There was a complicated story about a man named Hussein— "not Saddam Hussein of Iraq," Ilir laughed, referring to the Gulf War at the beginning of the year. This Hussein had promised them some papers, but I couldn't make it out. For what purpose? "Rap," Ilir said, "for the rap." There was something about videotapes, but I got it mixed up.

Then Zef and Pavli turned up for the evening at Vrioni's. I shook hands with Ilir's friend, but the farewell with Ilir was more elaborate, kisses on both cheeks, hand-holding, assurances that we must get together again. I was quite dazzled, infatuated of course. I don't think it was entirely sexual . . . well, who knows? Or, if I did know the extent of my desire, I preferred to keep my understanding of it inarticulate even to myself. It was just that it was so astonishing to come upon someone like him in this place.

Walking to Vrioni's, I must have babbled, telling Zef and Pavli about the boy. They seemed amused I was so taken, the way you are when a visitor comes to your hometown and enthuses about something there that you'd never thought of but that nonetheless leaves you pleased for both your visitor and yourself.

On the way, they reminded me that Vrioni had also worked for a time in the publishing house as a translator. In fact, at the time of Pavli's exile, Vrioni's name had also appeared on the list of those to be sent off to get "closer to the people."

"He was sent too?" I asked.

"He was meant to be sent," Pavli said, "but on special instructions from His Highness—"

"Who knew some French," Zef interjected.

"Who read his own books in French," Pavli continued, "and liked the way they had been rendered in French—"

"Because Vrioni translated his own works," Zef put in.

"There was no one who could translate his works as well as Vrioni did," Pavli added.

"So he was not going to saw off the branch he was sitting on," Zef concluded.

Vrioni lived in a detached two-storey house with a small front garden. His wife greeted us at the door. We were led into the living room, where Vrioni was waiting for us. He was a tall, elegant man. I was told later that he was seventy-eight years old, but I never would have guessed it from his looks or his manner. He was the son of a wealthy landowner and had been raised and educated in France before the war. When he returned to Albania after the partisan triumph, Hoxha had him jailed for thirteen years. Then he became a translator of books by Hoxha as well as those by Kadare.

His wife brought in a bottle of Johnny Walker, with glasses on a tray, and, after placing them on the low glass-topped table before us, retired upstairs, explaining that she wasn't feeling well. Our conversation was in French. Vrioni could speak English, but he made it clear that to discuss certain concepts only French was adequate. Zef and Pavli filled in for my deficiencies.

We hit it off right away. I mentioned that I liked jazz and uttered the name of the legendary Belgian jazz guitarist Django Reinhardt. Immediately, Vrioni lit up. He rummaged about beneath the sound equipment at the side of the room until he produced a cassette. The room filled with the instantly recognizable, unique arpeggios of the three-fingered jazz guitarist, joined by a violinist. It was Reinhardt's version of the "Marseillaise," accompanied by Stefane Grappelli, recorded just after the Allied victory in 1945, Vrioni told us. For a few minutes, we simply listened with pleasure and sipped our whisky.

Vrioni was most dubious about Albanian prospects. He began to tick off on his aristocratic fingers the reasons for his doubts in that precise manner of French intellectuals. First, the level of Albanian

culture was abysmally backward. I interjected that I had met a sixteen-
or seventeen-year-old boy in Tirana who was marvellously well versed
in contemporary music, having watched television from Yugoslavia.
My host was unimpressed. He continued his dissection of the country's
gloomy future.

I mentioned that I had seen his name in the American magazine
article about Kadare. It was clear that Vrioni had more than a propri-
etary interest in the Albanian writer. His translations into French had
made Kadare's reputation. Without the translations, which had so
pleased the French public, the great novelist might be unknown
today. There was a hint even that something more than translation was
involved. It was almost as if he regarded himself as Kadare's co-
author. And he had translated the Glorious Leader. Vrioni went to the
bookshelves on the far wall, and returned with a couple of volumes,
opening one to the title page. On it was Hoxha's inscription, in his
own hand, to his "Comrade" for his "tireless work" in rendering the
leader's writings into "perfect" French. Vrioni translated Hoxha's praise
of himself with considerable drollery, assuming our appreciation of
the implicit ironies.

I noticed that, on the low table before us, there was also a copy
of Milan Kundera's latest novel, which I had recently read. That led
to Vrioni's inquiring about a Mexican novelist he had only heard of
on his last trip to Paris. Did I know of Carlos Fuentes? I remarked to
him that this conversation might take place in any capital of Europe.
Yes, people were always surprised to encounter a cultivated Albanian,
Vrioni said. "Of course, you know Montesquieu's *Persian Letters?*" he
asked.

In that eighteenth-century work, the imaginary Persian, through
whom Montesquieu provides his portrait of the ills of contemporary
France, appears in a Paris salon and is asked, with near disbelief,
How is it possible for a Persian to be in Paris?

"I, too," Vrioni said, "have also been at a salon in Paris, and
upon identifying myself as an Albanian, I was asked, by a man who
knew his Montesquieu, But how is it possible for an Albanian to be
in Paris?"

For all his civility, even the charm of his vanity, there was something unsettling about Vrioni. I remembered the rasping voice of the
broken Trebeshina, the Don Quixote; at the name of Kadare, he had
spat the words "A collaborator." To be able to write, and to use his

fame as a platform from which to criticize the regime, however indirectly, had Kadare not also lent that renown to a justification of the regime? Had he not faced the moral dilemma of the person who sustains the culture, which he imagines as belonging to posterity, but only at the cost of semicollaboration with the totalitarian power, which he must persuade himself to believe is merely temporary? Was that not also true, albeit to a lesser degree, in the case of Vrioni? Here we were, in this comfortable home, with whisky on the table, the latest novels, and a modern sound system, and amid all these elements necessary to the maintenance of a civilization was the very hand of the Glorious Leader thanking his tireless comrade. I could have reached out and touched the signature of the dictator had I wished to do so.

Vrioni's ailing wife appeared at our departure. It was already night as Zef and Pavli walked me back toward the hotel. The martyrs boulevard was jammed with people on Saturday night, walking in family groups, sitting on the low wall along the park, milling about in conversation in the hot darkness. I was overwhelmed by the sheer physicality. When the ideological shroud is pulled away, what you're left with is warm, human sweat.

We wanted to arrange for a car for the following day. Ilir was with some friends in the congested driveway beneath the veranda of the Dajti. He dashed off into the shadows to secure a driver, soon reappearing with a man who appeared trustworthy enough. We agreed to meet in the morning, and Zef and Pavli melted into the throng of strollers on the boulevard.

I told Ilir that we were going to Durres the next day. "I also," he said. "For the swimming." But perhaps we could meet later in the afternoon for a soft drink. "Yes, yes," he said enthusiastically. His voice was like the chirring of birds. We would meet at five. The boy had a way of being almost constantly in physical touch, with hand-holding, an arm wrapped around you, a caress. Upon parting, an embrace, a kiss on each cheek, the smoothness of his skin.

In my room, I admitted that I had been conquered—I had let something into my heart. But what was the nature of such feelings? And what was the relationship between them and the more casual feelings I had had for the blond boy in Berlin? I recalled in Plato's works a conversation about profane and exalted loves. There were things I almost didn't want to know, moments when my desire seemed an abyss of the self. Yet desire, I knew, also belonged to the story.

In the morning, as the sun came in through the chinks of the half-pulled metal shade, I could hear the birds below in the otherwise empty garden. The driver proved to be reliable, and we were promptly on the road for our little holiday. As we passed buses jammed with like-minded weekenders heading for the sea, I found myself involuntarily glancing up at the windows of the packed vehicles on the unlikely chance that I might catch a glimpse of the boy on his way to the beach.

At Durres, we inspected the ancient Roman amphitheatre, first century I think it was. It had been semiexcavated, located right in the middle of a residential neighbourhood. The heat was stunning. It was a relief to duck into the shaded galleries and interior stairways. A Byzantine church had been installed into its midst in the Middle Ages; the whole place was a rockpile jumble of two millennia. We emerged at last into a portal overlooking the whole site. I can't recall if they had dug all the way down to the great half-circle stage of the theatre, but it was easy enough to imagine. When we finally clambered off the heap, I was grateful to our thoughtful driver, who had found a water tap that he ran for his parched inspectors of antiquities.

Then there was the local museum to see. It was across the street from a narrow beach at the sea's edge. I had only half an eye for the ancient statuary, for now I was longing for the Adriatic, which I could smell from there. "Where I come from," I said to Zef and Pavli, "it's considered good luck to dip your hand in the sea, if you're a visitor." I have no idea if that's true (though I live within sight of an inlet of the Pacific), but my hosts apparently thought we had fulfilled our duties as tourists and obligingly led me across the road. It was a scruffy beach, pebbles and shells mostly, but the Adriatic stretched out before us in a long, low succession of thin layers of wave. I reached into it and wet my hand, scooping up some water to my face while the sea ran over my foot.

I displayed sufficient enthusiasm for this natural wonder that Zef and Pavli decided to show me the beaches at the south end of town. It was a five-minute drive. Down the wide stretch of sand was an area of resorts and hotels where the workers and their families went for holidays and where the country's few tourists had been permitted during the old regime, to provide a source of foreign exchange. We stopped at one of the hotels to get a cool drink. We sat in a cavernous hall that gave out onto the crowded beach below and the

Adriatic rolling in and sipped an orange-flavoured concoction. Afterward, the three of us strolled among the mob of bathers, families, groups of boys playing football in the sand, bodies everywhere. Absurdly, I hoped to spy Ilir in this multitude, though I knew I wouldn't. But what struck me was that, when the ideological fog lifted, what you had were the people—not the abstracted version, as in "the people," but the physical fact of them—and these people, the Albanians, were not so different from the rest of humanity, not dissimilar to the Italians or Greeks, who were on their own beaches that Sunday afternoon.

In the car again—now we were travelling inland and north, to Kruje—the image of that human skin shimmering in the sun remained with me for some time. I turned to Zef and Pavli, sitting in the back.

"Communism never talked about the body," I declared.

"It never talked about the spirit either," Zef countered.

"But it had an equivalent to the spirit," I replied. "It had the notion of revolutionary consciousness. At least, that was a mental thing. But they claimed to be materialists, and yet they didn't speak—except mechanically—about the body." Yet, in the part of the world I came from, the body was relentlessly displayed, but for all its commodification it was rendered almost equally meaningless.

Of course, the return of the body is not the same thing as the birth of a citizenry, I admitted. The madman had broken many bodies here, but when the regime fell apart—for a variety of reasons, including the simple fact that it didn't work—the body of, say, old Trebeshina was, in a sense, replaced by that of the boy I was enamoured of.

Yet bodies, left to themselves, form only the relationships of a society—at best, the wisdom of the elders, at worst, the gangs of the cities. Whereas the dictionaries Zef and Pavli had made belonged to culture, even a universal culture, out of which citizens might emerge. I had no more idea how it might turn out in Albania than anyone else. But wasn't that true of so much else of that new entity that we referred to by the old name of Europe? For the moment, it was simply bodies that impressed themselves upon me. Bodies that, as Pavli had said, no longer had to turn their heads to see if someone was following.

At Kruje, in the mountains, there was a reconstruction of Skanderbeg's castle and a sweeping view of the valley below. We dutifully toured the site of the warlord's redoubt. Nearby was a little outdoor restaurant, and we sat in the walled garden by a fountain and feasted. Below us, at a table placed near the edge of a precipice, commanding a view of the valley, was a party of Italians. They were very jolly, yodelling out into the mountains, hoping to produce an echo. The waiter told us, however, that—far from being the frivolous tourists we imagined—they had taken in some Albanian young men who had fled to Brindisi—I remembered the footage of overloaded boats I'd seen on TV the previous spring—and now they had come to visit the parents, to bring them news of their sons.

Sheep wandered about the garden, eating bread from our hands or nudging up against our knees while we dug our fingers into their white, oily curls. But even as we feasted, dipping our bread into the dish of oil in which the olives soaked (Zef said, matter-of-factly, "I haven't tasted olive oil in two years"), and as the Italians holloed and yodelled, our talk strayed from the bucolic surroundings.

"What did you think the day Hoxha died?" I asked rather suddenly.

"It isn't very Christian," Zef answered, "but it was perhaps the finest day of my life."

"How did you hear about it?"

"We were not together at the time," Pavli said.

"First there was only classical music on the radio," Zef remembered. "And we thought something had happened. And, of course, the only thing that could have happened was that he died. So we waited for the official announcement, which was on the twelve o'clock news."

"I was travelling that day, to my hometown," Pavli recalled. "I took my little daughter with me. I went to see my father, who was sick. On my way to the train station, I met an old journalist. He approached me with sort of—I can't explain what his face was like when he saw me—but he desperately wanted to tell me something. He approached me with half a smile and said, 'He is dead and gone.' I got it immediately. When I reached home, I told my father, I gave him the news. He just rejoiced. 'I saw him go before me. I don't mind if I die now.' Those were his words."

Pavli fell silent. We listened to the water falling in the fountain.

Zef said, "We hoped that his death would be the end, but the regime lingered on for another six years."

"The true end of the dictator," Pavli continued, "was on that famous day when his ten-metre-high statue was brought down. My

wife was just walking with her bicycle in the square, and she saw
people gathering, rushing about, and the police throwing tear-gas
bombs. Nobody cared about their lives; they just rushed toward the
statue and managed to bring it down. Afterward, a tractor pulled it
to the campus, where the students were on a hunger strike. They cut
off his head, which was sent to the students. And then the body—"

"It was dragged along," Zef interjected, "like a dead crocodile."

"Without its head," Pavli added.

In the midafternoon, we went down from Kruje, back toward
Tirana. I was leaving the next day, so, though there would be a
farewell, this was, in a sense, the last of our conversation. And at the
end, as we had begun, we spoke of dictionaries. It was as if they
hadn't made themselves clear enough, hadn't got it right, and it was
somehow important to them that I understood.

"If we had been hot-headed, and just burst in a fit of passion
and told them everything we had in our minds, we would have been
content for a while, but our work would not have been done," Pavli
said. "Dictionaries are not our work. It is something which belongs
to the whole people, and people who make dictionaries are only a
few idiotic, I would say, hard-working asses who take upon themselves
the work of a lifetime."

"Eccentrics," Zef said, chuckling. "But it was some sort of justification."

"Or a revenge on our own selves," Pavli offered, alternatively.
"After having humiliated ourselves, serving him so devotedly, we
wanted to do something to atone for what we had done."

Zef disagreed. "I, for my part, didn't think of it as atonement. I
considered it only as a reply to people who, after liberation—I was
always hoping for liberation—to people who would ask me, and
during these years, what have you done? It was meant as a reply."

"So that you could say . . .?"

"I did something useful," Zef concluded as the car pulled into
the driveway of the Dajti.

I went down to the hotel veranda at five. Ilir was there, in a white
T-shirt and jeans. When we went into the bar to get mineral water and
soft drinks, he wouldn't let me pay; instead, he made some arrangement so that I was his guest. Upstairs, in my room, we sat on the
little balcony facing the electric sign. I coaxed him into shedding his
T-shirt, what with the heat. A fresh patina of tan acquired on the
beach at Durres that day burnished his torso.

Ilir was a dancer. His father wanted him to study law, I think it was, but he wanted to dance. We had some difficulty with language; we used Zef's dictionary to get through the rough spots—I would think of a word we needed in English, translate it into German, look it up, and show Ilir the corresponding word in Albanian, and then say the English for it. Cumbersome, but a bit like a game. He was in one of those folk-dance ensembles approved by the regime.

But the boy's passion was for ballet. Classical and modern ballet, though he called the latter "abstract." "Ballet abstract," he said. He told me the story of a ballet he was in at school—"The Silver Birds"—written by his teacher, his "choreograph." And then I finally got it about "the rap." What Ilir was interested in was "rap dancing." He'd seen this fellow M. C. Hammer, an American, a performer of rap dancing, on Yugoslavian television. And the famous Michael Jackson, of course. I hadn't paid much attention to any of that, though one absorbs it, because it's in the air, so I knew what he was talking about. The sound of rap was like the staccato of a firing squad, I'd thought. But Ilir's idea was this: he, too, wanted to be a choreographer, and the ballet he wanted to create would be a combination of classical ballet and rap dancing. Well, why not?

We sat on the balcony and chatted away for a couple of hours in the late afternoon. There were other stories. Something about his sister, or sister-in-law, wanting to flee Albania for the Italian refugee camps, how he'd pleaded with her not to go. And once he'd gone to Turkey for two or three weeks—I didn't quite get why—and stayed with a family, and they'd been very nice to him, but he'd gotten homesick.

It was all quite marvellous. I'd gone all the way to this benighted place, and I'd found what I'd been seeking, I suppose, in more ways than I'd expected. Ilir was outgoing, unself-conscious, his voice a little breathless. Perhaps all the pidgin-English and pidgin-Albanian made it seem much simpler than it was. I didn't think he represented the "spirit of Albania" or some such nonsense. There was a tempta-tion to make that of him, of course, because he was so full of his own light. But that's a dangerous sentimentality too. He was simply himself. But he was also of the place; he would have to live in Albania when Vrioni and Don Quixote and the translators had gone on. He might even make a ballet, if the place wasn't overtaken by chaos, if it didn't revert to hill banditry and blood feuds, if, against the odds, the musical body of this boy and the "deliberate belief" (as Conrad calls it) of the dictionary makers could forge a citizenry. Ilir wanted to see me again the next day, before I left. He would bring me a *regalo,* a gift. He'd come at nine the next morning.

That evening I took dinner in the hotel, in a large hall at the end of the long corridor, beyond the bar and breakfast room that flanked its length. Through the dining room windows, I could see the boulevard, filled with people passing up and down in the middle of the huge avenue. The pilgrims were at their cutlets. The Texans were at a table on one side of me. I gathered that they were off to Cairo the next day. Apparently, they'd done a deal for oil rights down at Flora, to the south, below Apollonia, the old Greek town—in return for which they would provide computer equipment (probably obsolete) from head office in Houston or Dallas. At the table on my other side was another businessman, with a woman, earnestly lecturing a local fellow, who seemed quite deferential before the pilgrim's sermon on efficiency and whatnot.

I took the air for a bit, among the strolling crowds, before retiring to my room. Before I nodded off, I saw the end of the story I was following here. When you're vouchsafed—in advance—a glimpse of the tale in its entirety, you simply shudder with gratefulness to the god for whom the Greeks named Apollonia.

Ilir arrived promptly at nine. The haze was just lifting from Mount Dajti. He had a plastic sack filled with *regalos:* a bottle of Albanian raki, another of wine, some candies, and a collection of video and cassette tapes—Beethoven, and a local singer, and M. C. Hammer, which he'd taken off the radio, TV footage of the visit of the American secretary of state to Tirana—even a snapshot of himself. He emptied his treasures upon me. Would I send him a video of Hammer or Jackson? "Yes, of course," I promised, "but there's one more *regalo* I'd like." He was puzzled. What more could there be? "I'd like to see you dance," I said.

"But where?" he asked.

"Here," I said. At first, he made the faintest show of resistance, but he was an artist and accustomed to performing. Beethoven is not really for dancing, he pointed out, even as he snapped the tape into my little interview recorder with the familiar dexterity of teenagers everywhere.

He placed himself in front of the gauze curtain before the window. It was embroidered with birds, and the faintest breeze moved the cloth. I pressed the button and symphonic strains emerged. At first, I didn't think it would come off. There was barely sufficient room to move between the bed and the doorway to the bathroom, three or four paces at most. I don't know what I expected—that it would be quite provincial, or crudely amateur, perhaps.

I needn't have worried. He struck a pose, this boy in T-shirt, jeans, and sneakers, and quickly found space to soar and plunge and turn. I don't know how to describe it. You could say, I suppose, that his terrible innocence took wing—if it was innocence, if it was terrible. What does Rilke say? "Every angel is terrifying"?

When the Beethoven ran out, Ilir immediately found the female pop singer on the tape and danced a mixture of Turkish and folkloric movements. For the finale, he rap danced to Hammer chanting the refrain "Can't touch this." It was one of those boasting songs from the American ghetto, full of rather aggressive sexual double-entendres and self-acclaim for the performer's artistry. Although I'd only paid annoyed attention to it when I'd seen it in passing on television, it now struck me as quite beautiful. I saw the art of it. Ilir simply viewed it as another form of modern dancing. For him, the elements of the culture had no gaping spaces. For his needs, Beethoven and Hammer were contemporaries. And the tiny room was as adequate as the stage in the amphitheatre at Durres.

At the end, he collapsed into the chair at my desk, heaving for breath. He was covered in a light sweat—it gathered in the trough above his lip and in the hollow at the base of his throat. I could smell him, breathe him in. He glowed. I offered him a can of cola. It was soon time for him to go; he had a test at school that day. Kisses, a hug in which I held that dancing body for a moment against my own. "Can't touch this," I said. "Can't touch this," he repeated with a grin.

The tires of the plane squeaked down onto the tarmac at Tegel airport in Berlin as I turned the last pages of Conrad's story. I was left at the end with Marlow, Conrad's yarn-spinner, his interminable voice having ceased, his face as impassive as that of a meditating Buddha.

I got up, reaching into the overhead baggage rack for my maroon-coloured gym bag. Coincidentally enough—and this was one of those thousand things you couldn't possibly make up—my seat companion was a riverboat captain just returning from some place in

Africa, where he worked for a German resource company. We wished each other well at the ends of our respective journeys.

That evening, I had a drink at the Café Einstein. When I said to a friend I'd run into there that I was just back from Tirana, he made me repeat the name and then tried it out himself, as if uttering the name of some place on the moon. I extracted Zef's dictionary from my bag as evidence that I wasn't lying. "But why did you want to go there?" he asked, tolerantly amused.

I soon took my leave, making my way in the cool and damp Berlin night across Nollendorfplatz, beneath the soot-stained nude statues embedded in the upper façade of the Metropol Theatre, into the web of narrow streets to the west of it where the bar I had frequented was located. It was late, and the blond boy wasn't there.

In his place was a rangy young man in his early twenties, tall, rather dark, athletic, not exactly my type. How quickly the sublime was replaced by the vulgar, I thought, slightly bemused, yet noticing that I wasn't tempted to exalt the former at the expense of the latter.

We struck up a conversation in broken German, the one language we had in common. He was from Zagreb, in Croatia, an economics student; his family had sent him to Berlin for safety in the midst of the Yugoslavian shooting. By chance, one of them, his mother, or perhaps a grandparent, was Albanian, and he seized with delight upon Zef's dictionary, which I had placed upon the bar between our elbows. When we encountered a word in German that was outside his vocabulary, we repaired to Zef's translation of it into Albanian, just as I had done with Ilir. I was a bit frightened of him, but in the cab he took my hand in his much larger one, reassuring and exciting me by circling his finger in my palm. At home, I satisfied him as best I could.

1992

| | | | | | |

Zoo Stories

| | | | | | |

Brian D. Johnson

| | | | | | |

INTERVIEWING CELEBRITIES IS, IN PART, WHAT I DO FOR A living. And it can get under your skin, all these fleeting encounters with familiar strangers. Stars have moved into my life. They drop by unannounced in dreams. They routinely invade my privacy. But I have to admit that I'm still not immune to the novelty, or even the thrill, of meeting an icon in the flesh. It's intriguing to meet famous people, sometimes for no other reason than because they are famous. It's like being able to walk around a sculpture after seeing only a photograph. I'm always curious to find out if a star's charisma "travels," or whether it diminishes when removed from the light of the screen, the way a pebble loses its lustre after being taken out of the water.

As a magazine journalist, I've done a couple of hundred celebrity interviews during the past dozen years. The list includes Madonna, Tom Cruise, Jack Nicholson, Michelle Pfeiffer, Dustin Hoffman, Harrison Ford, Robin Williams, Julia Roberts, Robert De Niro, Jodie Foster, Meryl Streep, Tom Hanks, Sharon Stone, Mel Gibson, Cher, Brad Pitt, Gwyneth Paltrow, Mick Jagger . . . there is almost no star left unturned. After a while, you start to lust after the names still missing from the portfolio, the unconquered peaks of celebrity. Brando, Dylan, even Schwarzenneger. And whenever another one falls into place—a trophy interview—there's a sense of completion.

Over the years, however, the celebrity interview has been industrialized to death by the Hollywood publicity machine. There is a glut of product on the market. Does anyone really need another cover story about Bruce Willis? And just what is at the bottom of our apparently bottomless appetite for show-business lives?

Our relationship with the stars is based on a mass delusion. By tracking stars through the media, we come to believe that we know them intimately, and what we don't know we like to imagine. Which is why, when Woody Allen does something unconscionable, we are shocked to discover that we don't really know him at all. Or why half the planet could grieve for Princess Diana as if she were a close friend or family member.

Stars see doing publicity as a necessary evil, a compromise. They covet their privacy, but at the same time they crave to be seen in the round. In bits and pieces, they improvise a public persona, one that conceals as much as it reveals. Through interviews, they compose a serial autobiography, one that is based on fact but behaves like fiction. In fact, celebrity journalism has become the pulp fiction of our age.

Interviewing stars is a sticky transaction, a blind date with a forced intimacy and an unnerving lack of equilibrium. Simply put, the star is rich and famous; the journalist is not. But professionalism requires that both parties overlook the differences and play the game. The journalist is automatically suspect, the sycophant with a switchblade up his sleeve. But as a star puts his personality on display to promote a movie, he too may feel the crawl of illegitimacy on his skin. Then—with both sides feeling estranged from the publicity machine that has thrown them together—they might find a common ground, if only in appreciating the absurdity of their encounter.

Sometimes interviewing a star is like taking out the garbage. But sometimes it has the alchemy of art—ideas flow, anecdotes fly, and as partners in an improvised playlet both sides leave the industry behind. Trust is established or denied within seconds, an exchange of glances, a brief volley of small talk. Protocol requires the journalist and the star to suspend disbelief, to slip into fictional roles. The star may use the occasion to express humility, to slip off the celebrity mask, whereas the journalist—playing the surrogate audience—has to assume an instant familiarity.

Some stars, such as Tom Hanks, seem to relish the transaction, using it as an invigorating form of public therapy. Robin Williams treats it as stand-up. Others, such as Jane Fonda (pre-Ted), are so insecure as to make the journalist feel strangely protective. There are stars like Jack Nicholson who use the interview as a grandstanding opportunity to speak in tongues. Then there are those who just plain refuse to play ball, such as Robert De Niro. Most magazine celebrity profiles are now dominated by coy, titillating, or smart-assed reportage of the writer's pretend relationship with the subject—the New Journalism reduced to postmodern formula. Celebrity profile writers behave like talk show hosts of the printed page, or like the star's new best friend. In *Vanity Fair,* Kevin Sessums and Sharon Stone lie naked, side by side on massage tables, while two masseuses work on their bodies. In *GQ,* Andrew Corsello goes roller-blading with Mira Sorvino, cooks shrimp paella for her, sits up past midnight in her candlelit living room until she is almost asleep under a blanket on the couch— then decrees that she has no sense of humour because she fails to laugh at his jokes.

As an entertainment writer who works for *Maclean's,* I sit at a certain remove from the Hollywood machine. When you have to pass through Customs with each trip to the capital of American pop culture, the job acquires overtones of anthropology. But no matter where you live, stars are another species.

Each time I return from a celebrity interview, friends are dying to know what this or that star is really like, as if I must have some information, or insight, that could not possibly be reported. Does it look like she's had a face lift? How did you get on with him? Were you nervous? Where did you sit? Was there anyone else in the room? How long did you spend with him? Did she flirt? Did he ask anything about you?

People are curious about the protocol. And what often sticks in my memory about an interview is the undocumented detail: the awkward question, the wriggle of subtext, the daydreamed observations that remain unspoken. Now, when I play back old tapes or sift through journals, some of the most telling moments are those that did not seem important enough to put in the magazine. What I remember most about interviewing Sting is sitting in his messy Montreal hotel room very late one night struggling to tear the cellophane off a cassette tape until, exasperated, he finally took it out of my hands and did it himself. What I remember most vividly about interviewing Kelly McGillis for *The Accused* is not the way she wept as she recounted her own horrific experience of being raped but noticing her the day before, wondering whether or not to approach her as she wandered alone and pensive on the hotel terrace at dusk (I didn't). And what I remember most about Madonna is her bedroom, and why she assumed I had an automatic right to see it.

Celebrity Habitat

I AM ALWAYS AMAZED WHEN A STAR INVITES A JOURNALIST into the home. For the writer, it is usually the best place for an interview. With the subject's taste on open display, there is no lack of stuff to describe. A car can be revealing too. Once Michael J. Fox drove me from the set of *Family Ties* to his house in a Porsche littered with beer cans at speeds of over 100 mph. That was before he had a family.

I was summoned to Madonna's house in 1989. It was the year of *Blonde Ambition* and *Truth or Dare,* when her fame was peaking. At the time, she lived in a small white bungalow behind iron gates at the dead-end of a road that snaked up through the hills above Sunset Boulevard. Melissa, an assistant, ushered me into a severely white living room relieved by paintings and cut tulips. Madonna appeared unannounced and shook my hand, firmly. Right away I was shocked by how small and plain she looked. Her bleached hair, with roots showing, hung limply. Red lipstick set off a bloodless complexion that was less than immaculate. Then I began to take in the clothes: the red Gaultier pants, and the white lace top that left her shoulders bare and her nipples visible through the fabric. After the introductions, she covered up with a plain black sweater.

All of these details would make their way into the magazine as part of the vicarious contact a reader expects from a celebrity profile. But what would go unreported was the odd feeling of power I had after entering her house. One way of overcoming any sense of intimidation in a star's presence is to overcompensate, and I acted offhand almost to the point of indifference. Madonna, on the other hand, seemed terribly anxious, as if she had an obligation to deliver. Even the way she displayed her body, then covered it up, seemed part of the presentation.

Throwing open French doors leading out to the pool, she sat down facing me on a gold divan. I produced a tape recorder and passed her the tiny microphone, which she clipped onto her necklace.

"All right," she said, "I'm wired. So here I am, and I'm going to spill my guts and try not to bore myself in the process."

With her legs crossed, her dancer's back straight, she talked for an hour and a half, choosing her words carefully and saying more than once that she did not want to sound stupid. She talked about Sean Penn's baby, Warren Beatty's endowment, God's bisexuality, Woody Allen's shyness, and her "itching desire" to give Michael Jackson a buzz cut. For an artist so fixated on sex, she seemed strangely cold. I had assumed that some token flirtation would be part of the package, but she was all business, answering every question I asked with the honest concentration of a student taking an exam. I never addressed her by name—"So, Madonna . . ." seemed both too formal and too intimate—nor did she use mine. Her blue-grey eyes examined me as she talked, but as if looking for validation in a mirror. She expressed no curiosity about me, and not once did we lapse into simple conversation.

At a certain point, it seemed polite to stop asking questions. With palpable relief, Madonna unclipped the microphone. She let out a long postperformance sigh, then leaned back on the divan, extending her body like a flying buttress and baring her midriff. I decided to push my luck and ask for a tour of the house. It began as a tour of the paintings, starting with the Frida Kahlo self-portrait, and ended in the bedroom. Like the house, it was smaller than you would expect. A white bed. A stuffed cat nestled on the pillows. "It's a good throwing cat," she said, picking it up and hurling it hard to the floor. We observed a moment of silence while I took in Madonna's bedroom.

Before leaving, I asked her assistant to take a snapshot of us together for the editorial page of the magazine.

"Is it black and white or colour?" asked Madonna.

"Colour."

"I hate colour. I love black and white. I would like to live in black and white."

Although she was not made up for the camera, Madonna relented and agreed to pose, as if she did not have the power of refusal.

Celebrity Skin

MADONNA'S APPEAL DID NOT SEEM OBVIOUS TO ME IN THE flesh, which perhaps makes it all the more impressive. Her beauty is not a lucky set of genes; it's a talent, a trick she does with the camera.

Many stars, up close, look shockingly ordinary. And, yes, many are smaller than you might expect, with heads that are often too big for their bodies (Mick Jagger, Mel Gibson, James Woods, Julia Louis Dreyfus, and Patrick Swayze come to mind).

Among female stars, nothing can enhance or destroy the illusion of glamour more immediately than skin. At close range, there is no hiding it. Jessica Lange, Michelle Pfeiffer, Gina Davis, Meryl Streep, Sophia Loren are all more breathtaking in person than on screen, and all of them have exceptional skin. Conversely, nothing makes a star seem mortal faster than an unradiant complexion. I met Mary Tyler Moore and Jane Fonda, separately, during the late 1980s, and both had complexions prematurely aged by a carefree affection for the California sun. I'm not sure if there is a link, but both women were also smaller than life and visibly nervous. It's strange when that happens. You walk into the room feeling that you should be starstruck in the presence of someone you've watched on TV or in the movies, someone you may have adored. Then you end up spending your time trying to put her at ease.

Some stars are perfect replicas of their screen personae. Steve Martin is pure Steve Martin. Clint Eastwood is appropriately slim and tall, although his chiselled features seem softer, almost feminine, off-camera. Sharon Stone has a mind as sharp as an ice pick, and she acts every inch the femme fatale. And Tom Hanks is the nicest guy in show business.

There are surprises. I was not overwhelmed by the prospect of interviewing Gregory Peck, but he turned out to be one of the most charismatic men I have ever met. As he talked, his baritone voice resonated through the years, reviving schoolboy memories of *Guns of Navarone* and *To Kill a Mockingbird,* the lost infatuation with simple heroism and paternal integrity. It was like having coffee with God. Paul Newman is another Olympian. When he walks into a room, everyone takes notice: his eyes project a cobalt-blue intensity that even the most scrutinizing close-up cannot entirely capture. Donald Sutherland, whose eyes are exceptionally large and liquid, has a devouring gaze.

Movie stars do tend to have more light in their eyes than the rest of us, which is only natural. Film is pure light. It is an art of projection, and so is acting. The camera registers the most subtle flickers of emotion through an actor's eyes. Harrison Ford has exceptionally busy eyes, the gaze of a man in the spotlight who is struggling to make up his mind if he is predator or prey.

The Anticelebrity

I FIRST MET HARRISON FORD IN A MANHATTAN HOTEL ROOM. He was promoting one of his less auspicious films, a personal drama about a brain-damaged lawyer entitled *Regarding Henry*. It was June 1991. The Gulf War had just ended, and New York's streets were jammed by a homecoming parade for the troops. I asked him about the war, and he began to tell me he was "appalled," but then there was an agonizing pause that I later timed on the tape at a full fifteen seconds. Finally, he explained his dilemma: "I would like to say a great deal about this, but I don't feel prepared to deal with it. It's very complicated. If that's what the subject of this interview was, if we could explore this in a colloquy that didn't have constraints of time and energy, we might reach something that I would be happy to live with. But an off-the-cuff comment. . . ."

Harrison Ford is the most anxious subject I've ever had the pleasure of interviewing. I say anxious, not nervous. He seems possessed by a deep fear of saying something inauthentic and by a simmering frustration that, no matter what he says, it will never measure up to his standards. As he talks, his hands work constantly— fiddling with the glass top of the coffee table, making it square and running his fingers around the corners for reassurance. Here is a man who cherishes right angles, and right answers, a carpenter searching for a clean plumb line. He is forever correcting himself, adjusting his words, and sometimes just crumpling up the whole train of thought and throwing it out.

"I've read a lot of articles about you," I begin, "and every one says you hate interviews."

"That says more about journalists than it does about me," he says without hesitation, like someone making a first chess move without having to think. "If you look at one hundred interviews and they all say I hate interviews, what they don't say is that I've given one hundred interviews. So I must not hate them so much. I'm not crazy about interviews. But I don't hate them. I don't hate the people who ask me the questions. And I don't mind promoting the films that I do."

Still, the business of being famous does not sit well with Harrison Ford. "I have an aversion to celebrity," he acknowledges. "I have an argument with the place that celebrity has in this country and in this culture. There's just too much celebrity babble out there."

Ford is a superstar, with credits in seven of the thirty highest grossing movies of all time. But he makes a fetish of humility. He insists he is a craftsman, not an artist. "I'm in a service occupation. I'm an assistant storyteller. It's like being a waiter or a gas station attendant. The guy in the restaurant is waiting on one to six people. I'm waiting on one to six million." Then he adds, "I have a problem with privacy. I would prefer to have the pleasure of anonymity, to be the observer rather than the observed. But generally the people I meet are generous and well intentioned—basically satisfied customers—and I try to keep it that way."

I've talked to Ford on three separate occasions, for the release of three different movies. Each time he spoke with the same thoughtful intensity, but by the third interview I noticed a change. There was no trace of anxiety. In its place was a leisurely confidence, as if he was the one in charge of the interrogation. Perhaps he finally had his media mask in place.

But this was also an interview for television—at the time, I was cohosting a TV arts show as well as writing for the magazine—and interviews for television are different. They are not raw material for a story; they are the product. They are much shorter. And many actors prefer doing television to print because their words and images reach the public unmediated. Television also invites performance—demands it, in fact—and an actor sitting in front of a camera cannot help but act. As an interviewer, you have to draw out the subject while worrying about your own performance on camera. You have to act friendly without looking sucky. Find the moment. Get the conversation up to speed in a matter of seconds. The questions count. They are part of the show, and they have to be simple, leaving room for an answer.

Sometimes dumb questions work best. My most memorable moment with Ford occurred during our second encounter, a print interview in a New York hotel to promote *Working Girl*. About halfway through, I started groping for a question about his iconic status and the nature of American heroism, finally sputtering, "I don't know what question comes out of all this except to say, how do you. . . ?"

"How do I get away with all this shit?"

He gave a hearty laugh, and for a moment all defences were down. We looked at each other with a giddy candour, two guys wondering how they ended up in their respective roles, having this dialogue. For a moment, Harrison Ford was not a Hollywood star or an action hero, just a smart actor with rugged good looks and dumb luck who had stayed honest and had a scar on his jaw, not from a fight, but from hitting a telephone pole in his Volvo while trying to put on his seat belt.

Up Close and Impersonal

THERE ARE INNUMERABLE WAYS IN WHICH STARS CAN BE "done." At the star's house or in a roundtable session at a hotel press junket. Free-range or factory-style. An interview can be stretched over a two-hour lunch or squeezed into a ten-minute phoner. And lunch is not always better than the phone.

I once had a remarkable phone interview with Meryl Streep. We got on, well, famously. There was an immediate chemistry, or so it seemed, with laughter ping-ponging back and forth, and after our time was up she just kept on talking—Meryl merrily yakking about this and that, until finally I was the one who had to cut the conversation short.

The next time I talked to Meryl Streep was for TV, at a media junket staged in rural Montana to promote *The River Wild*. Universal had flown in junketeers from around the continent, put them up at a hotel, and bused them into the woods. It was an idyllic setting, on a clear lake ringed by mountains. Then, despite all this expense and inconvenience, the crew shot the interviews on phony-looking sets, with rubber rafts and camp stoves arranged like props for some cheesy cable show.

There I was, face to face with Meryl Streep at a real lake, but I might as well have been in Cleveland. As the cameras rolled, she looked right through me. It was the end of the afternoon, and she was tired. For the umpteenth time that day, she talked about how women read rapids better than men and told her story of getting thrown from a raft and sucked into a hole. But I was just one in a day of interviews, another occasion to recycle her soundbites while trying to keep her performance fresh.

The Junket

IN DISPENSING STAR INTERVIEWS, THE INDUSTRY TREATS THE press as privileged fans who should be grateful for whatever access they get. And nothing formalizes this condescension so much as the studio publicity junket, an assembly-line ritual that has become the main engine of celebrity journalism.

Here's how it works. On a given weekend, several hundred print and TV journalists are flown in, at the studio's expense, to spend a weekend at a luxury hotel, usually in New York or Los Angeles. The stars spend a day doing print—playing musical chairs among round-tables of writers—and then doing private "one-on-ones" with the more influential scribes. The actors spend another day doing television. This time they stay put and the journalists rotate. Each interview subject sits in a hotel room that has been turned into a makeshift studio with two TV cameras in place. An actor will do as many as sixty TV interviews in one day. The interviewers file in and out on a strict schedule, usually five or six minutes per interview. The demands of the talent (for lighting adjustments, phone calls, cocaine breaks, etc.) delay the schedule and make the junketeers grumpy, but they can bide their time with mounds of shrimp and cheese in the hospitality suite. At the end of the day, the junketeers pick up their tapes along with a loot bag of souvenirs promoting the movie: a sweatshirt, a CD, a toy, and a shoulder bag (with a logo) to carry all the stuff.

Junket journalism is institutionalized payola. Most major news organizations, including the magazine that employs me, insist on paying their own way if they accept a junket invitation. But most junketeers travel at the expense of the studio, which puts them up in luxury hotels. Afterward, they are often asked to supply glowing blurbs for the film's advertisements. Many comply for fear of being cut from the studio's junket list.

In the age of virtual celebrity, of satellite links and website fan clubs, the ritual of the face-to-face celebrity interview now seems arcane, like a cash transaction in an age of plastic. And the industrial version of the ritual—the junket—is even more preposterous, this notion of slicing a star into hundreds of pieces so that everyone gets to go home with a personalized relic. For Hollywood, however, the junket offers one-stop shopping. It attracts the full media spectrum, from *Entertainment Tonight* to the regular pack of junketeers, who spend every second weekend of their working lives on the circuit, doing the stars. And they do talk about *doing* stars, as in "I'm doing Goldie after lunch," "I'm dying to do Mel," or "How many times can you do Demi?"

The junketeers are a frequent-flier club with their own social intrigues, gossip, and out-of-town affairs. And their routine proximity to the stars—as an itinerant court—breeds a weird hybrid of cynicism and sycophancy. The newspaper writers tend to be the cynics, although it is not unusual to see journalists at a print roundtable shamelessly ask for autographs. The TV folk, meanwhile, desperately want Mel or Clint or Arnie to like them, for the chemistry of those few minutes together on camera is, aside from the loot bag, all they have to take home.

Everyone's favourite: Robin Williams, because he lets the interviewer play straightman in a comic improv performance. Everyone's nightmare: Tommy Lee Jones, who is even more cold and unyielding in person than on screen.

There is not much fraternizing between the media and the talent. But instances of male actors hitting on female junketeers are not uncommon. For the record, I can't complain of having been sexually harassed by any of the stars I've interviewed. But one question does come up, no matter how much professionalism you invest in trying to ignore it: are you now, or have you ever been, romantically involved with the subject?

The Dream Interview

THIS IS THE ZONE WHERE FANDOM AND JOURNALISM OVERLAP. You find yourself sitting across from an actress you have imagined making love with, or a singer whose voice you have made love to, or a director whose film you would love to have made. But open adoration is unprofessional, unadvisable, and downright distracting, especially when beauty is involved.

I have always been fond of Michelle Pfeiffer, not just because of her beauty, but because she is such a good actor in spite of it. When I finally met her, the circumstances were less than ideal. It was at a junket in Los Angeles, a group interview for *Batman Returns.* She talked about the irony that Cat Woman might be the most demanding role of her career. She talked about her whips and the black rubber catsuit with the jagged sutures: "It feels like a second skin," she said, "but if you've had it on too long it becomes vacuum packed and a little painful—I got a skin rash once. When the suit started to deteriorate and get holes in it, it would start to cut into my skin around the hole, and that would get painful." In the room, you could almost hear brains whirring as the men tried to form a mental picture.

I could have watched Michelle Pfeiffer all day. She has a mesmerizing face, its angles constantly shifting between boredom and intrigue. At one point, she made steady eye contact with me while answering someone else's question. An undeniable frisson.

Later, at a junket for *Age of Innocence,* I had a one-on-one with Pfeiffer, but it was brief and for television. She was warm and animated until the camera rolled, and then a catlike wariness came over her, and her eyes, which had been so quick and casual, assumed a deliberate gaze that photographed well but gave nothing away. I felt I was talking to her through the bars of a cage. Her reserve lifted the instant the camera stopped. I didn't give it much thought. I'd got what I needed, which was simply her presence on camera.

Months later I had a dream that I was asked, on short notice, to do a one-on-one with Michelle Pfeiffer at her house. I had to drive into the hills to reach her home, up a winding road past cottage shacks with open yards spilling down to jungled ravines. There were animals everywhere: lions, tigers, mongooses, tapirs, baboons, zebras. It was messy and carnivorous. When I got to Michelle's place, I went into the backyard and started draping a big green plastic drop cloth over her back fence. Then I thought better of it and took it down. As I was gathering up the cloth, Michelle appeared, and from then on everything seemed badly timed. The photo shoot took forever. The photographer wanted Michelle to get on all fours and act like a cat. "It would be nice to get something thicker," he said, by way of explanation. I was unprepared for the interview. My tape recorder had been stuck in the "on" position, so the batteries were weak. An assistant ran out to get fresh ones from the Mini-Mart. Somehow I ended up sitting next to Michelle on her bed. She was confiding things to me in a whisper. We kind of drifted together until we were kissing. The photographer left, and then we were naked in a room with a dark blue floor. I couldn't believe my luck. But she was wacky. At one point, she took a rifle off a gun rack and started firing rounds into the ceiling.

Hollywood Bully

AT A CERTAIN POINT, I REALIZED I WASN'T JUST DOING THE stars. I was collecting them, like totems. And Jack Nicholson was a trophy interview. He is an actor who avoids the junket circuit. And on the rare occasions he does agree to talk, it soon becomes clear that what he has granted is not an interview so much as an audience. Most stars try to deflect fame with modesty, perhaps all too aware of a danger that John Updike once described this way: "Celebrity is the mask that eats into your face." Nicholson doesn't seem to worry about that. Like the Joker, he has happily let the mask devour his face and now just sits there, licking his lips. This is a man who enjoys being an icon.

We meet at his office on the Paramount lot where Nicholson, doubling as director and star, is putting the final touches on his laborious sequel to *Chinatown, The Two Jakes*. I asked his publicist how long we'd have. He smiled. "Jack likes to talk."

Nicholson is wearing a plain dress shirt and baggy black jeans that look brand new. He announces that he feels "a little light-headed" because he has been fasting for four days in an attempt to lose weight. He swigs from small bottles of mineral water and smokes Camels. "It's all I got left," he says, lighting a cigarette and letting out a long sigh. The familiar drawl is low and desert dry, the eyes fired with a look of manic complicity, which can turn into suspicion and paranoia in a twinkling. "I don't necessarily want to give you the interview you want," he warns at one point, as I try to redirect a line of questioning. "I want to give you the interview I want."

Nicholson speaks in the us-them syntax of a counterculture survivor, loquacious rants cut with garbled leaps of logic. "I did *The Postman Always Rings Twice,*" he told me, "because I knew feminism was getting so sappy at that particular time that it had to produce a desire for somebody who would step up and say, 'Hey baby! [smacking his fist into his palm] Let's cut out the bullshit with the newspapers. Let's deal with reality.' "

Huh? What newspapers?

There is no arguing with an icon. I listened, nodded, asked questions. Whenever I tried to turn the interview into a conversation, Nicholson's eyes narrowed into that crocodile gaze.

It went on for two and a half hours. Near the end, I took a bathroom break. Later, when I transcribed the tape, I strained to catch Nicholson's voice as he talked to a female assistant while I was out of the room. There was laughter, some flirting. "Let me take a look at you," says Nicholson. The assistant tells him he has twenty minutes before his next meeting. "Yeah," says Jack, "I'm going to just chat with the guy, now that I've pummelled him into the corner."

We did chat. We even argued, getting into a debate about money, which is what really divides the journalist from the star. And the disparity is so ludicrous—in economic terms, I'm shining his shoes—that both sides usually choose to ignore it. But when Nicholson declared that the white male is the only real minority in the world, I felt obliged to draw a line in the stardust.

"You're not oppressed the way other minorities are," I ventured. "You're richer, you're healthier."

"Waddya mean you're richer?" said Jack, who had pocketed $50 million for Batman alone. "Richer? What is that? My view of richer is that I don't want to work as much. Someone else's view of richer is they want a better job. What is richer?"

"Wealth."

"Wealth is based on the quality of life," he said.

"You're saying that money can't buy happiness."

"True. It's also true that the rich man doesn't want to swap places with the poor man."

"But the poor want to swap places with the rich."

"And they can't," said Nicholson. "I tell you. I've given people amounts of money knowing this."

"What do you mean?"

"I remember when I was twenty-something thinking if I just had $150,000 I'd never have to work again. You probably think if you had $150,000 it would—"

"It would solve some of my problems," I suggested.

"For how long?"

"I could get a year or two out of it. Write a novel. Pay the mortgage."

"I bet that don't cover your mortgage payments and everything else for two years. See how easy it is to dispel? You're a sensible man. The average guy thinks that $150,000 covers his life. At least you only think, erroneously, that it's going to cover two years."

"I live in Toronto. Perhaps if the money is in US funds. . . ."

"But what if you don't want to live in Toronto? What if your novel tells you you want to live somewhere else? What if you think in those two years, 'I'm disconnected. I have no juice.' Writing a novel, I go with Nietzsche. If you don't really want to write it in your blood, save us the space."

How could I argue with Nietzsche?

"Take Nietzsche off your back," Nicholson volunteered. "I don't want to be that spartan with you. I want to be as fair as I am with myself. But advice by writers tends to be: 'If you're a young writer who's hesitant about what he should write, indulge the impulse.'"

"Hesitate."

"Right. As a flip thing to do, I used to say, 'I'm the best writer, because I'm the only modern writer of my generation. I do it without paper.' That's just a twist on what a writer is, a gambit to have an interesting conversation. But in a sense it's true. I read a lot, and there is a tremendous amount of books that I read where I think, this person knows me and my work. This person is writing with sensibilities that have come through my collaborators and my efforts in the general dissemination of this."

So that's what I'm doing here, serving as conveyor for the general dissemination of Jack Nicholson. As he segues from unemployment to solar energy, from Reich to Tesla, from Gerald Ford to Madonna, from automotive design to neoimpressionism, I realize that I am listening to a star who sees himself as an oracle, who actually believes that the celebrity interview should be a pipeline for ideas, and opinions pour out of him like variations on a personal repertoire of jazz standards. "If you go back through my interviews," he says, "you'll hear almost everything I've said today articulated in some other way. I'm aware of this."

Satisfaction

I HAD NO DIFFICULTY KEEPING MY DISTANCE FROM JACK Nicholson. He did it for me. But when the journalist is also a fan, he can experience what psychiatrists like to call "boundary issues."

There is nothing in the world more banal than a Rolling Stones fan who believes he has a personal relationship with Mick Jagger. The Stones have built an empire on that delusion. And as a white male who was born in England, discovering the band in the 1960s was tantamount to discovering my ethnic roots, even if they had been swiped from black bluesmen. By the time I met Jagger, the idolatry phase was long past. I was too old, and so was he. But there was no getting around the momentousness of the occasion.

The first contact was a phoner to promote a Jagger solo album. As I sat in my office waiting for Mick Jagger to call me from England, I felt nervous and slightly ridiculous. I wrote to distract myself. When the phone rang, it was like being stung out of a dream. There was a scrabble of weird clicks on the line, and, exchanging pleasantries with the voice at the other end, I used all of my concentration to act normally. The cosy English drawl seemed instantly familiar, like warm flannel, and in no time I felt relaxed and thoroughly professional, as if interviewing Mick Jagger was just part of a day's work. Then, about ten minutes into the interview (which was to be printed as a Q & A), I looked down at the tape recorder and saw, to my horror, that the little wheels were not moving. I'd forgotten to turn the damn thing on. I agonized over whether or not to tell him. When I finally did, he was very kind, suggesting that we just go to the end of the interview and then run over the bits I'd missed. Before hanging up, I apologized.

"It's the first time it's happened to me," I said, as if explaining a sudden bout of impotence.

"Don't worry," he laughed. "You're not the first. It happens a lot."

I envisioned legions of starstruck journalists forgetting to push the record button.

I finally meet Jagger face to face in the summer of 1994, while the band is rehearsing its *Voodoo Lounge* tour in the gymnasium of a boys' private school in Toronto's north end. It is early afternoon. Waiting for the band to arrive in the school cafeteria, I chat with Jagger's handler, who tells me Mick does not like interviews to go beyond a "sprint" distance of about twenty-five minutes.

Jagger wanders into the cafeteria without warning. At first, I think it can't be him. He looks pale, dishevelled, impossibly slight. A bony, concave chest peeks through a half-buttoned shirt, pink and un-tucked, the rest of him disappearing into a lazy stroke of calligraphy in cream pants and sneakers. An indolent youth in old skin. The famous face seems to be almost hanging off him, like a mask in repose. The craggy ginger eyebrows, which don't quite go with anything else, remind me of my father's. There is a look of fatigue around the eyes, but the lines of his face are softer than in the gargoyle photographs.

The handler moves us to a barren, ruthlessly air-conditioned classroom with no desks and a map of France.

"Oh my gawd. This is serious," says Mick, surveying the room. "Are there any chairs?"

There are a couple in the corner.

"I'll take this plastic one," he says, like a schoolboy putting dibs on something.

I grab a plywood chair and carefully position it across from him, fretting about angles. This is not how I imagined meeting Mick Jagger.

He volunteers to test my tape recorder. He picks up the tiny clip-on microphone and holds it up to his mouth as if he is about to sing into a miniature stage mike. We play it back, and his voice—saying "one . . . two . . . three" in a bedroom whisper—sounds like a spooky signature. By now, the man knows his way around a microphone.

Watching Jagger talk, I keep getting lost in his face. It is like quicksand, morphing with expressions so strangely convulsive and exaggerated they seem beyond his control.

Later, when I listen to the tape, the voice sounds eerily famil-iar, wet with the cadences of English childhood. I realize that the sense of it eludes transcription. Ninety percent of the meaning lies in the inflection, in arabesques of erotic innuendo. Jagger speaks like a man in perpetual terror of boring himself, and he keeps lapsing into shorthand to avoid the obvious. The words are forever melting away in his mouth, consonants turning rubbery, vowels stretching like taffy. It sounds like I'm interviewing a musical instrument that plays only bent notes.

Jagger shrugs off the romance surrounding his band. "The Rolling Stones are a rock band," he says. "They make records, and they go on tour. You can't really expect them to do an awful lot more than that."

What do you ask Mick Jagger?

After Jagger, Keith Richards is a happy chatterbox. With his crevassed face and unmade hair, pirate eyes glinting like coals, he looks like a shrunken skull come to life. Keith is the Ancient Mariner of rock, the raconteur who lived to tell the tale, and he spins soundbites with practised relish. He also reinflates all the Rolling Stones romance that Jagger has taken care to puncture.

The visit culminates in an hour of watching the band rehearse, and the day passes like a dream. But as I drive back downtown, my excitement is tinged with a sense of loss. I've got everything I need, and more, but the fan in me feels betrayed. The journalist has sold off a piece of the personal fiction: he has gone around the magic door with a backstage pass, stared at his heroes, and got a saddening glimpse of mortality.

A week later, I attend a rare club concert in Toronto by the Stones. It is the first time the band has performed anywhere in four years. Jagger hits the stage, impossibly limber, like a delinquent on glue. His face, so slack a few days ago, is now savagely clenched, veins bulging from his neck. The mask has come to life. The sleepy eyes that squinted at me in that classroom are now downright demonic, and they're looking right at me. Strangely, that brief but undeniable flash of eye contact onstage means more to me than spending forty minutes alone with Jagger in a room.

Two years later, I ran into him at a party in Cannes for the première of *Trainspotting*. He was standing in a corner talking with friends and occasionally twitching to the music. There is a difference between seeing stars in the wild and in the zoo. I see them in the zoo all the time. But like anyone, I still get a kick out of seeing them— even minor ones—in the wild. Sam Shepard in a bar. Daryl Hannah on a plane. And like anyone, I go through the debate about whether to walk over and say something stupid. It's peculiar that we feel this need to approach stars and remind them of who they are. But perhaps that is the celebrity interview in its most elemental form, to say to a stranger, "Aren't you Susan Sarandon?"

I agonized over whether or not to go up to Jagger and reintroduce myself. Eventually, I did, just to end the deliberation. I'm a journalist, I thought. I have a right . . . a duty. To my surprise, he remembered me. We asked each other what we were doing in Cannes. We chatted about movies. It was brief, pleasant, and shatteringly normal.

Postscript ("It ain't me, babe")

IN 1965, FILMMAKER D. A. PENNEBAKER FOLLOWED BOB DYLAN
with a verité camera to create the classic documentary *Don't Look
Back*, a revealing portrait of a subject who did not want to be revealed.
At first, the camera can't find Dylan's face, which is glimpsed in pale
flashes as Dylan keeps turning from the lens, retreating into the
shadows of the black-and-white frame. Gradually, Pennebaker gains
his trust, and Dylan seduces the camera while pretending to ignore
it. He becomes most talkative in a scene where he refuses to talk.
Holding court in a hotel room with his ragged entourage, he rips into
a straight-laced *Time* magazine reporter who is trying to interview him.

Dylan: I know more about what you do—and you don't have to ask
me how or why or anything—than you'll ever know about me.
Ever. I could tell you I'm not a folk-singer and tell you why, but you
wouldn't really understand. All you could do is nod your head.

Time: You could be willing to try.

Dylan: No, I couldn't even be willing to try. Each of us really knows
nothing. But we all think we know something.

Time: You think you know more about what I do than I know about
what—

Dylan: No. I'm saying that you're going to die. You're going to go
off the Earth. You're going to be dead. It could be twenty years, it could
be tomorrow, it could be anytime. So am I. We're just going to be gone
and the world's going to go on without us. Now, you do your job in
the face of that, and how seriously you take yourself you decide for
yourself. And I'll decide for myself.

Time: Do you care about what you sing?

Dylan: How could I answer that if you've got the nerve to ask me?
I mean, you've got a lot of nerve asking me a question like that.

Time: I have to ask you that because you've got the nerve to question what I do.

Dylan: I'm not questioning you, because I don't expect any answer
from you.

1997

Mary of Canada

| | | | | | |

Joan Skogan

| | | | | | |

M ARY LIVES IN CANADA, I KNOW NOW. SHE HAS THE recipe for a certain life-giving tea made from the bark of *Thuya occidentalis*, the eastern white cedar. At her Marystown, Newfoundland, shrine, the Burin Peninsula's rising unemployment rate is on her mind, and in St. Norbert, Manitoba, she is Notre-Dame-de-Bon-Secours, keeping an eye on the Red River levels near the Métis wayside shrine. She works in Winnipeg's north end, and she steadies the wheel for tired drivers at Our Lady of the Highway on the road east of Vegreville, Alberta. Mary of Canada knows how to make ice miracles, how to soften winter and settle white water, whether these conditions are of the soul, or the Canadian landscape, or both.

I used to think Mary was easier to recognize at sea. She was near at hand there. She and the playmates pinned to the bulkheads were usually the only other women on board when I worked as an offshore fisheries observer on the west coast. On the joint-venture hake fishery in the deep waters off Vancouver Island, the Russian trawl fishermen kept her below decks in their shared cabins and tea corners, in colour magazine clippings of sixteenth-century Orthodox icons, pictures with softened edges in which the grave, gold-haloed head was fingered thin. On board the Polish fishing ships, the Byzantine Black Madonna of Czestochowa, as painted by Saint Luke himself on a plank from Mary's cedar-wood kitchen table, kept watch in the captain's cabin and the crew's mess. On one ship, she also hung over my bunk, guarding my well-being at the captain's insistence after the hawser line snapped when the fishermen and I were on the stern. Under her jewelled crown, the Madonna of Czestochowa's sword-scarred right cheek and straight-edged, sombre face seemed not unlike the look of the trawl bo's'n or the winch man or even me, some nights, when we hauled in the rain and dark.

Two hundred sea miles off the coast, on the *Lana Janine*, a Canadian black cod boat first rigged for tuna in the Gulf of Mexico almost fifty years before, Mary, left on board by the long-ago Mexican crew, lived in a locker on the top deck. The door by the ladder leading to the wheelhouse was inset with a blue glass cross. Beyond the sacks of potatoes and cases of root beer and Coke stacked in the locker stood an altar. On the altar, a hardwood arch. Under the arch, Mary. On the black cod grounds over the Bowie Seamount at the western edge of Canada's sea limit, Mary and the captain, the cook, the engineer, the deckhands, and I climbed forever up one side of *Lana Janine*'s slanted decks, then braced ourselves for the steep-angled descent down the opposite edge of the roll. The boat's heavy mainmast had been taken out to make more deck room for black cod traps, so she rolled on a following sea and when she was headed into swells. She rolled wallowing in the waves' trough and riding high in the spray. *Lana Janine* rolled when her main engines were running and when they were shut down for a few hours after midnight so we could drift and sleep. She rolled on both rising and falling seas, and on no sea at all, on calm water. Only one of the men spoke against her for this. "Roll, then, you bloody whore," he would say. "Roll your guts out." But she could not help herself. Even the latches on all her port and starboard doors were loosened from the strain of leaning.

In bunks built abeam, the men and I slid through the short nights, suffusing our heads with blood on one roll, jamming our feet into the bulkhead on the next. If the chapel door banged into my sleep on blowing nights, I would skitter across the slanted deck in bare feet to catch it before we heeled back. Against the shadowed bulkhead at the back of the locker, the Madonna's white plaster face was dark enough, then, to make her Mexico's Indian Virgin of Guadalupe. When *Lana Janine* lunged alone on the ocean at night, the figure of the woman with the rusted rosary swinging wildly on the portside lean seemed to be the boat herself, our lady of the north Pacific. She would bear us home, I thought, despite the desperate motion of her hull, and the long curve of the sea before the land would rise before us again. On those nights, I put my shoulder to the sanctuary door, pushed hard to secure the catch, then returned to my bunk to surrender again to the familiar, forgiven, head-to-foot sliding that slowly turned to sleep.

At sea, Mary was, like the rest of us on board, both familiar and foreign. The crew and I were our land selves; then, out of sight of land, with nothing to count on but the boat and the sea, with no one to help us but ourselves, and maybe Mary, we became something more, or less, than we had been on land. Mary, too, was both familiar—of and with the sea and the boat and us—and new—exotic, far knowing, and, for me, always from another country. She came from Russia or Poland or Mexico, and from somewhere else beyond those places. Offshore, she was necessary and inescapable, like the sea.

Onshore, she was harder to find. I missed her, or perhaps I only missed the sea. When I couldn't work on boats and ships any longer, I looked around for Mary on land, but she seemed to live only in churches, where her cheeks were too pink, and she would not look me in the eye. I read about other Marys: Egyptian Mer, whose name meant both "waters" and "mother love;" Aphrodite-Mari, born in the sea foam off Cyprus; Slavic Marzanna, Mari-Anna, who ensured the harvest; Saxon Wudu-Maer, Wood-Mary, goddess of the groves. Then I sent away for the *Novalis Guide to Canadian Shrines* and got in touch with Statistics Canada and the Canadian Catholic Archives in Toronto.

I learned that the 1991 census records more than forty-six percent of Canada's population, not including me, as Catholic, of both Western (Roman) and Eastern (Byzantine: Ukrainian, Slovak, and Greek; and Antiochean: Maronite) Rites. Eight percent of the population, sometimes including me, is Anglican. About .01% is Russian, Greek, Serbian, Coptic, or other Orthodox Christian. I learned that both Martin Luther and John Calvin loved Mary, that every mosque in Canada has a prayer niche dedicated to her because Allah says, "We have sent her as a mercy for the worlds." I learned that St. Joseph is the patron saint of Métis people, and of Canada, and that Mary is the patron saint of the human race. I learned that 659 churches in Canada are named for Our Lady or Notre Dame. Three hundred and forty-two are called after Mary herself. Immaculate Conception appears in seventy-six Canadian church names and Annunciation in thirteen.

Mary must have stepped outside church doors in Canada sometime, though. Before she was listed in the shrine guidebook, she inhabited the capes, bays, islands, rivers, mountains, streets, and towns named for her from coast to coast. She must have come ashore with other sailors.

I imagine that once upon a time a captain walked into the bush alone. It is always the captain who performs these tasks. Probably, his too-thin boots squeaked on the deep, crusted snow. Perhaps his thoughts chanted only "Here is not home, not home, not home," meaning that this place contained neither the foreseen sway of a ship deck nor the sweet, static comfort of known ground. He was forty-five years old, not unfamiliar with storms and war, but he might have been startled more than once by the gunshot snap of trees bursting in the cold.

Some way into the woods, well out of sight of the ship lying behind him in the river, the captain opened his cloak to withdraw the painting he carried. His hands and feet must have been numb with cold by then. Perhaps he stumbled as he set the painting, a portrait of a woman, into the branches of a tree in the snow-thickened forest that nearly enclosed him.

The woman in the gold-leaf picture frame was not surprised by the strange, cold land. She regarded the forest and the man kneeling before her in the snow with calm.

The captain's plea to her may have been an almost incoherent litany of need and fear: *Aidez-moi, aidez-moi, je vous en prie.* Help me. Help my men. So far from home. Help.

The man on his knees was Captain Jacques Cartier. The painted lady who already seemed to know the New World showed one shape of Mary, Mother of God, the same Mary who still lives at Notre Dame Junction, Newfoundland; on St. Mary Avenue and at St. Mary's Self-Serve & Carwash in Winnipeg; along the Virgin River in Saskatchewan; and in St. Mary's Alpine Park in British Columbia.

In mid-November 1535, Cartier and the crews of the small sailing ships *Emerillon* and the two *Hermines*—*La Grande* and *La Petite*—began their first Canadian winter in a log fort near present-day Quebec City. The ships lay fast in two fathoms of ice on the St. Charles River, smothered in snow higher than the hulls. By February 1536, twenty-five men had died of scurvy, and most of the others in the 110-man company were desperately ill.

The crewman who kept the journal of Cartier's expedition records that

> Our captain, seeing the misery and sickness so active had everybody put to prayers and supplications, and had an image of the Virgin Mary placed against a tree about a bow-shot distant from our fort across the snow and ice, and ordered that . . . all those who could walk . . . should go in procession, . . . while praying the said Virgin that it might please her to pray her dear Child that he would have pity on us. . . . [T]he captain bound himself a pilgrim to Our Lady who causes herself to be prayed to at Roquemado, [sic, Notre-Dame de Rocama-dour, Cahors, France] promising to go thither if God should give him the grace to return into France.

Grace appeared in the form of the Iroquois from Stadecona, who told Cartier he needed "the juice and refuse of the leaves of a tree" and sent "two women with the captain to fetch some of it, . . . and showed us how one could strip the bark and the leaves from the said tree and put the whole to boil in water, then to drink of it every other day and put the refuse on the diseased and swollen legs. . . . They call the said tree in their tongue *amedda*."

The *amedda* infusions and poultices, probably made from the vitamin-C-rich eastern white cedar, cured the sick men almost immediately. Cartier called the event "a real and evident miracle." The sailors were so grateful for their recovery that some of them insisted the grace of God, conveyed through Mary, the Iroquois, and the marvellous tree, had also eliminated their tertiary syphilis.

More than 1,500 years of Christian tradition joined an even longer spirit line when the results of Cartier's prayers linked Mary to a tree of life known all along by Canada's first people. The Madonna who listened to Cartier and his men praying in the forest also belonged, in part, to the sea. The Cartier expedition's prayers included the "Ave Maris Stella," a ninth-century invocation of the Star of the Ocean— "Show thyself a Mother / May the Lord divine / Born for us your infant / Hear our prayers through thine"—intended for sailors. Notre Dame de Rocamadour, the Virgin shown in the portrait Cartier placed in the tree, is a sailors' Madonna whose first home is the Cahors-district shrine, founded, in legend, by Saint Amadour, the Virgin Mary's servant who took ship for Gaul to work as a missionary. At another sanctuary dedicated to Our Lady of Rocamadour at Camaret-sur-mer on the Breton coast, the Lady caused her shrine bell to ring by itself now and then, signalling the deliverance of shipwrecked seamen who had commended themselves to her protection.

But in Quebec City, 462 years after Jacques Cartier's first winter in Canada, I might be starting to figure out the notion that he never doubted. Mary is here on land in Canada too. She lives not only on the high seas, and within Canada's 200-mile sea limit, but also in Canadian earth and rock and snow. She enters into living water and cedar trees of life. Sometimes she seems like the Mother of God, sometimes just mother, comfort in a blue cloak.

Wafik, the taxi driver who picks me up at Quebec City airport, knows Parc de la Jacques-Cartier but not the man himself, and he doesn't recognize Notre Dame de Rocamadour. But Mary, yes, he knows her. And, speaking about Mary, Wafik says he himself needs, urgently, to rest, rest in someone's arms. But, all the same, I get out of his taxi at St. François d'Assise Church at 1380 Rue St.-Martial, not far from the St. Charles River.

Here, in the church containing the Canadian shrine to Notre Dame de Rocamadour, Cartier, wearing decent Canuck boots now, still strides through the snow. In the huge painting hanging over a statue of Mary dressed in a peach-coloured robe, Cartier, followed by his limping, bandaged crewmen, stands before a picture of a fair-faced, crowned Madonna and child pinned to a leafless birch tree. Someone who might be an Iroquois crouches in the shadow of an evergreen on the left side of the painting.

On September 8, the Feast of the Birth of Mary, pilgrims' prayers in the sanctuary here still conclude, *"comme Jacques Cartier, je te remercie pour tes bontes,"* and the back wall of the church is lined with marble ex-voto plaques thanking the Virgin of Rocamadour for favours and blessings. The sun pouring through amber-coloured stained glass above the painting lights the snow, the birch tree, and Mary's face, but Mary has changed. Again. The fair-skinned, pink-cheeked Marys of the pilgrimage painting and the peach-robed statue do not resemble any image of the Virgin Cartier would have carried. The original

Notre Dame de Rocamadour is tall, white gowned, and dark, one of the oldest and most mysterious of the Black Madonnas who incorporate a long, possibly pre-Christian, past as part of their inheritance.

Outside the sanctuary, on the streets between the church and Cartier-Brébeuf Park on the river, a backhoe begins sidewalk repair. The Lincoln-Mercury dealer is open. The body shop is busy. And Wafik and his taxi are waiting on Rue St.-Martial. "Not much busy," he says, waving away my surprise. On the way downtown, Wafik, who says he was raised in Egypt as a Coptic Christian, wants to talk about the Mary his memory carried to Canada and the street in Cairo where you still cannot make bread. Here his right hand rises from the steering wheel and forms a bowl and bread dough in the air beside me in the front seat. But the dough will never rise on that Cairo street. To this day. Because on that street Mary was refused a piece of bread after she and Joseph had obeyed the instructions from the angel of the Lord to take their young child and "flee into Egypt" (see Matthew 2.13).

Parked in front of the Cathedral of Notre Dame des Victoires on Place-Royale in Quebec (American and English attacks defeated, thanks to Our Lady, Frontenac's guns, and fog in the Gulf of St. Lawrence), Wafik says, "No charge for this airport and the Mary and now this church." And, "Sorry about the resting in arms."

We sit together, silent, in the taxi for a minute or two. I wonder if I would have given Mary a piece of bread when I didn't know who she was. Before I get out, Wafik and I agree that Mary has tolerated much from most of us, in Egypt and Canada and everywhere. I can imagine another Mary now, smaller, maybe so tired the blue cloak drags in the dust, and hungry. She changes.

| | | | | | |

MARY MADE LAND IN CANADA LONG BEFORE SHE ACCOM-panied Jacques Cartier up the St. Lawrence and St. Charles Rivers in 1535. The Portuguese explorers Gaspar Corte Real and Prince Henry the Navigator, as well as other European sailor-adventurers set on the Grand Banks cod fishery, had already sprinkled Newfoundland charts with bays and harbours named for her. Basque whalers may have been working along the Newfoundland-Labrador shore as early as the 1400s. Every man in the Basque cemetery found in Red Bay,

Labrador, lies with his skull turned west, Mary's—and the moon's—way, the direction of the rose windows set around the Madonna's face or figure on the west walls of European cathedrals.

I am skimming across Canadian history, reading on the bus from Quebec City to the shrine at Cap-de-la-Madeleine farther up the St. Lawrence. Yearly now, Our Lady of the Cape receives a million visitors on the riverbank where the ice never formed in the mild winter of 1878–79 until she made an ice bridge in response to rosary prayers. The stone for her new church could then be carried across from the south shore with horse-drawn sleighs, and a shrine was dedicated to her, as promised. But Mary was busy in the land Voltaire termed "a few acres of snow, not worth a soldier's bones," for more than two centuries before the ice bridge. She worked at the Jesuit mission Ste.-Marie-among-the-Hurons in 1615, and she became Notre-Dame de Recouvrance to wrest New France from the English for Samuel de Champlain in 1630, then comforted Champlain on his deathbed and was the chief Canadian beneficiary of his will—500 livres for altar furniture at the Notre-Dame de Recouvrance chapel and 400 livres for masses to be said there for Champlain's soul. From 1642 on, she watched over the tiny colony called Ville-Marie, which would become the city of Montreal. As Notre Dame des Victoires, she despatched an American invasion in 1690 and sank most of the British fleet in 1711. In the countryside, she sometimes turned her hand to helping parishes too poor to spare a horse to haul church building stone. Mary, in white, would appear leading a black stallion, a devilish strong horse, whose bridle was *never* to be removed. Marius Barbeau's collections of early Canadian folktales and legends include stories combining

| | | | | | |

La Complainte de Cadieux

"[O]ne fine day, a young brave . . . arrived all out of breath in the midst of the families scattered among the huts, and cried: "The Iroquois! The Iroquois!" . . . There was only one way to escape: to try to run the rapids, a thing almost unheard of, for, as old Morache said, they are not thick and fast, the canoes that run the Seven Falls! . . . But that was not all, . . . someone would have to stay to make a diversion, drawing the Iroquois away into the woods. . . . Cadieux, as the most capable and expert of all, assumed the dangerous but unselfish mission.

. . . An hour had not passed before a rifle shot rang out. . . . During the struggle, in the noise of the shots, the canoes, caught up in the terrible currents, bounded through the bubbles and foam, plunged and rose on the crest of the waves that carried them into their course. . . . "I saw nothing in the Seven Falls," later said Cadieux's wife, who was a pious woman, "I saw nothing but a noble Lady in white who hovered over the canoes and showed us the way!"

Huron and habitant traditions, such as the tale of a "young woman ... beautiful as a dream" who appeared "out of the air" to "Hurukay, the ... Huron," carrying "the Child of all the people in this land, with straight black hair, dark eyes and a brown complexion. Its dress, instead of being linen embroidered in rainbow hues, seemed to be of tanned deerskin trimmed with rabbit. . . ." In the story, Hurukay reports that he saw the Child "under the Tree of Dreams."

Mary travelled west with voyageurs, *coureurs de bois,* missionaries, and settlers. By twenty years past the Plains of Abraham in 1759, her arms embraced a yet-unimagined country. On the coast that would become British Columbia, Juan Bodega y Quadra, despatched from the Spanish naval base at San Blas, Mexico, was charting lands and waters in the name of Nuestra Señora de los Remedios and the king of Spain. A bronze image of the Virgin of Remedy sailed with Quadra in 1779, on board the *Favorita,* the ship also known as the *Nuestra Señora de los Remedios.* In 1791, the Spanish naval officer Francisco Eliza's expedition explored west coast waters he named Ensenada de Nuestra Señora del Rosario la Marinera. The BC gulf and strait named for the Virgin of the Sailor's Rosary eventually settled, courtesy of Captain George Vancouver, for "Georgia."

At Cap-de-la-Madeleine, I am comforted by the bright width of the St. Lawrence with freighters in ballast, hulls high in the water, easing downriver past the shrine. There is also a huge concrete basilica, a cafeteria, a souvenir shop, a parking lot, and an information centre where the attendant and the Oblate Missionaries of Mary Immaculate priests who bless rosaries are kind to the English-speaking non-Catholic. The stations of the cross are set in peaceful gardens. The

... For three days the Iroquois beat the forest to find the tracks of the families, not even imagining they had been able to go down the rapids; for three days they also tracked the brave voyageur in the woods. Three days and three nights that were without sleep or rest for the unfortunate Cadieux! ... [H]ere is the lament of Cadieux which he wrote on bark at the Little Rock of the Seven Falls, after placing himself in the grave hollowed out by his own hands. . . .

Nightingale, go tell my wife
Tell my children that I take leave of them,
That I have kept my love and my faith,
And henceforth they must give me up.

It is here that the world abandons me,
But I have aid from you, Saviour of men!
Very Holy Virgin, ah, do not abandon me.
Allow me to die between your arms.

They were in the habit of keeping a copy of the lament as written on the bark fastened to a tree near Cadieux's grave at the Seven Falls portage. This was still done in my time, and it is in the same spot that I learned Cadieux's story, of which the voyageurs are so proud.

—*Forestiers et voyageurs,*
translated from Joseph-Charles Taché*

old shrine is still here, the stones-over-ice church where the statue of the Blessed Virgin once opened her eyes, which "appeared to be black, well formed and in perfect harmony with the rest of her face. Her look was that of a living person; it was partly severe mixed with sadness," said Father Frédéric, the Franciscan priest who was there on the miraculous evening in 1888.

Also here at the shrine is my weariness and a spring from which pilgrims fill plastic bottles, although the Notre-Dame-du-Cap information centre's site map clearly states that the spring is "from a natural source; has no miraculous origin." But when I drink from this spring at Cap-de-la-Madeleine, then lie down on the grass to rest, I remember other, older places where water is holy: the heads of the creeks in the Queen Charlottes, where Creek Women, one to each stream, call home the salmon; the spring below the oracle cave at Delphi, where I held my son's small hand to keep him from touching a coin and two icing-sugared, crescent-shaped cookies left on the rock beside the bubble of clear water coming from the ground.

Oh, Pat was an awful drunkard. The priest was always getting after him. One day he saw him drunk and he said to himself, "The rascal, he hasn't been to church for six months, an' he's always soused up." So he went up to Pat and says to him, "Say, Pat, when are you goin' to stop gettin' drunk, an' come back to church?"

Pat pulled out his watch an' said, "I'm goin' to pawn this, Father, an' pay off an IOU. Then after I do that, I will change an' become a good man."

The priest says, "Why don't you go in church and pray to the Blessed Virgin, maybe she'll send you the money."

Pat says, "That ain't bad. All right, I'll do it, Father." So he went in the church an' he prayed to the Blessed Virgin for ten dollars.

He prayed so hard the priest thought he really meant it. So he got up on a balcony and dropped down a five dollar gold piece. "There now," he said, "maybe that'll cure Pat."

I am grateful for the other water memories, and for other Madeleines, spilling from the spring on the ground the Jesuits called Blessed Mary's fief in 1659. First, M. de Magdelaine, the seventeenth-century landowner whose name gave reason for the presence here of Saint Mary Magdalene, a.k.a. Sainte Marie Madeleine. He lives now in photocopied pages from *Le Journal des Jesuites*, recorded September 11, 1646, as having "the concession" of this land at the cape. By 1653, the cape had been granted to the Jesuits and had become Cap de la Magdalene, also listed under Cap-de-la-Madeleine in the index to the Jesuit journal.

The parish of Sainte-Marie-Madeleine was recognized here by the first bishop of New France in 1678. When I am this far from the

Pacific, and farther yet from the Virgin Mary, the remote-eyed woman born without sin who stands inside the new basilica and the old shrine church, Saint Mary Magdalene is a relief. She is familiar, a woman from Magdala, a place the *Catholic Encyclopedia* describes as "a prosperous and somewhat infamous fishing village on the western shore of the Sea of Galilee." This Mary is easy to know. She was "a sinner" in Luke's gospel and a whore, the early Christian church decided. I decide that she is a hopeful woman whose faith surged as wide and deep as her sins, whatever they were. Besides, she drifted to good purpose. The story goes that after the Crucifixion Mary Magdalene drifted to the coast of France in a rudderless boat with no sails, then talked to people about Christ and Mary before becoming a holy hermit. I hope that Our Lady of the Cape shares her earth with Marie Madeleine/Mary Magdalene, sinner and patron saint of penitents and contemplatives.

After a long time lying on the grass beside the spring at Cap-de-la-Madeleine, Quebec, I remember Madeleine Dumont. Madeleine, sweetgrass and campfire-night supplicant of the Blessed Virgin Mary and wife who loved Gabriel Dumont. Gabriel, named for the angel who brought Mary news of her annunciation as Mother of God and for a mountain. Gabriel, who changed coats with a Cree scout to prove he could have killed him with his own knife but hadn't, who lies in the hill at Batoche, still thinking about Métis lands and battles and Louis Riel. Louis, who counted on Saint Joseph, patron saint of Métis people, and consigned himself to Mary's care before he was hanged for treason to Canada. A long way west from here.

Take the number 62 St. Norbert bus from the Eaton Place stop in downtown Winnipeg. Get off half an hour away at the corner of Avenue de l'Église and St. Pierre, across from the parish church. The Métis wayside shrine to Notre-Dame-du-Bons-Secours is near the bus stop, next to the house with the screened side porch and the basketball hoop out

But a few hours later a boy came up to the priest an' said, "Father, Father, shure an' Pat is comin' up the road beastly drunk."

The priest said, "The rascal, gone an' took my five dollars an' got drunk off'n it. I'll fix him." So he got a big sheet an' wrapped it around him. Then he hid behind a thorn hedge. Just as Pat come up, he jumped out an' said, "Hello!"

Pat looked at him an' said, "An' who are you, begorra?"

The priest said, "I'm God."

Pat said, "Begorra, I've been lookin' for you all day. Your mother owes me five dollars."

—"Pat and Mike Jokes from Nova Scotia," in *Folklore from Nova Scotia*, by Arthur Huff Fauset* back. The shrine is open to the street, but the neighbourhood noise of power saws and bike-riding children does not bother Our Lady of Good Help. She is standing at ease here in a blue cloak and sash beside an ex-voto sign for Chapelle du Bons Secours: "Elevated here by the Most Reverend Joseph Noel Ritchot in honour of our blessed Virgin Mary for her very special protection granted during the political troubles of 1869–70."

The chapel is in good repair. The nineteenth-century arched-ceiling panels showing translucent coloured scenes of Mary's biblical life are still in place. One of the eleven blue glass stars on the back wall is broken, but today there is no sign of the desperate need that caused Métis people from the Red River farms to plead for Mary's help in 1869. The bright, clean shrine contains no reminder of the barricade on the Pembina Trail, built and defended in fear of newcomers who wanted Métis land during "the political troubles," a.k.a. the Red River Rebellion and Louis Riel's provisional government.

The good help Mary gave in 1869–70 provided the inclusion of Métis land grants and language rights in the Manitoba Act when the new province joined Confederation in 1870, but Métis despair, and the Northwest Rebellion, rose in the South Saskatchewan River valley in 1885. Riel wrote to his mother from prison in Regina, assuring her that she had been good to him, that he would be brave at the gallows, and that he prayed her beseechings on his behalf would ascend to Mary. His body was taken to St. Boniface, the community on the Red River in eastern Winnipeg where he was born. Gabriel Dumont, who led the impossibly small Métis army for Riel, is buried at the Métis battle site at Batoche, Saskatchewan. Our Lady of Good Help knows where Madeleine Dumont lies.

Upstairs in the Public Rose Tavern

Reminded suddenly of her convent days by a sensibility still too conscious of the past, Heloise decided to take down the lascivious photographs that had been hung all over the walls of her room. Since her eyes were still lowered, Heloise was unable to make out anything of those naked, crouching figures bathing in the moonlight, offering in the quiet of their white hands, like pairs of lambs in some snowy retreat, immense white breasts, also victims of their own candor, over which, like the chaste locks of the Madonna, there tumbled heavy golden tresses, unsullied symbols, like the breasts, of an innocence about to be lost, a beauty soon to be consecrated in debauchery. Heloise was unable to make out anything in this depraved fairy landscape but the chaste foot of a girl who was depicted as spurning a pool full of toads—as in other pictures she had seen the Virgin spurn the head of a malignant serpent. . . .

—*A Season in the Life of Emmanuel,* by Marie-Claire Blais

Dried mud and grass are scattered on the chapel floor. Late in the afternoon, two swallows check the broken nest for an instant, ignore the rain-stained four of diamonds lying next to the fragments, and swoop up to the new nest and its hungry occupants hanging near Mary's head. The swallow was sacred long before it became the Madonna's bird, allowed to fly and nest within the great temples at Athens and Ephesus and believed to migrate to the moon. At Calvary, the swallow tried to fly away with the nails, and, in Russian tales, it fluttered around the cross crying "*Umer, umer,* he is dead" to persuade Christ's torturers to cease. In Scandinavian countries, the swallow is the Bird of Consolation, who *cries "Svale, svale,* console him" on Mary's behalf.

The only other visitor to the shrine is an elderly East Indian woman with a red dot on her forehead. She kneels long minutes near to Mary, leaves flowers on the altar, smiles at me, and walks stiffly back to the car where someone is keeping the motor running.

Mary, Our Lady of Good Help in St. Norbert, is watching out her open door when the number 62 bus back to downtown Winnipeg stops for me. She looks toward the Red River, running at peace right now below the dikes. But this Mary's firm mouth reminds me that she knows full well nothing stays the same forever. The waters will rise again. Only a splash of what might be river mud on her skirt suggests the spring 1997 Red River flood, but before that the river almost destroyed the Earl of Selkirk's Red River Colony on the Red and Assiniboine Rivers in 1826 and drove 100,000 people from their homes in 1950.

Mary knows water changes form. The river the Cree called *Miscousipi,* "Red Water River," from the colour seeping in its deep clay trench, flowed south, not north, before the last glacier receded. The Red River and its receiving Lake

Marmora's Miracle Web Site

http://205.206.169.2/amorcanada/miracle.htm

Individuals and groups saw manifestations in the sun, including images of Jesus, Our Lady, the symbol of the dove, the sacred Host and the Cross. Hundreds of people focused their cameras on the sun, and later discovered on their film silhouettes of the Blessed Virgin . . . . Visitors take away with them a bottle of water from the natural spring which was blessed by Our Lady for healing. . . . Another phenomenon observed by many visitors is that of huge golden energy fields in the sky encircling the hill of the Way of the Cross, as well as the lower level of the farm. These sights have been witnessed by adults and children alike. Within these energy fields, Steven Ley said he saw the magnificent features of angels, some of whom were six feet high.

Winnipeg are left over from Lake Agassiz, the glacial lake that used to cover much of Manitoba, northwest Ontario, and parts of eastern Saskatchewan, North Dakota, and northwestern Minnesota. But before rivers and lakes, before the ice, Manitoba lay under a sea. Lamp shell and sea lily fossils star the marine limestone at Stony Mountain, Manitoba. Our Lady of Czestochowa, the Black Madonna I saw on the Polish fishing ships, has a shrine in Polonia, south of Riding Mountain National Park in southwestern Manitoba. The original Czestochowa icon was most likely painted from a fifth-century Constantinople image called the *Hodegetria,* the "One Who Leads the Way," the Madonna revered by ships' pilots. At sea, she always faced the bow.

These water-wise, dry-land Madonnas give me a means to consider Mary everywhere in Canada, no matter how she shifts form and place. The sweet familiarity of the vessel names—*Ste. Marie Sur Mer No. 37,* port of registry Bathurst, New Brunswick; *Star of the Sea III,* port of registry Vancouver, British Columbia; and the *Stella Marises* on both coasts—seems not so far from the grasslands. In Manitoba, centred between the Atlantic, Arctic, and Pacific Oceans, I can convince myself that Mary of Canada survives, even thrives, on travel and transformation.

She smiles to see herself in the Winnipeg phone book, listed with Catholic schools and a cathedral, an Anglican church, a Montessori school, garden centre, dry cleaners, carwash, gas station, and St. Mary's Polish National Catholic Church. She knows we smile, except sometimes in the dark, about the serenely incandescent, white-plastic-robed Virgin Mary night light with the four-watt bulb, $1.50 plus GST and PST. She is present in the Winnipeg Native people's parish named for Blessed Kateri Tekakwitha, Lily of the Mohawk. Mary doesn't mind that she and Kateri and their sister Edith share the woman's role in Leonard Cohen's *Beautiful Losers.* She doesn't even mind that Cohen caught Edith and her lover injecting themselves with liquid from "Perpetual Lourdes Water Ampoules . . . and Tekakwitha's Spring" rather than a little heroin. She knows she'll

Kwakiutl man's prayer while gathering fronds from young yellow cedar as medicine for his wife

. . . *Please have mercy on her and, please, help each other with your powers, with our friend, acrid roots of the spruce, that my wife may really get well. Please, Supernatural One, you, Healing Woman, you, Long Life Maker.*

—as quoted in *Cedar,* by Hilary Stewart

be a mother again in poems by Charles G. D. Roberts ("When Mary the Mother Kissed the Child"), Jay Macpherson ("The Natural Mother"), and Marjorie Pickthall ("Mary Tired").

Mary, the shape-shifter, recognizes herself in the 1671 *Assomption* portrait, painted at Jesuit headquarters in Quebec City by Frère Luc, who took the name of the patron saint of artists when he joined the Recollet order. But that's her, too, in Thoreau MacDonald's 1926 *Pine Tree Madonna* and in the contemporary Annunciation drawings and paintings by Winnipeg artist Richard Williams. Williams says that his Marys, who are sometimes short-haired, often naked or vulnerable in a torn cloak, and occasionally holding a Pepsi (the drink for a new generation), "should not be confused with religious icons" rather, "they try to dismantle the bloodless image underlying the visceral polemics of gender politics. Ancient hatreds may threaten her, but enduring love, generosity of spirit, faith, hope and forgiveness are at the heart of the story. . . ." His artist's statement for his Mary Had a Dream exhibit emphasizes Mary's nearness: "My Mary has been removed from a distant past and is shown in the here and now. She is as human as we are, and dreams of better times. Listening to the promise of an angel, she agrees to risk everything in order to help reinvent her world."

That's Mary with the strong bones, full lips, and wide, direct-gazing eyes in the stained-glass windows that Toronto artist Sarah Hall made for Immaculate Conception Church in Woodbridge, Ontario. The same, but different, Mary rests in the almost cave-painting lines of the Mother and Child window that Hall made for the All That Glitters Mural in Toronto's Scotia Plaza.

And here she is again, in William Kurelek's children's book *A Northern Nativity Christmas Dreams of a Prairie Boy,* safe from the snow and the night, placing a radiant child on packing straw in a boxcar in the 1930s CNR freight yards in Winnipeg. On another page, Mary waits with her baby in the passenger seat of a broken-down car on the road beside the slag heaps at an iron mine. The car is green, maybe a '62 Chev. A worried-looking Joseph peers under the hood. But all is well on Christmas Eve in Flin Flon, Manitoba. The ore truck has stopped up ahead, and the driver is on his way back to the holy family with a tool kit.

Now Mary is on a construction site in Regina, Saskatchewan, surrounded by cranes and concrete forms, safe and warm with her baby on her knees in the night watchman's trailer. Joseph stands over a fuel-drum fire outside the trailer, talking with the watchman. Mary wears a Ukrainian embroidered blouse.

The Nativity-dream paintings of William Kurelek, who grew up on a dairy farm in southern Manitoba, show sixteen Canadian Christmas Marys, always the same round-faced woman now, alight with joy, bending over the child. She and Joseph and the holy child find shelter in a country church in Prince Edward Island; at the Star Service gas station in a small Alberta town where the New Bethlehem Motel shows a "No Vacancy" sign; in trappers' camps and fishermen's sheds and other places of refuge among ordinary Canadians.

Mary finds herself in W. D. Valgardson's *Sarah and the People of Sand River*. The picture book begins before Sarah was born at an Icelandic farm near Lake Winnipeg, when a Cree woman from Sand River across the lake "took a pendant of Mary and the Christ child from around her neck and gave it to Sarah's grandmother. It was made of brightly coloured beads stitched on deer hide. 'It is all I have,' the woman said. 'But always wear it. If any of my people see it, they will know you are a friend.'" As Our Lady of Guadalupe, the Mexican Indian Madonna, Mary was declared Patroness of the Americas by Pope Pius XII in 1946. She knows that the Sand River bead pendant, and the place that she is sometimes given in Cree sacred pipe rituals and in the dance for the ancestors at Fox Lake in the Little Red River area, are among her truest forms. Mary sees herself as a Canadian Indian woman with her head bowed in grief, beside a tormented Christ with a broken eagle feather fastened to his braids in Native artist Alex Twin's stained-glass windows at the church on the Ermineskin Reserve in Hobbema, Alberta.

Mary hears something of herself in the Toronto rock band Our Lady Peace, although she doesn't get into music stores often. In Canada, she

Let Me Fish off Cape St. Mary's

Take me back to my western boat,
Let me fish off Cape St. Mary's

Let me sail up Golden Bay
With my oilskins all a'streamin' . . .

From the thunder squall
—when I hauled me trawl

And my old Cape Ann a gleamin'
With my oilskins all a'streamin'

Take me back to my western boat,
Let me fish off Cape St. Mary's

—"Let Me Fish Off Cape St. Mary's," by Otto P. Kellard, in *Historic Newfoundland and Labrador*, Department of Development and Tourism, Province of Newfoundland and Labrador

shops at Holt Renfrew, not Winnipeg's Portage Avenue store but the branch on Bloor Street in Toronto. In Deborah Porter's play *No More Medea*, Mary not only shops at the Toronto Holt's, but she also responds to Medea's accusation that she has "a particularly sanguine legacy. Immaculate conception. Virgin birth" by saying, "The lies of legend. Don't you think I see it? Live with it?"

I believe you, Mary. You can see how earthly girls and women exhaust themselves trying to live up to the perfect-female version of you. In the author's foreword to her *Sacred Hearts* script, playwright Colleen Curran notes, "My cousin had a record based on the movie *The Song of Bernadette*. I traded her a Beatles 45 for it and whenever we wanted to put on a 'serious' show we played the record and lip-synced the story with actions for family and friends we had forced to be our audience. I think that we all secretly wished we could be Bernadette or the little children of Fatima and be the recipients of a miracle—a divine message. But we never thought of the consequences."

Curran's play, performed at the Alberta Theatre Project, the Blyth Festival, and the Centaur Theatre in Montreal, reveals the Canadian small-town consequences when Mary spins on her stone pedestal to prove that she *is* responding to an ordinary woman's failure and confusion and to her prayer for hope.

Denise Boucher's *Les Fées ont soif*—"The Fairies Are Thirsty"—casts three Marys. Marie is the housewife who sings, to the tune of "I'se the Bye That Builds the Boat,"

I'se the gal that scrubs the wash
And irons every Monday
He's the bye that makes the dirt
And kicks my ass on Sunday.

The Madeleine character is a hooker. I halfway know by now that Madeleine has to be a whore in the theatre of the Madonna, a whore played here, I hope, by an actress with hair red enough to match the bright mop supposedly flaunted by

Matt and the Anchor

Larry also went fishing with . . . Matt Howard. Early one season Matt lost an anchor; his wife, when he told her, said she would pray every day to the Blessed Virgin Mary for its return. Months later, he and Larry hauled in their nets and sure enough, there was the anchor, corroded but still recognizable. We can imagine the transports of joy and thanksgiving at home when Matt reported his luck to his wife, because sometime later someone asked Larry how the day's fishing had gone and he replied:

'Tis to the Virgin we must pray
And every day must thank her;
Matt went out to fish today
And caught his little anchor.

—from *Larry Gorman: The Man Who Made the Songs*, by Edward D. Ives*

255

Mary Magdalene, a.k.a. Sainte Marie-Madeleine. In the play, round-heeled Madeleine is afraid of getting fat and being alone. She wishes she were a mother, or a virgin again.

The third Mary is the statue, holding a chain instead of a rosary between her fingers while she recites

As for me, I am an image. I am a portrait.
My two feet stuck fast in plaster.
I am the Queen of Nothingness. I am the door to the abyss.
I am the priests' wet dreams.
I am the white sheep, the white ewe unshorn.
I am the star of the bitter sea.
I am the dream of ammonia.
I am the daughter of Mr. Clean.
I am the mirror of injustice.
I am the seat of slavery.
I am the sacred vessel, never lost and still unfound.
I am the darkness of ignorance.
I am the eye of the white tornado.
I am the refuge of imbeciles, the succour of the ineffectual.
I am the tool of impotence.
I am the rotting symbol of rotten abnegation.
I am a silence heavier and more oppressive than any words.
I am the yoke of those jealous of the flesh.
I am the image imagined. I am she who has no body.
I am she who never bleeds.

At the beginning of Boucher's play, the Marys sing the refrain "Have mercy upon us. Have mercy on you" to introduce the frequent switching and eventual transformation of their stereotypes. The last word of the last scene, spoken by each Mary in turn, is "Imagine!"

I like to imagine that Mary knows Montreal poet Mary di Michele meant to write "The Moon and the Salt Flats" not for Utah but for Manitoba, and for me:

. . . the pulse of the earth was white, the sky, marine.
The Indians spoke of it in their red dream language
of clay and old blood. Sailing for me is the angel of tenderness.

It had been promised in books that if I were good
and prayed to the right gods I would find my heart
netted in blue pacific light, but I'm perched

unsteadily on spindly doubts and can't run.
They call me bitter tears, Mary means,

without the trace of the sea I hear in *Maria* like a shell.
Only the salt of that forgotten ocean's biography
remains a relic of powdered bone, chalk white,
Saint Sea who still can make the earth's eyes here moist.

| | | | | | |

Maybe Mary of Canada remembers that this country is the world's largest per capita consumer of salt (the snow and ice on the roads) and that much of it lies underground in southwestern Manitoba.

Maybe Mary remembers the *Lana Janine*. I imagine she was there Monday, March 16, 1992, about 0800 on the west coast of Haida Gwaii, Queen Charlotte Islands, British Columbia. I imagine she saw, perhaps even felt, the flames flying out of the engine room and across the main deck. She would have heard the shouting, would have heeled with the boat one last time to slide the lifeboat off the deck. She would have seen, I hope, the Fisheries patrol vessel *Arrow Post* steaming full speed over an otherwise empty sea to pick the raft and the men known to me— the deckhands, the cook, the engineer, and the captain—out of the choppy water.

If the top deck lasted until *Lana* went under, the Mary in the storage-locker chapel by the wheelhouse ladder is 400 fathoms down now, lying on her side while the chapel

Barbara Martin's Show Towel of 1876

. . . shows the motif of the Lady in the Rose Bower. Who is this Lady? In medieval south Germany, she was the Virgin Mary, with her Child close by, who sat in the rose garden. . . ."

—Joseph Schneider Haus Canadian Mennonite Collection, Waterloo County, Ontario

My Madonna

I hailed me a woman from the street,
Shameless, but, oh, so fair!
I bade her sit in the model's seat
And I painted her sitting there.

I hid all trace of her heart unclean;
I painted a babe at her breast;
I painted her as she might have been
If the Worst had been the Best.

She laughed at my picture and went away.
Then came with a knowing nod,
A connoisseur, and I heard him say;
"'Tis Mary, the Mother of God."

So I painted a halo around her hair,
And I sold her and took my fee,
And she hangs in the church
of Saint Hillaire,
Where you and all may see.

—Robert Service

Remember

—to prevent rain on your wedding day in Canada, pin a rosary to the clothesline the night before.

door, surely burst from its latch again, stirs back and forth in the dark water. If the plaster Mary burned with the superstructure of the boat, then her dust is there in the sea.

Now imagine Mary is here in the beer parlour at the Patricia Hotel on Main Street in the north end of Winnipeg. She is listening to a man from Conne River near Bay d'Espoir, Newfoundland, who says he's looking for the Virgin Mary. "She's about twenty-nine," he says. "She's supposed to be out tonight. Bartender over at the McLaren—he keeps an eye out for her too—he gave me a call, said she was in there, but she was gone by the time I got there." Now silence.

In time, alternating slow speech, pauses, and hurried words, the Conne River man, part Micmac, tells this Mary's story. Hugeness and pain in the night. Pink dresses and new sweaters to reward an eight-and then nine- and ten- and eleven-year-old girl. Sometimes money, sometimes Mae West pies, soft, round, and sweet in cellophane, in return for silence. Now other rewards from strangers.

"She tries," he says, "for weeks, she tries, but she can't keep out of the life." He looks across the table now. "I tell her," he says, "but she doesn't believe. I tell her she's still the virgin Mary. It was taken away from her. She never gave it up. She's still the virgin Mary." Mary of Canada looks back at him and nods.

The Mary who is country born and makes courage and consolation possible would do no less. Our Lady of Good Hope at the edge of the ice on Stuart Lake in northern British Columbia; Our Lady of Good Counsel in Toronto; all the Ladies of Help, Sorrow, Mercy, Compassion, Capes, Highways, and Refuges of the Canadian east, west, and arctic coasts and the earth between would do no less.

Mary, who lives here in Canada, gives her full consent to snow and ice, to fresh and salt water, to cities and cedar trees (eastern white and western red), to change, and to us.

1997

| | | | | | |

*The excerpts from *Forestiers et voyageurs*, *Folklore from Nova Scotia* and *Larry Gorman* can also be found in *Folklore of Canada*, by Edith Fowke.

Looking for Richard

| | | | | | |

Ian Pearson

| | | | | | |

IN THE WOMB, A CHILD BEGINS TO HEAR ABOUT FOUR
months into term. Diligent parents will expose the foetus to Brahms
or Joni Mitchell or songs of the humpback whale in hopes of incul-
cating their own civilized tastes into their offspring. My parents weren't
musical, and at best I might have sprung into the delivery room with
the soundtrack to Oklahoma hardwired into my cerebellum. There was
certainly no prenatal exposure to the music of Richard Thompson, who
was four years old at the time and, as he would be many times in his
career, without a recording contract. But perhaps some sonic accident
instilled a yearning for all the kinds of music that come together in a
little-known British singer-songwriter who moonlights as a guitar god.

It would have been a chilly fall evening in 1953, and my mother
would have been knitting with me safely curled in her belly. To keep
my brother and sister occupied, she would have let them play with
the yellow Bakelite Marconi radio. At night in Edmonton, you could
receive signals from as far away as Salt Lake City and Vancouver. As
the two children twirled the dial, all sorts of music would have reached
my foetal ears. Some diddle-diddle-di Irish music, some bagpipes
and a Scottish ballad. Some early rock'n'roll from Vancouver: Jackie
Brenston performing "Rocket 88" or some Louis Jordan. A jazz guitar
special with Django Reinhardt and Les Paul. From a distant country
station, Hank Williams singing "Move It On Over," Hank Thompson
singing "The Wild Side of Life," and some Cajun music. Polka hour

featuring Jimmy Shand playing "The Bluebell Polka." Later, on one of the public stations, some Louis Armstrong and Erik Satie.

However the music may have imprinted itself, I had an instant sense of belonging when, as a teenager, I encountered Richard Thompson's music. I found a musician who drew elements from all these musics and more. My interest began with his work in the 1960s with Fairport Convention, the British folk-rock band that forged a union between British traditional ballads and electric instruments. It gathered speed with the six recordings he made with his angel-throated wife, Linda, in the 1970s, and it accelerated with the consummate musicianship and accomplished songwriting of his solo career in the 1980s and 1990s.

What began as mere fandom eventually bloomed into full obsession, albeit a mildly embarrassing one. "Richard Thompson fan" doesn't have the same cachet as "Bruckner aficionado" or "devotee of Louis Armstrong." When Richard Thompson fans (or RT fans, as they call themselves) begin to explain their enthusiasm, they mumble apologetically, because being a fan of a popular musician is not a respectable pastime for an adult. Being a fan of an unpopular musician may be even worse, for there are always nagging doubts about why he can't reach a wider audience. Tags such as "England's best-kept musical secret" and "Why isn't this man famous?" will follow him to the end of his days.

Still, obsessiveness is not entirely a bad thing. An obsession is like something foreign encased in your body. Childish whims will disappear like pimples. (Or you hope they disappear: I live in fear that someone will uncover a review I wrote in grade 10 in which I proclaimed that Cat Stevens's *Tea for the Tillerman* is a work deserving comparison with Bach or Beethoven.) More depraved obsessions become malignant and can eat away reason and sanity, as illustrated by the disturbing cases of Mark David Chapman and Lou Reed fans.

But obsession can also be something that feeds you. Did anyone ever suggest to James Boswell that his role as secretary of the Samuel Johnson Fan Club was damaging his legal career? Did Richard Ellmann's friends think that this James Joyce thing had gone too far? Did someone pull aside Köchel as he catalogued Mozart and say, "Hey, get a life"? An obsession can be less like a growth and more like a beneficial organ—with Boswell, it provided his very heartbeat. Thompson's work may be something like a pancreas, not essential, but you're glad you have it. Thompson is obviously not a Johnson or a Mozart. He'll be remembered as a superb craftsman, not as an iconoclast or an innovator. But his relationship with his small legion of followers illustrates the special aesthetic that develops between a living performer and his audience. Occasional stumbles are forgiven in light of the vast body of work behind them and the promise of rewarding work to come. Thompson's music has taken risks, soared, hit ruts, and evolved much like the lives of his fans over the past thirty years. We're passengers on a roller coaster left to us by Miles Davis and Pablo Picasso fans. That our chosen artist may not be destined for immortality doesn't matter one whit. It's the ride that rewards us.

| | | | | | |

"GOD, THEY ALL EVEN LOOK LIKE HIM!" OBSERVED A FRIEND as we entered a 1993 Richard Thompson concert in Toronto. Looking around, I spotted an inordinate number of men with bald heads and beards. Maybe eight or nine before I stopped counting, but the rest of the audience was certainly dominated by men older than thirty-five. I knew that they were fully functioning human beings who were probably excellent teachers, librarians, engineers, fathers, lovers. I also knew during the moments before Thompson took the stage that these otherwise splendid minds were cluttered with RT minutiae: the date of the 1985 bootleg version of "Calvary Cross," the merits of the shelved version of "Shoot Out the Lights" versus the official release, the pins he wears on his beret, whether or not that beret is really a balmoral, the guitar tunings for "Keep Your Distance," the source of the Archibald MacLeish quotation he used as the title of his *Rumor and Sigh* CD, the great lost songs, the continuing influence of Islam on his life and his mysterious two-year retreat to an Islamic community from 1975 to 1977, the name of his girlfriend who was killed when the band's van crashed in 1969, the echoes of his hobby of bird-watching in his lyrics.

To an outsider, it would all be rubbish, stored in the same bin in the brain that stubbornly holds on to baseball statistics (Steve Barber, 20-13, 2.75 ERA), former girlfriends' birthdays (March 15, April 12, July 4), and locker combinations from grade 3 (23-32-8). But when the show started, every piece of trivia was gloriously validated.

Thompson bounded on stage, his bald pate covered by a balmoral, his blue eyes twinkling, a grin coursing across his bearded face. A tall, athletic man (he is now forty-nine), he had a military-erect bearing as he held his acoustic guitar. He got a standing ovation before he uttered a word or strummed a chord. "Thank-you. I'm the opening act," he joked to the audience, awaiting his electric backup band. A pick held by his right thumb and forefinger slammed a driving rhythm from the lower strings while his three free fingers plucked lightning-fast notes in concert with the string-bending octopus of his left hand on the fretboard. If you closed your eyes, there were indisputably two guitar players on stage. (His prowess drives other guitarists to despondency: Bonnie Raitt was so humbled by his guitar playing at a recent performance that she wanted to go home and break her wrists.)

"I ride in your slipstream," he sang in a taxed baritone. "I wear your reflection / I echo your heartbeat / in the wind." It's a song about a spouse, a parent, a stalker, or God, depending on how you hear it. One of the strengths of Thompson's songwriting is its ambiguity—the better songs assume varying shades of meaning over time. Many fans thought his 1982 song "Shoot Out the Lights" was an expression of rage wrought by a broken marriage because it coincided with his stormy breakup with Linda. Thompson later revealed that he had been inspired by an account of Leonid Brezhnev shooting out lights in an alcoholic rage following a Soviet setback in Afghanistan. One composition becomes different songs to different listeners.

Neophytes in the audience were enjoying an affable singer-songwriter putting on a display of wizardry on an acoustic guitar. They could even forgive his limited singing ability, which has improved over the years to the point where he can actually quaver. His self-deprecating humour often leavened the darkness of the songs. (Thompson refers to his penchant for gloomy themes as "Celtschmerz.") He cautioned at the beginning of one number: "The guitar break in this one sounds like film music. It would be a good time to take that, ahem, break you need. You, sir, over there." He pointed to a man who had been heckling him with song requests. "You can go point Percy at the porcelain. Or catch up on your sleep. If you nod off, people will just think you're emoting."

When Thompson was joined by his band and switched to electric guitar, no one was going to nod off. His electric solos scream with emotion, and he makes the instrument a commanding second voice to the lyrics. His jangly excursions on the Fender Stratocaster can be as mantric and mesmerizing as Coltrane improvisations and as forceful as bagpipes. After his first long solo built, climaxed, and let us down gently, I was grinning from ear to ear. I felt the same kind of physical elation I get from a good ski run.

My friend, who had been enchanted by Thompson's acoustic performance, said, "I just don't get guitar solos." Thompson switched back into his literate folkie mode and soon had her in the palm of his hand again. The rest of the show mixed fiery electric songs with elegant acoustic gems, with elements of Cajun, morris dance tunes, rockabilly, and Arabic music thrown in.

After the show, I muttered a bromide I had said probably a dozen times over the years: "That's the best I've ever seen him play." It had been about the twentieth time I had seen him perform, but the happy-go-lucky guy on stage remained a mystery to me. All these contradictions arose: a teetotalling Moslem who has spent much of his working life in bars, a staunch supporter of British traditions stranded half the year in California (where his second wife runs a travel business), a middle-aged, content family man playing (sometimes) ferocious rock'n'roll and writing sombre songs about the edges of life. He is someone you have to keep watching to see what will be revealed.

It's Thompson's almost wilful obscurity that brings out the crusading spirit in his fans. A couple of years ago, a classified ad in the fan newsletter *flypaper* offered for sale something called "Richard Thompson Decorating Tips." I sent away a dollar to Cambridge, Massachusetts, and got back a sheet suggesting that, during his next tour, I get a map of the continent and place "colorful push pins" in every city as he performed there. "Soon your wall display will be full of colorful highlights—the longer the tour, the better it gets," said the brochure. "For devotional purposes, place a votive candle in front of or near the map. Keep it lit for the duration of the tour."

Only Deadheads carry the same sense of mission about their heroes. (The warped idolatry of fans like the ones pinning the maps suggests that the appellation Dickhead might be appropriate for Richard's fanatics.) Longtime followers have the satisfaction of having stuck with someone who had a few rocky patches and always emerged with better work. As well, the music carries such resonance. The Fairport Convention songs are connected to centuries of British ballads before them. Thompson's original songs ring with British, American, Andalusian, and Arabian precursors. And his newest songs are wrapped in the echoes of three decades of his own work.

| | | | | | |

THE TRUTH IS, I BOUGHT MY FIRST FAIRPORT CONVENTION album because of the cover and a girl.

She was a Mia Farrow look-alike a couple of years ahead of me in my Edmonton junior high school. She worked in Hurtig Books on Jasper Avenue, easily the coolest summer job in town. We knew each other's name and not much more. It was 1969, and I was fifteen, working in a warehouse for the summer. I could afford one record a week because I was too small and nerdish to have any dates. Edmonton's best record store, Opus 69, was directly across the street from the bookstore.

One Friday evening, I was eyeing the new Rod Stewart album when Michelle walked in. I quickly replaced plebeian Rod and headed for the import section. She loitered by the folk section. I flipped past a couple of psychedelic albums that would have been too garish to impress her. The Nice—too pretentious. The Move—too much of a risk. Then an album with a strange photograph on the cover. An English country garden with a tweedy middle-aged couple standing by their brick fence. In the backyard, a motley group of hippies sitting on the lawn and sipping tea. No print on the front cover—the back cover revealed it as *Unhalfbricking* by Fairport Convention. Obscure band, weird cover, even some Bob Dylan songs—perfect!

I went to the cash register, where Michelle was buying a James Taylor record. "Hi Michelle!" I said boldly, laying down my prized new discovery to impress her.

"Oh, uh, hi," she said, embarrassed at forgetting my name. She glanced at me, glanced at my record, gave a slight shrug, and headed out the door. I was just as remote to her as some record she'd never heard of.

The clerk, who looked like Rick Grech on the back photo of *Blind Faith,* had not noticed my romantic disappointment. He gazed into the Fairport Convention LP as into a mirror. "Fucking amazing album," he said, and he was right.

| | | | | | | |

That night, I went to bed sans Michelle with side 1 of *Unhalfbricking* on the record player. I drifted off to sleep to "A Sailor's Life," a traditional ballad rendered contemporary by Sandy Denny's pure vocals, Dave Swarbrick's jolly Jack-tar fiddle, and twenty-year-old Richard Thompson's spidery electric guitar. The music emulates the ocean, the guitar and fiddle repeating the cycle of crashing waves and catching melodic lines like a billowing sail catching wind. The duet reaches a crescendo and finally descends into a dead calm.

Not your ordinary psychedelic clatter. "Mysteries to be uncovered here," I thought as I nodded off. Twenty-nine years later, I can still feel the mystery in the music.

I knew nothing about Thompson at the time. He was just a name on the album jacket, and he wasn't even identified as the lead guitar on the Fairport Convention albums I owned. I must have learned from a review that he was the source of the glorious guitar work. At a time when Clapton was God and Jimi Hendrix was something ineffably greater, Richard Thompson (who is now recognized as a member of the rock guitar pantheon) was almost anonymous. Following his career has been like cheering for the world's best fastballer who has been stuck pitching for the Cuban national squad.

Unhalfbricking was Fairport's third album (it took me years to uncover the first two in import bins). The next (and last) two albums Thompson made with the band invented a new genre of music—British folk-rock—and confirmed one direction of my life.

I was sixteen, in a boys' boarding school, and I carved out my identity in part with my record collection and my status as the only subscriber to *Rolling Stone* in the school. (This was 1970, when the magazine stood for something.) I had a lot of Dylan and Rolling Stones albums, like everyone else, but I also had a few oddities such as the Bonzo Dog Band and Captain Beefheart. The defining album of my high school years was *Liege and Lief* by Fairport Convention. After the successful experiment of "A Sailor's Life," the band unearthed more British ballads and launched traditional characters such as Tam Lin and Matty Groves on electric excursions. Where other British bands used the rhythms of American black music as a foundation, Fairport looked to its native musical roots for inspiration. When the band played the Troubadour club in Los Angeles in 1970, a heckler demanded that it play some rock'n'roll. Thompson replied, "This is English rock'n'roll."

To a sixteen-year old, it was magical stuff. I loved the stories—Matty Groves's death from innocent lust; Tam Lin's monstrous transformations in the arms of his lover, Janet; Crazy Man Michael killing a raven, which becomes the corpse of his true love. I went to *The Norton Anthology of Poetry* and found some of the lyrics—Fairport taught me the power in those words. At a time when I was equally proficient in science and the arts, I decided to study English. Richard Thompson may have saved the world from one more computer programmer.

| | | | | | |

FOR A FEW YEARS, THOMPSON DISAPPEARED FROM MY LIFE. During university, I still played Fairport records occasionally, but my tastes had veered into jazz, blues, and a bit of classical. I loved traditional ballads and tunes, but I found much of British folk-rock precious. I'd take a Howlin' Wolf song about a backdoor man over any song with the word elf in it. Although Thompson's first solo album and the first two albums with Linda had received critical acclaim in Britain, I didn't even know he was still recording. (His 1972 solo album *Henry the Human Fly* earned the distinction of being the lowest-selling album in the history of the Burbank-based Reprise record label.)

Then in 1976 I read a review of a record called *Pour Down Like Silver* by Richard and Linda Thompson. The reviewer identified Thompson as the whiz guitar player from Fairport Convention who had now made three sparkling albums with his wife. I soon caught up on all his recordings and fell hard for them. An anthology called *Guitar, Vocal* gave me a first taste of his furious live performances, and two extended guitar solos—"Calvary Cross" and "Night Comes In"—became personal mantras. The thistly spikiness of his playing created an intricate hypnotic swirl of sound. I found it difficult to play anything else after the Thompson solos except more Thompson music. As a result, I went through two or three copies each of his records.

Richard Thompson reciprocated my devotion by retiring to a Sufi community in Norfolk. On my first trip to England, in 1977, there was no mention of him in the punk-addled music press, and I didn't meet anyone who had heard of him. He seemed as unknown in his native country as he was in North America. On a rainy stopover in Guernsey, I indulged myself by listening to *Guitar, Vocal* on headphones in a record store. The clerk probably wondered why a lonely twenty-three-year-old Canadian backpacker asked to hear an obscure record no one had asked for before. But she was probably used to the isolated souls who haunted the listening booths and used the headphone cords as lifelines. Thompson's records were the sort you listened to when you were alone. In a way, I've never taken off those headphones, because there's too much of myself at the other end of the line.

When I returned to Canada, my enthusiasm for Thompson remained mostly private. A few friends appreciated his work, but no one shared my obsessiveness. Richard and Linda Thompson emerged from isolation in the late 1970s and produced two lacklustre albums. My respect for his body of work was constant, but my hope that he would recapture his former fire waned. New enthusiasms such as Talking Heads and Abdullah Ibrahim took over the turntable, and they offered the promise that Thompson appeared to have lost. At age twenty-five, I stored away my fanaticism like an old record on a bottom rack.

IN 1982, A SMALL AD APPEARED IN THE *TORONTO STAR*: "Richard and Linda Thompson Band, Horseshoe Tavern, May 26." Those words gave me the same jolt of excitement that winning numbers give lottery ticket holders. I was delighted but puzzled that they were touring North America for the first time. A couple of days later, I discovered their new album, *Shoot Out the Lights,* which was both their breakthrough and a valediction for their dissolving marriage. The eight songs alternated between the male and the female voice, each song presenting a different position of romantic anguish. Richard was a man in need whose desire to hit the road overtook his duty to his family. Linda was a woman walking on a wire who was falling. Thompson said speculation about the autobiographical nature of the album, particularly by *Time* magazine, was "baloney, *National Enquirer* standard." But ensuing events made it hard to hear the album as anything but a harrowing document of a breakup.

The concert was to begin at 9:30 p.m. I lined up at 5:30, first in line and with a duty to grab a table for ten. (These were friends I had indoctrinated over the years, a couple of Brits who were Fairport fans, and a girlfriend who was more interested in watching me watching my dream come true than in watching the band.) Around 6:00 p.m., those bent, sly notes came peeling off the Stratocaster and spilled onto the street, where about a dozen diehards had gathered. It was the sound check, and no one was allowed into the bar. From the doorway, I revelled as Thompson roared through a medley of surf-guitar hits: "Pipeline," "Walk Don't Run," "Hawaii Five-O." The sound adjusted, we were allowed into the bar. As I went to the basement washroom, I passed Richard Thompson sitting alone disconsolately at a table with a small blue bottle of Ramlösa water in front of him. In the washroom, I decided I would make a fool of myself and tell him how much his music meant to me. When I went back upstairs, he was gone.

A setlist (these are lists kept by the most trainspotterish of fans) of that evening will tell you the band played the following songs.

A Man in Need	I Want to See the Bright Lights Tonight
Walking on a Wire	I'm a Dreamer
Lonely Hearts	Hard Luck Stories
New-Fangled Flogging Reel-Kerry Reel	Withered and Died
Honky-Tonk Blues	Don't Renege on Our Love
Dimming of the Day	Pavanne
I'll Keep It with Mine	Sloth
You're Gonna Need Somebody	Backstreet Slide
Shoot Out the Lights	Genesis Hall
It's Just the Motion	Living on Borrowed Time
For Shame of Doing Wrong	Down Where the Drunkards Roll
[INTERMISSION]	Danny Boy

A bootleg tape will reveal to you scorching guitar solos from Richard and from-the-gut vocals by Linda. But only an eyewitness can tell you how Richard and Linda were at each other's throat all evening. Richard completed a make-your-jaw-drop solo on "For Shame of Doing Wrong," Linda stepped up to the microphone to sing the closing verse, and Richard cut her off with an additional two-minute guitar break. Linda (who had recently given birth to the couple's third child) sat on a chair at the side of the stage with tears coming down her face before she composed herself to sing again.

At intermission, one of the Brits at my table said, "There's something horribly wrong between them. She's bawling her eyes out. He's being a complete jerk."

"Oh no," I insisted. "It's just that the songs are so sad, and they're such emotional performers."

In the second set, even I had to admit that the Thompsons were in trouble. Their personal torture resulted in some great music, but it was painful to watch such bad chemistry on stage. One published account says Linda hit Richard over the head with a Coke bottle after the Toronto show. Another says she got drunk (she had spent years as an Islamic abstainer as well) and stole a car. She left the tour for a couple of days before rejoining the band for a final two or three gigs to fulfil contracts.

The marriage was effectively over before the tour. Richard had met an American woman (now his second wife) earlier in the year and fallen in love. Linda and Richard had decided to tour North America for the sake of their future separate careers, but in Toronto the marital fission broke them. That performance was one of their last shows. Once again I was caught being a fan of something elusive.

| | | | | | |

"HOW CAN YOU LISTEN TO THAT GUY AFTER WHAT HE DID TO his wife?" a female friend once asked me.

I replied that marriages do break up and that Richard and Linda, both in solid second marriages, were again on amiable terms.

"But he dumped her with a baby in her arms," she insisted.

"I can't defend either of them, and I don't know the details," I said. "But some great songs came out of the breakup."

"That makes it worse," she said, "capitalizing on his wife's distress."

"The songs are more universal," I explained. "Thompson says they're not about him at all. They're like short stories that sometimes happen to be told by creeps."

"And you enjoy that?"

"Many of them, though some of them suck."

This friend reluctantly accompanied me to a Richard Thompson concert and fell in love, not with me, but with the performer.

"I never realized he was so funny. He's so completely charming," she said, leaving the concert.

"And not a gloomy misogynist?" I suggested.

"The songs are so different when he does them live," she said. "But he should wear a baseball cap instead of that beret."

"It's not a beret, it's a balmoral," I replied. "Besides, I thought you were Linda's big defender."

"All I'd need is three days with him," she said. "Then he could go back and do whatever he wants to however many wives he has."

SHOOT OUT THE LIGHTS WAS AN ASTONISHING CRITICAL success and provided a launching pad for Richard Thompson's solo career. Partial residency in California gave Thompson the opportunity to tour North America regularly. For the fans, the ground had shifted. No longer was our hero remote and unproductive. He would play major cities such as Toronto every year or two and release some sort of recording about every year. (The first CD I bought was Thompson's *Across a Crowded Room* in 1985, even though I didn't own a CD player.) In the 1970s, it was impossible to get the slightest shard of information about him. By the mid-1980s, there were frequent articles and interviews, two newsletters, and a concert video; by the early 1990s, there was an Internet mailing group. Before, being a fan meant hunting down all his records in import bins. Now that the floodgates were open, it was a matter of collecting every piece of information.

For me, this led to a mountain of music that I otherwise wouldn't have discovered. Through the newsletters, I found exciting experimental musicians Thompson played with (David Thomas, The Golden Palominos), some great Cajun sessions (with Michael Doucet and Beausoleil), three of Loudon Wainwright III's best albums (Thompson co-produced two of them), and bizarre appearances on a Japanese electronic album and with a Swedish folk group. I tracked down some of the wonderful obscurities who were Thompson's favourite musicians, such as Louisiana jazz singer-pianist Nellie Lutcher, 1950s rockabilly chick Sparkle Moore, Northumbrian piper Billy Pigg, and the 1930s German vocal group Comedian Harmonists.

I started amassing a collection of bootleg tapes. I had one CBC recording of a Thompson concert and used it as the seed of a collection that now includes about 100 shows from various stages of his career. The live tapes are essential to understanding his music, because there are about twenty of his own compositions he's never recorded; there are dozens of cover versions that proudly show his catholic taste; there are the hugely adventurous electric solos and the fabulous wit between songs.

The newsletters also compiled a discography of every record Thompson had ever appeared on. The present count is about thirty-five of his own (or with a group in which he plays on every track), around 100 of other artists', as well as two tribute albums to Thompson in which artists as diverse as R.E.M., Bonnie Raitt, Bob Mould, David Byrne, Los Lobos, the Five Blind Boys of Alabama, and Dinosaur Jr. paid their respects to a favourite songwriter. In the early 1970s, Thompson played guitar on numerous sessions in Britain, mostly for folksingers (though if anyone has a copy of his 1969 session with South African sax player Dudu Pukwana, please call me!). He was often paid as little as thirteen pounds for these sessions, which were a matter of popping into a studio and playing a few bars. Occasionally, these records contain some splendid examples of Thompson's guitar work, but often his presence on the records is perfunctory. The records popped up serendipitously at garage sales and in cutout bins in record stores. They included such cornerstones of popular music as *Tigers Will Survive* by Ian Matthews (one dollar in a garage sale), *The Electric Bluebirds* (two dollars in a Buffalo record store), and *Urban Cowboy* by Andy Roberts (four dollars in a used-record store). My finest discovery was a compilation album in a Toronto record store that included the first single recorded by Fairport Convention ("If I Had a Ribbon Bow"), in effect Richard Thompson's first recording. My delight was amplified by an Opus 69 sticker on the sleeve, a talisman from my favourite record store of my teen years—a record I had possibly physically flipped over twenty-five years earlier.

Collecting was a harmless enough pastime, because it was easy and inexpensive to ferret out the products of a lesser-known performer (by contrast, an Elvis Costello fan estimated that a collection of every Costello recording in every format would cost around $100,000). But the discography noted several rare British albums by long-forgotten artists such as Gary Farr, Shelagh McDonald, and Mick Softley. I sent for a catalogue from a British collector and found some of these records available for exorbitant prices. I hesitated until a friend said, "If you're so close to having everything, you might as well continue."

I sent off a money order for thirty pounds for *Strange Fruit* by Gary Farr, possibly twice the amount Thompson was paid for performing on the session. The record is on the turntable as I write this, and it is a truly dreadful affair. Insipid blues serve as a foundation for bad poems with titles such as "Revolution of the Season" and "Down among the Dead Men." Thompson's guitar only appeared on a couple of cuts.

But I'm glad I bought it. I'm glad I own this unrefined memento of hippie trash as a reminder that all 1960s music wasn't magnificent Hendrix solos and perfect Beatles riffs. The album cover I hold in my hands is perhaps one of a couple of dozen that may survive around the world, and I appreciate the curiosity value. If I present it to the *Antiques Road Show* in the year 2016, curator S. Frith may sniff, "Ah yes, the session where Thompson met those chaps from Mighty Baby who turned him onto Islam. I would suppose it might fetch about, hmm, thirty-one pounds."

I'm also glad to hear it because it generates more questions about Thompson. Did he enjoy these sessions, or did they drive him nuts? Was Gary—who appears on the cover in a buckskin jacket with a twelve-string guitar, a blond hippie wife in a dashiki, and his young boy, naked except for cowboy boots—as much of a dork as he appears on the cover? How did the erudite Thompson deal with him?

Perhaps to make up for the dubious music, cosmic forces aligned to make my Gary Farr purchase worthwhile. In June 1997, I was in a nightclub called Casey's in Billings, Montana. On a bulletin board, the club owners had posted newspaper clippings extolling the food and music of Casey's. One was a 1989 letter to the local paper from a Welshman who had moved to Los Angeles eleven years earlier (a good eight years after the recording of *Strange Fruit*). He had spent a few weeks in Billings on a film shoot and said the music scene in town had pleasantly surprised him. The letter was signed "Gary Farr, Los Angeles." It had to be the same guy. Obsessiveness creates its own coincidences. Or illusions.

| | | | | | |

MY BURGEONING COLLECTION OF RT MATERIAL ALLOWED
me to assemble my own Richard Thompson. I compiled tapes that
showcased either the rock'n'roll raver or the insightful balladeer. I
made one tape with only novelty songs: Thompson singing in
Okinawan; covers of songs by George Formby, Buck Owens, and
Plastic Bertrand; his operatic parody "March of the Cosmetic Surgeons,"
with the chorus "We nip-and-tuck and we nip-and-tuck and we nip-
and-tuck and we nip-and-tuck all day / We liposuck, and we liposuck,
and we liposuck, and we liposuck all day."

Most of all, I used tapes to proselytize. I perfected the 100-
minute introduction to RT, balancing Linda's tender set pieces with
Richard's rawer stuff. It showed off his dazzling wordcraft, such as the
killer line "I feel so good I'm going to break somebody's heart tonight."
It demonstrated his ingenuity with rhyme in a song about a jealous
man going through his lover's photographs of her old flames: "This
one's a poet / Bit of a wet / Bit of a gypsy / Bit of a threat / Wonder
if she's got over him yet." It threw out romantic sucker punches such
as "Trouble becomes you / It cuts you down to my size."

The RT tape became a sort of calling card. If I was talking to a
man about his musical enthusiasms, the Thompson tape became a hard
return volley. It said "My musical hero is better than yours, and let's
see John Hiatt/John Cale/Robyn Hitchcock come up with 100 minutes
of music so varied and powerful." With women, the message was
different. The tape was an extension of me, an advertisement promising that beneath the quiet exterior lurked a passionate romantic and
a raging soul worthy of those guitar solos. A friend once told me he
met a woman who knew me. He couldn't remember her name, and
I couldn't place whom he was talking about. "She said you were very
nice," he said, trying to provide more details. "Oh yeah, and she said
you made her a tape."

That could have been Daphne or Heather or Sarah or Ruby. Or
Trish or Ellen or Mary or Shelley. There have been a couple of dozen
women over the years. Most seemed to like the tapes, and I did turn
a couple into long-term fans. The strongest reaction to a tape came
from another man, a jealous ex-boyfriend of a woman with whom I
had been on one or two dates. When he found the Thompson tape
in her apartment, she admitted that a guy had given it to her. He tore
the tape from the spools and cracked the cassette shell in half. The

cassette was the 1980s equivalent of a dozen red roses, and the spaghetti of tape in his hands was his way of blighting my troth. His technique worked. Recognizing such danger and ardour in the flesh rather than on tape, she soon resumed her relationship with him.

I picture some of those tapes lying on shelves, encountered once or twice a year by accident, and provoking some pleasant memory or at least the thought, "Hmm, wonder how Ian's doing?" In the best case, she'll play the rollicking live version of "Tear Stained Letter" and start dancing around. Some essence of what I believe in will be coming through those speakers. In the worst case, she'll look at the tape with bafflement and wonder why that music meant so much to that guy.

| | | | | | |

OF COURSE, A WOMAN IS NOT AS LIKELY TO LET A MUSIC collection play a large role in her life. I recently visited a "collectible record and CD fair" in Toronto, and in the course of two hours I spotted only one or two female customers in the throng of hundreds of music-hungry men. A fellow on the Richard Thompson Internet mailing group tried to nail down the gender differences about music collecting:

> I remember sitting in a bar with a male and a female friend, and her being completely mystified as he and I batted back and forth the names of which musicians had appeared on other people's albums, who'd produced whom, etc. She asked why men were so interested in that stuff, and my improvised answer was that maybe there was something anthropological to it: Didn't men in traditional societies have to know and be able to recite their kinship (for example, as a sign of status)? If there's some biological underpinning to that skill/interest, maybe it transfers over to knowing the "lineages" and connections of musicians, baseball players, etc.

Or, as a female record store proprietor suggested to me, women just don't have the money to throw away. Another view says that men are acting on an atavistic hunting impulse, that a yearlong search for the rare Thompson EP *Reckless Kind* is the same instinct as spending a hunting season chasing an albino stag through the woods.

More likely, it boils down to a difference of emotion between the genders. Women display more emotion than men—men need a surrogate badge to show that they're feeling something inside, even if they can't express it. A live recording of Otis Redding wailing his pain or Richard Thompson busting his heart on a melancholy ballad does the trick.

Music collecting is also about longing. A Bobby Bland song can put me in a black juke joint in the late 1950s, a place I couldn't and wouldn't visit. The early Fairport Convention songs capture the innocence of the late 1960s, a decade I was old enough to observe but not to participate in. Music collecting allows middle-class men to revert to their crassest instincts: if you have no experience, buy it.

Hence the moonscape of bald heads at Thompson concerts. Women who attend the concerts enjoy the performances and might buy a CD or two. Men pounce on the experience as something they have to own, something far too important to let slip away after a two-hour concert.

| | | | | | |

WHEN I DISCOVERED THE RICHARD THOMPSON MAILING LIST on the Internet in 1995, I felt a mixture of fulfilment and unease. Every day, fans from around the world post messages about Thompson. About 800 people subscribe to the list, and they generate from fifteen to fifty messages a day. (When Thompson was asked what he thought about the list, he said, "They're worse than real critics, they're amateur critics. Haven't they got anything else to do with their lives?" A T-shirt bearing the former statement soon adorned hundreds of fans.)

I scanned these messages every morning (still do), more interested in information than opinion. At first, it was satisfying to know that others shared my most picayune interests, but the more we talked about this tape and that song and those rumours, the more I felt I was losing something. My fascination with Thompson was fuelled by unanswered questions, and too many of those questions were being answered.

Compared with these major-league obsessives, I was a mere punter. Some of them projected a lot of unwarranted importance onto a musician who has never asked for it and found ludicrously deep meanings in the simplest of lyrics. One fan expostulated that Thompson's choice of the name Sergeant McRae for a minor character in the song "Vincent Black Lightning 1952" was a reference to the Greek goddess Rhea and the Gaelic word meaning "son of grace." I think Thompson was somewhat clumsily trying to find a rhyme for the word *robbery* at the end of the next line in the song, but I didn't want to enter rudely into a flame war.

Still, I occasionally threw some piece of Thompsoniana into the electronic ether that was too arcane even for my fellow travellers. (I still haven't received a response to my observations that the melody for the Thompson B-side "Living in Luxury" was filched from a minor Everly Brothers song called "The Facts of Life" and that the Everly Brothers' song "The Ferris Wheel" was an important influence on the Thompson classic "Wall of Death.")

The list members were generally intelligent, humorous, and courteous. (An extraordinary number seemed to be librarians and teachers.) A sophisticated musician deserved an equally sophisticated audience. I exchanged messages with a few of them but couldn't sustain an extended correspondence about RT. Too many of them were just like me. When I saw their excesses, I recognized my own. Theories about the genesis of the nomenclature of Sergeant McRae were embarrassing because they reminded me of too many of my own half-cocked theories. I could keep the element of embarrassment at bay only by hiding away my obsession.

ON THE COVER OF RICHARD THOMPSON'S 1994 RECORDING *Mirror Blue,* a lawn ornament replica of the guitar hero sits in a mirrored box. On the foldout sleeve of the CD, a sequence of photographs shows the Thompson lawn ornaments fresh out of the box, in a garden, on a disused dresser, in a garage sale, and in a box of junk. On the back cover, the lawn ornament lies smashed in half in front of a bust of Elvis.

Thompson created the cover concept to show the brittleness of idolatry. He based it on the Koranic story of Abraham sneaking into the temple and breaking up all the idols except the largest, in front of which he left an axe. It was a direct message to his fans: "Don't make too big a deal about what I do." Even more telling was

Thompson's act of ordering the manufacturer, Mr. Mick of Hollywood, to destroy the seventeen custom-made statues after the photo shoot. Thompson knew damn well that, in spite of his satire on idolatry, diehard fans would deluge Mr. Mick with orders for RT lawn ornaments of their own.

Had I been able to get my hands on one, I would have happily planted an RT lawn ornament in my own garden. It would have been a parody of a parody. I understood what Thompson was spoofing, but my own lawn ornament would be a sign that I was *in on the joke*. Thompson knew better. Fans like me would blithely ignore what he was saying just to get our hands on a backyard idol.

When desirous thoughts of RT lawn ornaments lodged in my head, I was worried that my fandom had travelled too far from the music. The last time I saw Thompson perform, I fretted beforehand that I wouldn't be able to enjoy the concert because I was crushing enthusiasm with analysis. As well, I found his latest album *You? Me? Us?*, wildly inconsistent. (I was quite roundly flamed on the Thompson list when I suggested there were a couple of colossal duds on the CD.) I also noticed that in recent years he had become more predictable on stage—extremely professional and engaging—and less willing to take chances. The CD had received few local reviews, and the concert had little publicity—I didn't want to see him humiliated by an empty house.

When we entered the Phoenix club in Toronto that night in late October 1996, the place was packed. Thompson doesn't need a barrage of publicity to sell a concert for him—the faithful will always show up. Any fears of being jaded or bored were wiped clean once Thompson plugged in with his roaring Stratocaster. The high point was "Shoot Out the Lights," a mainstay of Thompson's electric shows that serves as a platform for the most sublime of guitar solos. Thompson finished singing the final chorus, which set up the solo, and exploded on the high end of the fret board. About fifty feet from the stage, a tall man in a white shirt yelped and threw his glass of beer into the air. He charged through the standing crowd to the stage and grabbed the monitor at the bass player's feet. He started banging his head against the monitor as Thompson, who had stepped back a metre, continued his solo. The freaked-out man wasn't rushing Thompson.

As threatening as he seemed, he wasn't pursuing the musicians. By butting his head against the monitor, he was trying to get inside the music, to crack open his own rage and wash it into the angry torrent of the solo. An alert bouncer grabbed the miscreant and threw him out of the club. Introducing the next song, Thompson coolly said, "Hmmm, seems like some members of the audience were given the wrong address for the Metallica concert."

My own reaction was somewhat more sedate. After two and a half hours of musical bliss, I once again shook my head, pulled the string in my back, and said, "He keeps getting better."

After the show, a friend who knew the promoter invited me backstage to meet Thompson. "No, no," I protested. "I'd make an idiot out of myself. I know him well enough already. I don't need to meet him." She persisted and dragged me into a backstage lounge. There record company types were introducing Thompson to record store managers and a few media hangers-on. In spite of his rigorous performance, he was unfailingly convivial in his compulsory glad-handing activities.

I was desperately trying to think of something that would mark me as a kindred spirit, that would elevate me in his eyes from being just another fan. I remembered his interest in Jimmy Shand, the Scottish accordion player ("the Lawrence Welk of the Glens" Thompson calls him). He had said in an interview that he had collected Shand records, and out of curiosity I had picked up a couple of Shand LPs at the bargain bin in Sam's. Both were Canadian releases, targeted at the kind of sentimental Scot who faithfully attends the White Heather show every year. I decided to offer them to Thompson, hoping he'd cherish them as I value an obscure Thompson release.

Thompson finally worked his way around the circle of industry people and stood in front of me. He was taller than I had expected and grinned bemusedly with an expression that said, "Oh yes, another fan." I introduced myself (or more possibly I didn't), congratulated him on the show, and blurted, "I've got some Canadian Jimmy Shand records, if you'd like them."

"Ah, yes, Jimmy Shand," he smiled. "I've got dozens of Jimmy Shand records because fans keep giving them to me. Bloody awful stuff. Can't stand it, really." He laughed, and a record company flack guided him out of the room.

I laughed too at my feeble attempt to ingratiate myself with him. But I felt I'd been party to a little confidence, Richard letting me in on a secret he wasn't spilling to other fans. Or else he was simply taking the piss out of me. It didn't matter. I didn't want to become good friends with Richard Thompson. I wanted to *be* Richard Thompson. But maybe it was best to leave the job to the man himself.

1997

Outrunning
the Sun

| | | | | | |

Mark Abley

| | | | | | |

A DAMP FEBRUARY AFTERNOON IN MONTREAL, MILD enough for smokers to huddle in small groups outside McGill University's tobacco-free arts building. Just a few hundred metres downhill, a plaque proclaims this the site of the Iroquoian village of Hochelaga, whose residents once discovered, welcomed, fed, and puzzled over Jacques Cartier. Inside the building, hundreds of people have packed an amphitheatre. It's the windup of a three-day meeting looking into the doubtful fate and many recommendations of the Royal Commission on Aboriginal Peoples. Set up in 1991, when memories of masked Mohawk warriors confronting heavily armed soldiers were fresh in the public mind, the commission had taken more than five years to produce a gargantuan, 3,537-page report.

A man with a dark blue shirt, ponytail, and suspenders bounds to the podium. He stands there, eyes half-closed, as the crowd noise slowly lessens. Then he begins to speak—in the Kanyen'kehaka language, otherwise known as Mohawk.

The surprise is palpable. The man doesn't stop after a single sentence; his words flow out into the baffled audience like the unexpected music of a dream. A neoconservative columnist on the stage leans forward, pushing his head into his hands. A former prime minister listens impassively. You can almost feel the anxiety, even among many of the indigenous people in the room: *How long will this go on?*

Not long. A minute or two after he began, Ernie Benedict—a traditionalist leader from the Mohawk community of Akwesasne—kindly switches to English. Mine is not the favoured language for the *ohenton karihwatehkwen*; even so, a version of the great thanksgiving address can be given in it. "We have had the help of all creatures from our Mother, the Earth," Benedict says. "We will now return that love in thanks and greetings." They are greetings with a difference. He sends a ritual salutation to the plant creatures, the animal creatures, the bird creatures, the sun. . . . By the time the speaker reaches "our grandmother the moon, who, we believe, is faithfully performing her task," Andrew Coyne's mood is looking as dark as his elegant suit.

It is a symbol, and a symptom, of the condition of Mohawk that Benedict's opening words should have aroused such consternation. In a city, a province, a country where two European languages jostle for power and prestige, no Native language is defined as official. On the contrary, the cadences heard uninterruptedly across this land for millennia have been consigned to the shadowy realm of "heritage languages" and the shark-infested waters of multiculturalism.

Mohawk is one of roughly fifty-five Native languages still used in Canada ("roughly," for the mere act of classification can breed vicious dissent among linguists). Until recently, the figure was one higher, but the death of an old woman named—in English—Angela Sidney wiped the Yukon language of Tagish off the list of the living. The list will go on shrinking, because many of Canada's indigenous languages are no longer spoken by the young. Not just most of the young, I mean; all of the young. Linguists say that only three of the fifty-five (Cree, Inuktitut, and Ojibwa) appear sure to survive far into the twenty-first century. Some languages are now hanging by a desperately short thread: the minds of a few elders.

Cécile Wawanolet is one. She lives in a modest house in the riverside village of Odanak, an hour's drive east of Montreal. When she dies, the Abenaki language will be nearly extinct. I met her a few years ago—a spry lady in her mid-eighties—attempting to instil the tortuous grammar of her mother tongue in the heads of a tiny class of adult students once every week. For teaching aids, she had chalk and a blackboard. After a couple of hours poring over verbs in the village's cultural centre, her ageing pupils would return to their lives in French.

"When you're young, you don't think about language," says one of her students, a former Radio-Canada researcher named Monique Nolett. "We grew up hearing the old people speak Abenaki. It was like music, but we didn't think of it as a goal for ourselves. Later on, we realized that we should have learned it."

At first glance, the only people for whom this linguistic erasure could possibly matter are the Abenaki themselves. And there aren't many of them left to care: a few hundred in southern Quebec, a couple of thousand across the U.S. border. Their population, ravaged by European diseases, was further pared in 1759 by a volunteer Yankee militia. Robert Rogers and his Rangers burned Odanak, killing dozens or hundreds of Abenaki—a slaughter conveniently absent from the histories I read in my youth. The militiamen were acting on the orders of Jeffery Amherst, a British general in the Seven Years' War who would later tell an underling to "infect the Indians with sheets upon which smallpox patients have been lying, or by any other means which may serve to exterminate this accursed race." Montreal, where I live, has a street named after the man.

THE IDEA OF PHYSICAL GENOCIDE WAS OUT OF FASHION IN Canada by the twentieth century. But the notion of cultural genocide took longer to disappear. It is, indeed, still with us, though mostly in discreet and well-tailored cloth. Certainly, the poet Duncan Campbell Scott harboured no regrets about his assimilationist work as an Ottawa bureaucrat. "We have arrived within measurable distance of the end," he wrote in 1914. "The happiest future for the Indian is absorption into the general population, and this is the object of the policy of our government. . . . The final result will be this complete absorption. The great forces of intermarriage and education will finally overcome the lingering traces of native custom and tradition."

Scott saw education as a means to vanquish tradition. Those who relied on Native tradition could not be wholly educated, still less absorbed. That idea, that weapon, was crucial to Canada's long-standing system of residential schools. "Prison schools" might be a better phrase. Over the past decade, we've become painfully aware of the sexual and physical abuse endured there by thousands of indigenous children. But as yet, few non-Natives have understood that the schools also inflicted a systematic linguistic abuse.

As the Ojibwa author Basil Johnston has written,

If a boot or fist were not administered, then a lash or a yardstick was plied until the "Indian" language was beaten out. To boot and fist and lash was added ridicule. Both speaker and his language were assailed. "What's the use of that language? It isn't polite to speak another language in the presence of other people. Learn English! That's the only way you're going to get ahead. How can you learn two languages at the same time?" . . . on and on the comments were made, disparaging, until in too many the language was shamed into silence and disuse.

Teaching a language only at night school, as Cécile Wawanolet does, will never retrieve it from the deepening silence. Unless she can somehow reach the children of Odanak, Abenaki may soon join the ghostly company of Tagish—not to mention the lost tongues of the Beothuk, the Huron, the Hochelagans. The 1991 census showed that more than a million people in Canada are of Aboriginal descent, yet only 190,000 reported having an indigenous language as their mother tongue, and just 138,000 said they continued to speak it at home. The astonishing thing, though, is not that a few languages have died, but that the vast majority remain alive.

Knowing the importance of education—their style, not Duncan Campbell Scott's—some Mohawks are making strenuous efforts to keep Kanyen'kehaka alive among the young. The language has an honoured place in their immersion schools and survival schools. Even so, it's a constant fight against fatigue, attrition, despair. If you're struggling to master the language, there are a thousand other things you're not doing. Many Mohawks consider it all a waste of energy and time, though fewer will say so in public. In the end, why bother?

The question has many possible answers. But on the lips of those who are actually waging the battle, one of the prime motives is religious.

Among the Mohawk-language advocates at Kahnawake, just over the Mercier Bridge from Montreal, is a man who used to be called Peter Taylor—and still is, for the most part, though he prefers to go by Katsitsanoron. He produces a weekly talk show in Mohawk on the community's radio station, K-103. The station's other programming—like most of the daily conversation in Kahnawake—takes place in English. Katsitsanoron could easily abandon the struggle. So far, he has resisted.

"The language needs to survive," he tells me, "because contained within it is who we are and how we identify with the universe. It helps us place ourselves in terms of nature and the world. We are not who we think we are without our language. Our ceremonies and rituals must be conducted in our language. Without it, the Creator can't identify us—can't separate us from the rest of the din."

To Katsitsanoron, it's essential to preserve a feeling of Mohawk difference. For him, as a fluent insider, Aboriginal languages lie at the heart of Aboriginal culture. Culture is more than language; yet culture relies on language. It's a key concept, but one on which absolutely no consensus exists. To an outsider like myself—a poet, someone whose craft and pleasure unfold in words—Katsitsanoron's words also suggest a second issue: the true significance of the immense distances between different languages, different language families.

| | | | | | | |

PEOPLE WHO WANT LANGUAGES TO SURVIVE DON'T BASE A serious argument on picturesque vocabulary—the famous wealth of Inuktitut words for "snow," for instance. Instead, they look deeper, to what underlies all words: syntax and structure. They suggest that a language—any language—shapes both identity and thought. New words can be invented if the old ones are lost. But new syntaxes?

The critic George Steiner was perhaps guilty of overstatement when he declared that "an entire anthropology of sexual equality . . . is implicit in the fact that our verbs, in distinction from those of semitic tongues, do not indicate the gender of the agent." Still, you have to wonder what Steiner would deem implicit in the fact that most indigenous languages do not show gender at all. "The male-female-neuter hierarchy is entirely absent," Cree playwright Tomson Highway has written. "So that by this system of thought, the central hero figure from our mythology—theology, if you will—is . . . neither exclusively male nor exclusively female, or is both simultaneously." That hero, Nanabush, must be played by a man in one of Highway's plays, a woman in another.

Yes, but what of the real world?

"The 'real world,'" wrote the great linguist Edward Sapir in 1929, "is to a large extent unconsciously built up on the language habits of the group. No two languages are ever sufficiently similar to be considered as representing the same social reality."

His student Benjamin Lee Whorf took the concept of linguistic relativism even further. In a late essay called "Languages and Logic," Whorf addressed his fellow speakers of English:

> We are constantly reading into nature fictional acting entities, simply because our verbs must have substantives in front of them. We have to say "It flashed" or "A light flashed," setting up one actor, "it" or "light," to perform what we call an action, "to flash." Yet the flashing and the light are one and the same! The Hopi language reports the flash with a simple verb, *rehpi:* "flash" (occurred). . . . Hopi can and does have verbs without subjects, a fact which may give that tongue potentialities, probably never to be developed, as a logical system for understanding some aspects of the universe.

Sapir and Whorf were both fascinated by Nootka, a member of the small Wakashan family of languages. Nootka is spoken on southwestern Vancouver Island, today by fewer and fewer: a thousand at the most optimistic guess. Whorf noted that, for the English sentence "He invites people to a feast," Nootka needs but a single word: *tl'imshya'isita'itlma*. Literally, "Boiling result eating those go to get somebody." (Add a few nuances, invert the order, and you get "He, or somebody, goes to get eaters of cooked food.") Sapir remarked on how the Nootka play games with their language—adding sibilant noises or meaningless consonants, for example, when talking to, or about, children, fat people, short people, left-handed people, circumcised males or people with eye defects. The game is different in each case. Or it used to be.

For me, as a resident of English, a regular visitor to French, and a bungling tourist to German and Spanish, the sheer strangeness of all this is amazing. I can imagine, with some effort, what it is to inhabit Russian or Bengali; like English, they form part of the far-flung Indo-European language family. That guarantees, at some level, a sense of familiarity, a verbal kinship. But what is it like to live in the imaginative world of Nootka? I have no idea.

"We are just as much in a prison-house of culture as they are," the anthropologist Dominique Legros told a Concordia University newspaper. He has spent years in the Yukon, working with the Northern Tutchone people. "Even as an atheist, my mind is still imbued with our cultural notion of God, so I had difficulty conceptualizing a religion in which the Creator was not a supreme being, but a bird-man who made the world by trial and error."

Tutchone, like Nootka, has fewer than a thousand speakers left. Its prison-house is getting smaller by the decade. Ours, by contrast, keeps growing and growing until the iron bars seem nothing more than a trick of digital light. This, too, is an illusion.

Canada is far from alone in facing the imminent extinction of languages. The number spoken in the world is a matter of dispute— between 6,000 and 6,700, it appears. Of that total, some linguists warn that a mere 600 are likely to flourish a century from now. Once lost, the other thousands will be lost forever; no amount of nostalgia, software, or scholarly papers will bring them back. Soon we may have the power to clone a herd of Javan rhinos. But we will never have the power to clone a dead language.

Indeed, the standardization of human speech may be happening at an even faster, more dramatic rate than the above paragraph suggests. A few giant languages—English, above all, but also Chinese, Spanish, Arabic—are rapidly altering the structure and vocabulary of almost every tongue they touch. Career ads in the *Frankfurter Allgemeine Zeitung*—for jobs in Germany, aimed at Germans—often bear titles such as "Junior Product Manager," "Holding Controller," "Pharma-Marketing-Trainee." Halfway around the world, the *Far Eastern Economic Review* has described English as "Asia's premier language," "part of the identity of a new Asian middle class," and "Asia's unifying tongue and its language of opportunity." As far back as 1983, linguists realized that Basque education students in Bilbao (the stronghold of the unique and isolated Basque language) had a weak, Spanish-influenced vocabulary, were making serious errors in grammar, and had begun to adopt a Spanish word order when speaking or writing their mother tongue. But as Spaniards have painfully learned, the threat of cultural standardization may foster intense political resistance.

Bigger—in linguistics as in almost everything else that matters— does not equal better. In his superb book *After Babel,* George Steiner observed that "we have no sound basis on which to argue that extinct languages failed their speakers, that only the most comprehensive or those with the greatest wealth of grammatical means have endured. On the contrary: a number of dead languages are among the most obvious splendours of human intelligence."

The sun
over the hill,
   I saw it go down.
I started out running,
   started out running.
That's how I was,
   I didn't go slow,
      ha na.

That's not what I did;
I wasn't that way,
   that way,
I ran fast,
   ran fast.
I got home quickly,
   got home quickly,
      ha na.

| | | | | | |

ANDREW COYNE HAD COME TO MONTREAL TO DENOUNCE. The Royal Commission on Aboriginal Peoples had recommended, among much else, a concerted effort to keep traditional languages and cultures alive in Canada's First Nations. But to the Southam columnist, its report marked "a fundamental departure from liberal-democratic values." By highlighting the value of cultural difference, the commission displayed "the folly of identity politics"—a folly that leads to "the elevation of identity above other concerns like fairness or freedom." The report appeared to accept that "real nations are ethnic or cultural ones"; Coyne disagreed. There is, he argued, "something narcissistic" about the claims of both Aboriginal peoples and Quebecers. Above all, the report placed an unacceptable stress on collective rights and called for "a retreat into a traditional culture that is ill-suited to the demands of an industrial economy."

There were scattered cries of "Shame!" when he sat down. But at heart, I think, nobody was too surprised. Coyne had said, clearly and forcefully, what a host of non-Natives have always thought. Our law is the law. Our language is the language. Rights are individual. Differences will eventually fade away.

Such an attitude has a long history. I think of S. Hall Young of Alaska—"the mushing parson," he was admiringly called—an influential Presbyterian missionary in the early years of American rule. In 1867, the United States had purchased a huge territory whose Russian overlords had begun to encourage Native literacy; but the Bureau of Education soon changed that. Young was in line with the government. When his mission board asked him to translate the Bible into Tlingit and to compile a Tlingit dictionary, he refused, saying:

> I learned [of] the inadequacy of these languages to express Christian thought. . . . We should let the old tongues with their superstition and sin die—the sooner the better—and replace these languages with that of Christian civilization, and compel the natives in all our schools to talk English and English only. Thus we would soon have an intelligent people who would be qualified to be Christian citizens.

Even by the standards of the late nineteenth century, Young's belief that Christian civilization could exist in but a single language seems remarkable. Was he a racist? Not exactly. But he was a "linguicist"—to use a disparaging word deployed by the Language Rights Movement (a group, founded at Roskilde University in Denmark, that campaigns for a universal declaration of linguistic human rights). And the mushing parson has powerful heirs.

"Traditional culture is dead," wrote the Canadian journalist William Johnson in 1992. "Indians now depend on cars and television, guns and automobiles, central heating and medicine. The challenge they face is the same challenge which was faced by people all over the Earth when confronted by the dynamic, technologically superior European culture: adapt or risk degradation." In another of his Montreal *Gazette* columns, Johnson warned that "Native people and our governments sooner or later must learn to talk the same language and draw up their final treaty." That treaty, needless to say, will not be composed in Dogrib or Blackfoot.

YET THE ESSENCE OF TRADITIONAL CULTURE IN OUR HARSH
landscape was always an ability to adapt to change. Most Inuit hunters
now use guns and snowmobiles—but they also maintain profound
links to tradition. The quality of difference they embody has spiritual
depths and overtones; it's born of an intimacy with land and place that
has survived the blessings of our age (central heating, antibiotics) as
well as its curses (substance abuse, teenage suicide). Johnson confuses
the surface details with the inner truth. He fails to see that there's
nothing traditional about a bullheaded refusal to change.

"Our traditions define and preserve us," the Chickasaw author
Eber Hampton has written. "This continuity with tradition is neither
a rejection of the artifacts of other cultures nor an attempt to 'turn back
the clock.' . . . It is the continuity of a living culture that is important to
Indian education, not the preservation of a frozen museum specimen."

Given a chance, a language can adapt. Native people have been
busy adapting for centuries. Tiorahkwathe—a band councillor and
former teacher who is also one of the few middle-aged men to inhabit
Kahnawake in an Aboriginal language—has translated the country
songs of Hank Williams and Charley Pride into Mohawk. *Back to the
Rez*—a recent memoir by Brian Maracle, a Mohawk writer who might
almost be called a "born-again traditionalist"—describes the author's
move from Ottawa to the Six Nations Reserve in southern Ontario and
his joy in rediscovering Mohawk customs. Maracle's favourite festival
at Six Nations, Noyah, takes place on New Year's Day. But the custom
and even the name have nothing to do with Iroquois antiquity; they
emerged from the *Nieuw Jaar* celebrations of the seventeenth-century
Dutch. Even so, Noyah is now a valued part of Six Nations tradition.

All this is to the good. "Mélange, hotchpotch, a bit of this and
a bit of that is how newness enters the world," Salman Rushdie once
observed. "It is the great possibility that mass migration gives the
world, and I have tried to embrace it. *The Satanic Verses* is for change-
by-fusion, change-by-conjoining. It is a lovesong to our mongrel
selves."

Fusion is one thing; obliteration, another. Mass migration can
mean both. To many indigenous Canadians, it meant fusion in the eighteenth and nineteenth centuries, when travelling white men still had
need of Indians. The Métis were born of that need (often, admittedly,
it shaded over into the exploitation of women). "Conjoining"—

Rushdie's word—implies a partnership, not a takeover. So does the fashionable idea of mongrelization. But today, in Native Canada, "a bit of this and a bit of that" is also how differences get rubbed away. The force and allure of English seem unavoidable. An hour surfing the Net, an hour watching *NYPD Blue,* and an Aboriginal teenager has fallen one step closer to permanent change-by-media.

The significance of such a change depends, in part, on whether the capacities of the human brain are used differently in different language systems. Some scientists deny it. At the Massachusetts Institute of Technology, Steven Pinker—a protegé and popularizer of Noam Chomsky—condemns the relativism of earlier linguists. Whorf did "not actually study any Apaches," Pinker claimed in his book *The Language Instinct;* "it is not clear that he ever met one. His assertions about Apache psychology are based entirely on Apache grammars—making his argument circular. Apaches speak differently, so they must think differently. How do we know that they think differently? Just listen to the way they speak!"

Chomsky's theories of generative grammar and deep structure appear to pose an intellectual barrier for defenders of Native languages. The royal commission defined language as "the principal instrument by which . . . members of a culture communicate meaning and make sense of their shared experience." But if, at some unimaginable Ur-level, all languages are alike, why should it matter if most of them die out? In *Aspects of the Theory of Syntax,* Chomsky boldly stated: "It is possible to convey any conceptual content in any language."

Hmm. I can express the conceptual content of a Shakespeare soliloquy (or a Cowboy Junkies song) in a few sentences of paraphrase. That doesn't mean I will have grasped its entire meaning, let alone its emotional resonance. To change the metaphor: you can convey the melodic content of Mahler's *Resurrection Symphony* on a solo ukulele as well as with a massive orchestra. Yet the meanings will not be the same.

Whorf, like Chomsky, heard indigenous languages from a distance. But what of those who work and play inside them, bringing the words to life in their mouths?

"Indigenous people view reality as eternal, but in a continuous state of transformation," the law professor Sake'j Youngblood Henderson has said.

It is consistent with the scientific view that all matter can be seen as energy, shaping itself to particular patterns. The Mi'kmaq language affirms this view of the universe, building verb phrases with hundreds of prefixes and suffixes to choose from, to express the panorama. The use of verbs rather than nouny subjects and objects is important; it means that there are very few fixed and rigid objects in the Mi'kmaq worldview.

Henderson emphasizes difference. Chomsky suggests, by contrast, that an extraterrestrial would see all humans as speaking a single language. Pinker presents this fanciful image as though it were a fact, basing it on the "discovery that the same symbol-manipulating machinery, without exception, underlies the world's languages. Linguists have long known that the basic design features of language are found everywhere."

But DNA underlies all the world's plant and animal species, too, and even an extraterrestrial might have a hard time seeing an elk and an orchid as similar—basic design features or not. Chomsky and Pinker are not linguists in the old sense of the word; their work is grounded in American English. As George Steiner has pointed out, Chomsky claimed that "exciting results on universal grammar" arose from his book *Sound Patterns of English*. But many of his examples, far from being universal, didn't even apply to the language as spoken in Britain. "Might it be," Steiner asked, "that the transformational generative method is forcing all languages into the mould of English?"

Steiner is severe in his critique, suggesting that Chomsky's theories "could account, with beautiful economy and depth, for a world in which men would all be speaking one language, diversified at most by a moderate range of dialects." In fact, though, our small planet is home to more than 6,000 languages—a number that defies any simple idea of survival benefit to the species.

Why this fantastic diversity of human tongues, making it difficult for communities, often . . . similar, to communicate? How can such exceeding variety have arisen if, as transformational grammar postulates and biology hints, the underlying grid, the neurophysiological grooves, are common to all men and, indeed, occasion their humanity?

No one has come up with a satisfactory hypothesis, and it is a central weakness in generative grammar that Chomsky and his colleagues do not recognize the full scope and importance of the question.

When I talk with Tiorahkwathe, the band councillor from Kahnawake, I ask him after a while why it matters that Mohawk should survive. Gradually, he gives me a range of answers. They veer from the aesthetic ("Our language is very picturesque, everything is descriptive") and the religious ("Most people even forget to thank the waters each and every day") to the psychological-cum-sensual: "When you're speaking in the language, it's like having a three-flavoured ice cream: vanilla, chocolate, raspberry. But when you do the translation, you take out two of the flavours." Yet his initial response—"So that we don't become part of the melting pot"—was political.

> *I outran the sun;*
> *I outran the sun.*
>   *That's what I used to do.*
>   *That's how I was,*
>   *how I was,*
>   *ha na.*

> *I didn't sleep late,*
> *didn't wait for the sun;*
>   *that's not what I did.*
> *I wasn't that way,*
>   *that way,*
>   *ha na.*

| | | | | | |

"MY VOICE HAS BEEN ANGRY FOR QUITE A WHILE," OVIDE Mercredi said. He was talking quietly, but there was an edge to his tone, and the crowd caught it. The national chief of the Assembly of First Nations never looked directly at Andrew Coyne, who had preceded him to the mike, but most of what he said was a clear response.

A bitter response, too. Coyne had attacked the royal commission's call for a third order of government—an indigenous order—as threatening Canada with something alien: a racially based system of authority. "I don't have any difficulty with the idea of racial government," Mercredi retorted. "I see it every day of my life. . . . The so-called institutions of government that Canadian society values are based on two colonizers, the French and the English. Those institutions are racially based."

The longer he spoke, the angrier he seemed to become. A few minutes after he began, Mercredi launched into a series of rhetorical questions: "Have you seen us win anything lately? Are we getting our land back? Our resources? Are our languages guaranteed in your laws? Is the money spent on English and French being spent on the Cree language, the Ojibwa language, the Inuktitut language, and other indigenous languages of Canada?"

I was reminded suddenly of another, very different Native leader: a man whose office I'd visited a few years before. Max Gros-Louis was the beefy, big-voiced chief of the Wyandot, or Huron—a people with a tragic history. Nearly 350 years earlier, Iroquois soldiers, armed with new weapons and old hatreds, had destroyed Huron civilization, expelling the survivors from their lands in what's now central Ontario. The refugees split up. One remnant drifted into Michigan, only to be banished to Oklahoma; another fled into Jesuit protection just outside Quebec City. Its descendants are still there, apparently well integrated into the Quebec mainstream. On the wall of Gros-Louis's office was a laminated cover of *Paris Match* showing him with the singer Roch Voisine.

Never mind his slightly goofy, floppy-bellied appearance: Gros-Louis is a shrewd man. I asked him about a quixotic attempt by a few in his community to revive the Huron language, unspoken in Quebec for nearly a century, unspoken anywhere since the 1960s. "We are a nation that doesn't have a language," he replied. "That is almost shameful. It would be a matter of pride to take our language back."

For Gros-Louis, even a limited rebirth of Huron would heighten and legitimize his people's tenuous claim to nationhood. Except, perhaps, for a dusty reservation in Oklahoma, their sole home is this suburban outpost of Quebec City, complete with souvenir shops and a sorry-looking totem pole or two. Gros-Louis believed, rightly or wrongly, that the recovery of an old language would give his few thousand people a new sense of power. An unkind observer might see this as the *reductio ad absurdum* of ethnic nationalism.

| | | | | | |

WHAT WOULD IT TAKE FOR HURON TO RISE FROM THE DEAD? Thanks to the linguistic skill of Jesuit and Recollet friars, enough texts survive in the language that a rich vocabulary still exists. A harder task would be the creation of a groundswell of desire among the Huron themselves. Only desire allowed Hebrew to be reborn, not just as a religious language but as a medium of daily speech in a new homeland. By contrast, *A Handbook of the Cornish Language* was published by a Cornish nationalist in 1904—yet no child today learns Cornish as a mother tongue. Henry Jenner had some Celtic romantics on his side, but he lacked the dedicated support of most Cornish people.

Writers, linguists, dreamers, anthropologists, even Native politicians: no matter what they desire, a language can't flourish without popular support. Brian Maracle is refreshingly clear on who should be held responsible for the widespread lack of interest in Aboriginal languages at Six Nations: the community itself. "If there's one thing that people here revere," he writes, mother tongue in cheek, "it's their tax exemptions. So, if the people could somehow be required to speak the language if they wanted to remain tax-exempt, hundreds and thousands of people would stampede to sign up for classes, and the preservation of our mother tongue would be assured."

Language allows us to feel at home in the world. But language can provoke alienation too. The onslaught of English is affecting not only cultures whose languages are in evident decline but also cultures whose languages seem relatively strong. In his recent book *Returning to the Teachings,* the lawyer Rupert Ross explored some of the vexed encounters between Cree and Ojibwa people in northwestern Ontario and the Canadian justice system. Those encounters are made harder, Ross insists, by the differing worldviews that underlie our languages: "My Aboriginal friends talk a great deal about what it's like to have to use English all day, and they generally describe it as a strain. If we truly recognized that we occupy a universe of constantly transforming things, people and relationships, they suggest, then we would have no choice but to discard our heavy reliance on nouns to capture and describe it."

It's not just in Canada's endless debate over Quebec that nouns have political weight. And it's no coincidence that Quebec—for all its difficulties with Native demands, especially in the event of sovereignty—is the province that has gone easily the furthest to encourage the use of Native languages. Quebec, unlike English Canada, has no trouble accepting the principles of collective difference and collective rights. Its policy statement "Safeguarding and Promoting Aboriginal Languages in Quebec" commits the government to "facilitating the restoration of the aboriginal peoples' sense of belonging to their culture, through official recognition of the legitimacy and value of their mother tongue."

By its profound effect on how we understand and confront public issues, language itself is political. Whatever else Quebec nationalists may not understand, they do grasp the kinship between language and power. Ray Conlogue had French in mind when, in *Impossible Nation*, he wrote: "To be at risk of losing your first language is one of the great human traumas, particularly in the modern world where language plays a larger role than before in the definition of human identity." But his perception applies equally well to any number of First Nations languages. In small language groups, the trauma is not only individual; it is also collective.

Some would argue that the greatest threat to Native identity is not cultural but economic. In northern Canada, the survival of a partially hunting and trapping economy can seem a more urgent concern than the survival of any particular language. But the distinction may be more apparent than real. Economic and cultural life are of a piece—you can't rip them apart and expect either one to flourish.

That's one of the messages I take from a bilingual 1995 book called, in English, *Gathering Voices: Finding Strength to Help Our Children*. On each facing page, the text appears in Innu—fittingly, because copyright belongs to the Innu nation. The book offers the testimony of the people of Davis Inlet, Labrador, before a "people's inquiry" of their own and before the Royal Commission on Aboriginal Peoples. Out of a battered squalor, the Innu produced a document rich in detail and plentiful in ideas.

Most of their recommendations entail a return to Innu tradition, which has been weakened by alcoholism, social breakdown, and the appalling living conditions of Davis Inlet. The return would be, at once, cultural and economic (it would have political implications too): "We could depend more on hunting for our food. Men and women should work with the children to teach them how to do Innu crafts. We need to produce books on culture and language for the school. We can make our children happy by teaching them our traditional games." These sentences may seem disconnected, but in the Innu world they follow each other without strain.

| | | | | | | |

THIS IS A LOT MORE THAN JUST PLAY-ACTING. YET CRAFTS AND traditional games go only so far. Even if they salvage many of their traditions, the Innu can't go back to a world without money. For those without work or any prospect of it, alcohol beckons, gasoline beckons, glue beckons. Across Canada, unemployment on reserves is a prime reason why so many young people drift to Main Street, Yonge Street, East Hastings Street. City lights hold the flickering promise of money, glamour, escape.

Celia Haig-Brown, a professor at Simon Fraser University, relates a telling story in an anthology called *The Circle Unfolds*. British Columbia is home to about twenty-six First Nations—half the national total. Understandably, the common language at the Native Education Centre in Vancouver is English. A few years ago, some of its students decided they wanted to learn a Native language. But rather than favouring Nootka, Shuswap, Okanagan, or any other language of the region, the centre offered them a night course in Cree—a language, indeed a member of an entire language family (Algonkian), that is not spoken west of the Rockies. Cree does, however, stretch from Alberta to Quebec. The night course soon petered out.

You can tease several implications from this story. The first involves the students' sheer hunger to speak an indigenous language— their feeling that, if their voices remained confined to English, some essential trait of identity might be lost to them. The second, by contrast, is the extreme difficulty of answering this hunger. Without local roots and a living context, weekly night courses in a foreign language have no chance of success. A third, related point has to do with demographics. Each of British Columbia's Native languages is spoken by a few hundred or, at most, a few thousand people. Some are more vibrant than others; but the cruelty of numbers and the omnipresence of English suggest that none has the power to expand beyond its own small towns or villages. In the country as a whole, only Cree, and perhaps the related Algonkian language of Ojibwa, enjoy that potential. Together, 80,000 Canadians may still speak them at home, as well as a few thousand in the United States.

One possible future, indeed, would involve a strengthening and streamlining of Cree, seeing it eventually become something close to a national Indian language. Cree speakers now make up more than two-fifths of all people in Canada who have an indigenous mother tongue. Not enough has yet been written in Cree—but still, far more than in most Aboriginal idioms. Cree already hybridizes with other languages; the former mayor of Sioux Lookout, for example, has put out a CD of country music in which he sings partly in English and partly in "Oji-Cree." Besides Ojibwa, there are other tongues that are, I'm told, near cousins of Cree, just as Spanish is a cousin of Italian. Is it their destiny to be gathered up into a kind of super-Cree?

But for more than forty of this country's indigenous languages, such a gathering is inconceivable. They belong to ten other language families: most of them known to a minute number of people, all of them entirely foreign to the widespread Algonkian group. The extraordinary and isolated language of Kootenai, for example, stands at an immense distance from Cree. Its classic grammar was written by an Italian Jesuit in 1894—in Latin. Kootenai is now spoken at home by just a few dozen people in southeastern British Columbia. Of all the non-Algonkian languages, only Inuktitut—by virtue of its isolation, its majority status in the Arctic, and its confident use by Inuit children— seems certain to endure beyond the next generation.

"I'd like to learn the language," admits Russell Wallace, a young Vancouver composer and writer who belongs to the Lillooet people— a small group of Salish whose ancestral home lies in the southwestern interior of British Columbia. His parents left the reserve in the 1950s. Their sufferings at residential schools induced them not to pass on the language to their children: "They would speak it between themselves, but they felt it would hinder us in school."

Now, decades later, Wallace feels its absence. Slowly, he has begun to grasp some of his ancestral language through its music. He, his mother, and his sister sing in Lillooet—or, to call it by its own name, Stl'atl'imx. Ceremony and art may well give the language a last breath, even when it is no longer used in everyday life. "I think there's a resurgence," Wallace says. "Some people my age do speak the language, though not fluently." Hopeful words—though if the 1991 census was accurate, the plight of Lillooet and all other members of the Salish family is grim. According to the census, its eleven languages are used on a daily basis by only 835 people.

| | | | | | |

IT'S A SWEET ILLUSION TO SUGGEST THAT LILLOOET OR ANY other of Canada's endangered languages could somehow attain a status akin to Latin and ancient Greek: dead tongues that still have the power to nourish and inform living languages. After all, Greek and Latin were written for centuries and studied for millennia. Moreover, they belong in the family tree of English and French: they're central to our linguistic heritage. But the indigenous languages of the Americas don't grow on that particular tree. They don't even grow in the same part of the forest. Except for a host of place names and a much shorter list of nouns (tipi, moccasins, inukshuk . . .) that English and French have already adopted, they will leave no trace on mainstream speech.

The best hope for the small languages ("hope" is perhaps an exaggeration) may lie in a determined brand of cultural separatism. In *Back to the Rez,* Brian Maracle admits that some people at Six Nations now suggest ending the political wars over tradition "by physically creating two separate communities." A divisive, heart-rending choice. But several models exist. It's by isolating their children from the modern world that the Amish and old-order Mennonites have survived for centuries in eastern North America, speaking an archaic form of German. Hutterites do the same on the Prairies. And in a few of the continent's major cities, close-knit enclaves of Hasidic Jews are keeping Yiddish alive.

All these groups have chosen the path of collective isolation as a means to God. Salvation, they believe, springs from linguistic difference. They have, of course, paid a tremendous price. To embrace the mainstream is to pay another price: in North America at large, German and Yiddish exist only on the lips of the old.

Such worries may seem remote to the Cree. Yet even though their language has so far avoided numerical freefall, many of its speakers look ahead anxiously. Dialects are eroding. Rare words are being lost.

The plays of Tomson Highway—whose mother tongue was Cree—pay sharp, unsettling testimony to a language conflict in the mind. English is not only the language of power in our society; it has also become the vehicle of Highway's art, the conduit of his fame. But the plays suggest a profound guilt, as though by turning his back on Cree, Highway has offended against his own sense of the sacred.

In his second play, *Dry Lips Oughta Move to Kapuskasing*, the drunk and half-crazed Simon Starblanket hears the androgynous voice of the trickster hero Nanabush. "*Weetha,*" he says. "Christ! What is it? Him? Her? Stupid fucking language, fuck you, da Englesa. Me no speakum no more da goodie Englesa, in Cree we say '*weetha,*' not 'him' or 'her.' Nanabush, come back!"

But Nanabush does not come back, not yet, and Simon spirals downward. Spitting on an image of Jesus, he cries: "Fucking goddamn crucifix yesssss . . . God! You're a man. You're a woman. You're a man? You're a woman? You see, *nineethoowan poogoo neetha.*"

Meaning, "I speak only Cree." The printed text tells me this; a live production would not. As the scene ends, Simon shoots himself. Soon after, big Joey launches into a bilingual hockey commentary in which the Cree language keeps getting undermined:

". . . *Igwa aspin sipweesinekwataygew.* Hey, *k'seegoochin!* How, Number Six Dry Lips *Manigitogan igwa soogi pugamawew anee-i* 'particular puck' *ita* Number 66 Little Girl *Manitowabi.* . . ."

Highway's previous play, *The Rez Sisters*, also has a death near its end. After the materialist frenzy of "the biggest bingo in the world," Marie-Adele Starblanket collapses into the arms of a silent Nanabush. Her last words mingle Cree and English: "*As-tum* . . . *as-tum* . . . *pee-na-sin* . . . wings . . . here . . . take me . . . take . . . me . . . with . . . *pee-na-sin.* . . ." The lighting changes, and the surviving women hum a funeral song in Ojibwa around Marie-Adele's fresh grave. Yet despite its sombre ending, *The Rez Sisters* is a much funnier and more effervescent play than *Dry Lips*. Conscious of its bleakness perhaps, Highway chose to conclude the second play with an image of resilience and hope: a naked man holding up a naked baby, the wife/mother laughing nearby. The final words are in Cree.

| | | | | | |

AT THE MONTREAL CONFERENCE, MERCREDI HAD SPOKEN FOR more than fifteen minutes, but he still seemed preoccupied by Coyne. He kept going back to what he had just heard, or, at least to what he thought he had heard: "'You'll never survive on this land unless you assimilate to our society. Speak like us, dress like us, think like us.' This is what is called individual universality. There's other names for it, like cultural genocide and racism." Near the end of his speech, Mercredi switched languages. Like Highway, he had grown up speaking Cree in the pine forests of northern Manitoba. Mercredi made some remarks in his mother tongue, then gave a rough translation: "I live different from you. Not that I hate you. But because I like the way we live ourselves, as people. The future must be different."

With Cree words behind him, his anger dissolved. "I apologize for my tone of voice," he finally said. Someone in the crowd shouted "No!" When Mercredi sat down, most of his listeners stood up. A few metres away from Coyne's right ear, a woman beat a huge drum.

The dawn,
when it came,
I saw it.
I got up,
I got up.
The dawn,
I ran toward it,
ha na.

I thought I'd always be that way;
that's how I used to travel;
I thought I'd be that way forever
but now my strength is gone.
I thought I'd be that way forever;
that's how I was.
Listen to me,
ha na.

| | | | | | |

JOE CLARK HAD A DIFFICULT TASK. AFTER THE SPEECHES by Coyne and Mercredi, he wryly observed, "I thought there might be some need for the calming influence that I have become so well known for." But he didn't really mean to induce tranquillity; he wanted to challenge complacency. It was, in a sense, the classic liberal dilemma of a sympathetic, well-meaning outsider. I felt for him. Writing this essay, I feel in a similar rhetorical position.

In Clark's eyes, the royal commission's report offers Canada a new chance. Its proposals are radical, he agreed, "but on this unusual issue, there is a very broad sense in the country that what we are doing is wrong." Actions flowing from the report could renew "a country that many of us feel we are at risk of losing. The larger issue we are dealing with has to do not so much with constitutional provisions as with a sense of spirit and a sense of pride. We need to recapture a sense of the spirit, the traditions and the pride." That was the good news. The bad news was this: "We live in a very impatient time. If this report becomes one more failure, the results could be incendiary."

Clark is widely travelled, widely respected. Not only has he talked; he has listened. Even so, at some level the issues remain abstract for him. He cannot know what it is to *feel* Ojibwa or Onondaga. Neither can I, writing in the language of the usurper: the language of Walt Disney and Bill Gates. On the first page of my notebook for this essay is a sentence I copied from the Chickasaw writer Eber Hampton: "As I prepared to enter a sweat lodge ceremony in Minnesota, the leader of the sweat said, 'Eber, I know you can't pray in Indian, but pray in Indian in English.'" In capital letters, I added: IS THIS POSSIBLE?

Native people give opposing answers. Here is one, from Maracle's *Back to the Rez:* "Without the language, our ceremonies, songs and dances will cease. . . . The Confederacy will cease to function. . . . The names themselves will lose their meaning. Without the language, we will lose our traditional way of thinking and our distinctive view of the world."

But here is another, seven pages earlier, from the same author and the same book: "Just because we started speaking English doesn't mean we also started playing cricket and eating kippers. No, we still play lacrosse and eat corn soup and we still have an attitude regarding the future that is hard to pin down."

I'm interested in that "we." Is there an ambiguity about it? If "we" means "Mohawks," it also means "not Cayuga, Seneca, and the rest of the Iroquois Confederacy." If it means "members of the Six Nations," then it also means "not Cree, Dakota, and other indigenous peoples." But if "we" means "all of us Indians," then it suggests a hybrid Native culture that transcends the barriers of language.

I remember attending a pow-wow on a sultry July day at Kahnawake. The host drum was beaten by a group of Assiniboines from southern Manitoba; the master of ceremonies had moved from Pennsylvania to Navajo territory in Arizona; the head male dancer was a Michigan Ojibwa. According to my souvenir program, one of the sponsoring businesses was East of Texas Westernwear in Kahnawake (Visa accepted). The program described the Grand Entry Song as "probably an imitation of rodeos and Wild West shows." A mélange, a hotchpotch, a bit of this and a bit of that; something old, something new, something culturally impure.

The pow-wow bore the name "Echoes of a Proud Nation." But what, exactly, was the nation: Mohawk, Iroquois, or pan-Indian? Speakers of Mohawk and all other Iroquois languages call themselves Onkwehonweh—"the real people." Haida, Innu, Inuit, Dakota: these names also mean "the people." Indigenous languages preserve a sense of privacy and exclusion that many Native people would no longer see as desirable or even possible. Yet if the mongrelized future for a newly public, inclusive Aboriginal culture can be symbolized by ersatz rodeo songs and East of Texas Westernwear, it won't be only white poets who feel a huge sense of loss.

Let's face cruel facts. We live in an age when almost any political choice requires economic justification. But it's no good searching for financial benefits in a profusion of languages. So far, Ottawa has refused the royal commission's call to create an Aboriginal Languages Foundation: a body whose mandate would be to document, conserve, publish, and, where possible, revitalize Native languages across the country. Such a foundation would cost taxpayers money, of course—the commission suggests $50 million, spread over five years. But it would also entail a commitment by the federal government to take indigenous languages seriously. It would require a policy; it might even create an issue.

When economics fail, aesthetics remain. But to make an argument for preserving Native languages on aesthetic grounds is very dangerous. One risks appearing like a mere connoisseur, or somebody who condescends to admire the quaint behaviour of exotic locals. I have tried to avoid that—at the risk of understating the true value of what may be about to vanish.

Just two quotations, then. The first comes from one of Canada's finest poets, Robert Bringhurst, a man who has spent many years studying the Haida language and translating Haida narratives that were, almost miraculously, recorded a century ago. The totem poles and other carvings made by West Coast peoples are now regarded by many non-Natives as a national treasure. But as Bringhurst writes, "It seems clear that Haida oral literature had the monumentality, subtlety, gravity, restraint and the sly, involuted humour of Haida and Tlingit visual art. . . . The best of the extant Haida narratives, like the best of the extant rattles and poles, are, as the Haida say, *nagwighagwi q'ita*: they are fluently and deeply carved."

The second quotation is more succinct. It comes from Kenneth Hale, a colleague of Noam Chomsky at MIT: "Languages embody the intellectual wealth of the people that speak them. Losing any one of them is like dropping a bomb on the Louvre."

And that gives me the power to care—even though, as a speaker of English, I can only stand and watch as the bombs fall like rain all over the planet. Colonialism proved to be a useful armament; the internal combustion engine, another; but today the power of Microsoft and MTV is unprecedented, incalculable, almost unimaginable. Michael Krauss, the founder and director of the Alaska Native Languages Center, has said that "the battle of the living room will be fought with what I call 'cultural nerve gas'—insidious, painless, and fatal." Satellite TV may finish a job that residential schools only began.

SOME PEOPLE, I GUESS, APPLAUD THE DEATH OF LANGUAGES. They see it as evidence of progress. From an economic standpoint, they're no doubt correct. It would be useful to IBM and Coca-Cola if all the consumers in a global monoculture could read their propaganda. But as someone who cherishes diversity—who finds value, rather than threat, in our differences—I insist on my right to mourn. This is not an aesthetic judgement; it's a declaration from the heart.

"The old people say that if you lose the language, you also lose the culture," says Marrie Mumford, director of the Aboriginal Arts Program at the Banff Centre. "I believe that. We're in an age where the young people are starving to know who they are, and to speak their language. The children are hungry." Despite those words, Mumford herself—a middle-aged woman of mixed Ojibwa, Cree, and white ancestry—speaks no indigenous language well. (She has studied Cree and Ojibwa enough to understand many words and concepts, and her daughter is now learning Cree.) But although the program at Banff brings together indigenous artists from across the country, working in a collaboration that depends on the use of English, Mumford still asks that when people of different origins gather and introduce themselves, "those who have their language speak it first. Because that means they have a deeper understanding of the culture than those who have been deprived of the language. Those who are only in English learn from those who have their language."

Mumford suggests that the acquisition of a Native language can help to free indigenous people from a crippling feeling of inadequacy, restoring to them a sense of value. It is, if you like, a healing circle. For a sense of value is a prerequisite in any effort to save and strengthen a heritage. And in the end—no matter how positive or negative the reinforcement that emerges from mainstream society—that sense must spring from Native people themselves. Hence the importance of such disparate entities as the En'owkin Centre in Penticton, the Cree Cultural Centre in Timmins, and the Woodland Cultural Centre in Brantford. Sure, if Ottawa were to set up an Aboriginal Languages Foundation, and to pour intelligent resources into Native education and media, the chances of linguistic survival would multiply. But no amount of money alone can do the job.

From his long experience in Alaska, Michael Krauss writes: "With adequate Native-language programs in the schools and on television and radio, the basic responsibility for the survival of the Native language is more clearly seen to be where it has always been, with the parents to speak it to their children. Not bilingual education, not even bilingual television can themselves keep Alaskan languages alive; only parents speaking the languages to their children can do that, as has always been the way."

Standing at the McGill podium, Joe Clark was trying not to sound defeatist. It would be "a great tragedy," he warned, if the royal commission's report were simply shelved and forgotten—if it, too, were to become a dead language. "Yet there is an expectation that this could very well become another lost opportunity." Clark kept resorting to the imperative: we must do this, we need to do that. Usually, his "we" seemed to mean non-Natives. If we do not have respect for Native Canadians, he finally said, "it is not possible to have respect for ourselves."

> *I thought I'd live forever,*
> *thought I'd travel forever;*
> *that's how I was.*
> *I thought I'd always be that way*
> *but now my strength is gone,*
> *ha na.*

> *I'd always be with the mountains,*
> *it seemed;*
> *that's how I was,*
> *that's what I believed.*
> *I felt*
> *so proud.*

> *I thought I'd be that way forever.*
> *But now my strength is gone.*
> *I thought I'd be that way forever.*
> *That's how I was,*
> *how I was,*
> *ha na.*

| | | | | | |

THE LAST WORD SHOULD GO TO AN INDIGENOUS CANADIAN. Somehow it makes a difference. Here, then, is what Basil Johnston of the Ojibwa nation says about what the loss of language means to Native people:

> They can no longer understand the ideas, concepts, insights, attitudes, rituals, ceremonies, institutions brought into being by their ancestors; and, having lost the power to understand, cannot sustain, enrich, or pass on their heritage. No longer will they think Indian or feel Indian.

And although they may wear "Indian" jewellery and take part in pow-wows, they can never capture that kinship with and reverence for the sun and the moon, the sky and the water, or feel the lifebeat of Mother Earth or sense the change in her moods; no longer are the wolf, the bear and the caribou elder brothers but beasts, resources to be killed and sold. They will have lost their identity, which no amount of reading can ever restore.

Bagey dispayva,
mate ?eyamo,
> *nyevo geyome, bene.*
Gayaj mu?evaga:
> *wamejemavɛga*
>> *banm.*

| | | | | | |

NOTE: The italicized words between sections of this essay come from a traditional "Song of Farewell" known to the Havasupai people of what is now Arizona. The entire song, translated by Leanne Hinton, appears in Coming to Light: Contemporary Translations of the Native Literatures of North America *(Random House, 1994). The last verse is in Havasupai.*

With respect to vocabulary, I have chosen to step through a linguistic minefield as though it did not exist. Therefore the terms "indigenous," "Indian," "Aboriginal," "Native," and "First Nations" all appear in this essay. If nothing else, this adds variety. I hope it does not also cause offence.

This essay was written in 1997. In June 1998, Heritage Minister Sheila Copps announced that the federal government would spend $20 million, spread over four years, in an Aboriginal Languages Initiative.

1997

| | | | | | |

| | | | | | |

Biographies

| | | | | | |

Mark Abley

Mark Abley is a poet, journalist and travel writer. Born in England in 1955, he grew up in northern Ontario, southern Alberta, and central Saskatchewan, and was a Rhodes Scholar at Oxford University. His book *Beyond Forget: Rediscovering the Prairies* was published in Canada, the United States, and England. He is the author of two books of poetry, *Blue Sand, Blue Moon* and *Glasburyon*. For the last decade, Abley has worked at the *Montreal Gazette* as a feature writer and as the book review editor. He won a National Newspaper Award for critical writing and was shortlisted in the same awards for international reporting. Before joining the *Gazette*, he wrote and narrated four series for CBC Radio's *Ideas* and was a contributing editor to *Saturday Night* and *Maclean's*.

"Outrunning the Sun" was published in an abridged form in the *Gazette* in 1997. A full version appeared in *Brick* in 1998.

| | | | | | |

David Carpenter

David Carpenter lives in Saskatoon, where he writes full time. In the 1980s, he published three books of short fiction: *Jewels, Jokes for the Apocalypse*, and *God's Bedfellows*. His first novel, *Banjo Lessons*, won the City of Edmonton Book Prize in 1998. Many of his personal essays are about seasonal rituals around home. They are collected in *Courting Saskatchewan*, which won the Saskatchewan Book Award for non-fiction in 1997. Most of Carpenter's literary essays, including "Hoovering to Byzantium," appear in *Writing Home*.

Dan David

Dan David is Mohawk (Kanienkeha:ka), Bear Clan, from Kanehsatake, near Oka, Quebec. He has worked for CBC Radio as a national Native broadcaster and as a reporter and writer for CBC-TV news. From 1995 to 1998, he held the Chair of Diversity in the School of Journalism at Ryerson Polytechnic University. David won National Magazine awards for "Anarchy at Kanehsatake" and "All My Relations," both of which first appeared in *THIS Magazine*. David is currently the head of TV training at the Institute for the Advancement of Journalism in Johannesburg, South Africa.

| | | | | | |

Kim Echlin

Kim Echlin published *Elephant Winter*, a novel, in 1997. It was nominated for the Chapters/Books in Canada First Novel Award and has been sold in the United States, Italy, and Germany. She has written for the *Canadian Forum*, *Quill & Quire*, and the *Globe and Mail*. Echlin was arts producer at the CBC for *The Journal* and freelanced for *Witness* and *Life & Times*. She is currently fiction editor at the *Ottawa Citizen*.

Echlin has a PhD in English literature (her thesis was on the Ojibway trickster). "Fiddle and Bow" was first published in the *Weekend Magazine* of the *Ottawa Citizen*. Echlin currently holds a McGeachy fellowship in support of her new fiction.

David Hayes

David Hayes is an award-winning journalist who has written or co-written four books, as well as scores of magazine articles for Canada's premier publications, including *Saturday Night,* the *Globe and Mail, Report on Business, Canadian Business, Chatelaine, Equinox,* and *Toronto Life,* where he served as the magazine's media columnist in the late 1980s.

A graduate of Ryerson Polytechnic University's journalism program, Hayes began his freelance writing career in 1981. Since then, Hayes has written on a variety of subjects, although his area of specialization has been media/communications and the arts. His non-fiction books include *The Lost Squadron, Power and Influence: The Globe and Mail and the News Revolution,* and *No Easy Answers: The Trial and Conviction of Bruce Curtis.* He has also co-written a book with international figure skating choreographer Sandra Bezic called *The Passion to Skate: An Intimate View of Figure Skating.*

Hayes also teaches magazine writing in Ryerson Polytechnic University's School of Journalism.

| | | | | | |

Michael Ignatieff

Michael Ignatieff is the author of eight books, fiction and non-fiction. He has won the Governor General's Literary Award for non-fiction and the Gelber Prize for writing on international affairs. His biography of Isaiah Berlin is published by Penguin Canada.

Marni Jackson

Marni Jackson is a Toronto journalist and author of *The Mother Zone,*
a bestseller nominated for the Stephen Leacock Award. She has written
for the stage, worked as a story editor on films, written a teleplay for
the CBC, and published articles in all the major Canadian magazines,
as well as for *Rolling Stone* and *Outside* in the United States. With
the Clichettes, Jackson co-wrote two stage shows, "Half Human, Half
Heartache," which toured Canada, and "She-Devils of Niagara." Her
columns for *Toronto Life* won two National Magazine awards. For
two years, Jackson was also co-host of the TV Ontario book show,
Imprint. Random House U.S. will publish her next non-fiction book,
on the subject of pain.

| | | | | | |

Brian D. Johnson

Brian D. Johnson is senior entertainment writer and film critic at
Maclean's. Born in England in 1949 and raised in Toronto, he received
a BA from the University of Toronto, where he was editor of the
Varsity. After working as a reporter at the *Gazette* in Montreal (1970–74),
Johnson left journalism to devote five years to music. He toured,
recorded, and composed percussion soundtracks for two documentary features. At *Maclean's* since 1985, Johnson has also written for
the *Globe and Mail, Saturday Night, Toronto Life, Chatelaine, Flare,*
Equinox, Take One, and *Rolling Stone.* He has won three National
Magazine awards. Johnson appears frequently on radio and television,
and co-hosted CBC Newsworld's *On the Arts* for three seasons.

Kyo Maclear

Kyo Maclear has spent equal amounts of time by the Pacific and Atlantic oceans. She has travelled widely in Japan, Europe, and North America, and has published non-fiction and poetry in *This Magazine, Toronto Life, Fuse,* and *West Coast Line*. Born in England in 1970, Maclear received her MA in 1996 from the University of Toronto (Ontario Institute for Studies in Education). She has worked as a staff editor for *MIX Magazine* and Bruce Mau Design. She continues to devote her energies to freelance writing and book illustration.

Maclear's first book, *Beclouded Visions: Hiroshima-Nagasaki and the Art of Witness,* was published in 1998. "Race to the Future" first appeared in *Brick*.

| | | | | | | |

Barbara Moon

Barbara Moon is an editor-at-large at *Saturday Night* and, until 1998, was a senior editor for the Creative Non-fiction and Cultural Journalism Program (formerly Arts Journalism) at The Banff Centre for the Arts. A nationalist and a lifelong journalist, Moon is the author of hundreds of major articles in magazines such as *Maclean's* and *Saturday Night* and features in newspapers such as the *Globe and Mail*. She has also written dozens of television documentaries—among them several segments of the experimental CBC-TV *Images of Canada* series— and books, including *The Natural History of the Canadian Shield*. Among relevant honours, Moon holds a Maclean-Hunter first prize for Editorial Achievement, the University of Western Ontario's President's Medal, and the National Magazine Foundation's Award for Outstanding Achievement.

Don Obe

Don Obe is a professor in the School of Journalism at Ryerson Polytechnic University. He is a former chairman of the school and founder of its acclaimed magazine, *Ryerson Review of Journalism*. His professional experience includes editor-in-chief of the *Canadian* magazine and *Toronto Life,* and associate editor of *Maclean's.* For the past nine years, Obe has been a senior editor in the Creative Non-fiction and Cultural Journalism Program at The Banff Centre for the Arts. He has won a gold medal for ethical writing in the National Magazine Awards and, in 1993, his industry's highest honour, the National Magazine Award for Outstanding Achievement.

| | | | | | | |

Ian Pearson

Ian Pearson has worked as a writer, editor, and radio and television producer for the last twenty years. He was associate entertainment editor at *Maclean's* in the early 1980s, and ended the decade as articles editor of *Toronto Magazine* at the *Globe and Mail.* After a flirtation with film as a development officer of the Ontario Film Development Corp-oration, Pearson spent three seasons as books producer for CBC Radio's *Morningside* and later worked on CBC-TV's *Gzowski in Conversation.*

Pearson has written for most major publications in Canada, including *Saturday Night,* the *Globe and Mail, Destinations, Toronto Life, Toronto, Maclean's,* and *Quest.* He has been nominated five times for National Magazine awards, winning a silver in 1993. "Looking for Richard" was originally published in *Saturday Night.*

Stan Persky

Stan Persky teaches philosophy at Capilano College in North Vancouver, British Columbia and is a book columnist for the *Vancouver Sun*. He has written several books, including *Buddy's: Meditations on Desire, Then We Take Berlin,* and *Autobiography of a Tattoo.* An earlier version of "The Translators' Tale" appeared in *Then We Take Berlin.*

| | | | | | |

Joan Skogan

Joan Skogan was born on the west coast and received an MPA from the University of British Columbia. She has written features for CBC radio, *Saturday Night, Border Crossings,* and *Georgia Straight.* Her book *Voyages at Sea with Strangers* is a memoir of working on foreign ships offshore as a Canadian fisheries observer. *Skeena: A River Remembered* is an aural history of the Skeena River fishery.

Besides her work as a journalist, Skogan has published short stories and prose poems in *Grain, Prairie Fire, West Coast Review,* and other magazines. Her stories are included in the *Journey Anthology* and other collections. Her books for children are *The Princess and the SeaBear and Other Tsimshian Stories, Grey Cat at Sea*, and *The Good Companion. Moving Water*, her first novel, appeared in fall 1998. "Mary of Canada" was originally published in *Saturday Night.*

BIOGRAPHIES

Rebecca Solnit

Rebecca Solnit is an essayist, critic, and activist based in San Francisco. Her books include *Secret Exhibition: Six California Artists of the Cold War Era, Savage Dreams: A Journey into the Hidden Wars of the American West,* and *A Book of Migrations: Some Passages in Ireland.* "Lise Meitner's Walking Shoes" was originally published in *Savage Dreams.*

Solnit is a contributing editor to *Art issues* and *Creative Camera;* a columnist for *Grand Street;* a regular contributor to the environmental magazine *Sierra;* the author of essays in numerous museum catalogues and books, such as the *Whitney Museum's Beat Culture and the New America* and the Denver Art Museum's *Visions of America: Landscape as Metaphor in the Late Twentieth Century;* as well as a political activist involved in nuclear, environmental, and human rights issues.

| | | | | | | |